FROM THE PEACE
TO THE FRASER

Newly Discovered North American
Hunting and Exploration Journals

1900 to 1930

Prentiss N. Gray
1884-1935
Here, Gray hunts blacktail deer in Northern California in 1900.

FROM THE PEACE TO THE FRASER

Newly Discovered North American
Hunting and Exploration Journals

1900 to 1930

by

Prentiss N. Gray

A BOOK OF THE BOONE AND CROCKETT CLUB
CONTAINING THE HUNTING AND EXPLORATION TRAVELS
OF PRENTISS N. GRAY AS HE CROSSES ALASKA, MONTANA,
NORTHERN CALIFORNIA, UTAH, WYOMING,
AND MANY CANADIAN PROVINCES.

Edited by

Theodore J. Holsten, Jr. and Susan C. Reneau

1994

The Boone and Crockett Club
250 Station Drive
Missoula, Montana

FROM THE PEACE TO THE FRASER
Newly Discovered North American Hunting and Exploration Journals
1900 to 1930

by

Prentiss N. Gray

Edited by Theodore J. Holsten, Jr. and Susan C. Reneau

ISBN Number: 0-940864-21-5

Library of Congress Catalog Card Number: 94-78743

Published in October 1994
First Printing

Published in the United States of America
by the
Boone and Crockett Club
Old Milwaukee Depot
250 Station Drive
Missoula, Montana 59801-2753

(406) 542-1888

This book is dedicated to Sherman Gray
who loaned his father's journals to the Boone and Crockett Club
and made this entire project possible.

Ten original journals, written by Prentiss N. Gray from 1900 to 1935 and shown here against a whitetail deer pelt, were loaned to the Boone and Crockett Club by his son, Sherman Gray, for the production of this book. The photographs in this book were taken by Gray using a variety of cumbersome, but state-of-the-art, cameras from the early 20th century.

Foreword

THEODORE J. HOLSTEN, JR.

During the period between 1893 and 1933, a series of general hunting, exploration and conservation anthologies were published by the Boone and Crockett Club. The first of these books was titled, *American Big-Game Hunting* and the driving force behind its publication were the efforts of its editors, George Bird Grinnell and Theodore Roosevelt.

Grinnell continued to line up original material by Boone and Crockett Club members and was principal editor of all seven books in the series. The last book in the series, *Hunting Trails on Three Continents*, was co-edited by Prentiss N. Gray. It was only a short time after its release that Gray died in a tragic boating accident.

In the sixty years since the release of *Hunting Trails on Three Continents*, no additional anthologies were put together, although there certainly were many prominent Boone and Crockett Club members who could have contributed interesting material. We thought it would be worthwhile to re-explore the concept and to solicit original material from our current membership. This led directly to the discovery of the unpublished hunting and exploration journals of Prentiss N. Gray.

At the Boone and Crockett Club annual meeting in Chicago in December of 1993, I happened to be conversing with Prentiss N. Gray's son, Sherman, who is a current member of the Club. Sherman indicated that he had considerable unpublished material written by his father, and we discussed the idea that I should meet with him for lunch when next in the New York City area, to see if some of the material could be used in the new Boone and Crockett Club anthology.

In March of 1994, I scheduled a trip to New York and contacted Sherman to see about setting up the planned meeting. I suggested he bring the material to our meeting and I would take it back with me to my home in the Minneapolis area and consider including some of it in the anthology being developed. Sherman asked if I really wanted to take it with me since it would fill a couple of large, heavy boxes. We decided rather than meet, to have Sherman ship the material to me, despite his concern about its safety.

Imagine my surprise when the boxes arrived and instead of loose notes and photographs, I found more than twenty large, leather-bound volumes of original journals, beautifully typed and including hundreds of his original (never-before-published) photographs placed appropriately throughout the various episodes. Prentiss N. Gray had meticulously written up his field notes, and was an outstanding writer as well as a photographer. His observations of the wonderful places he visited on his many trips to remote places could not be described better! It is no wonder that Sherman was concerned about safety in shipping these precious journals.

Because there was so much wonderful material in the Prentiss N. Gray journals, we decided to postpone the planned anthology in favor of a book devoted entirely to Gray's writings. Indeed, there was so much material, that we have concentrated on his North American adventures in this book. Prentiss N. Gray traveled extensively to Africa and other remote places and this may represent an opportunity for another book in the future.

We are indebted to Sherman Gray for allowing the Boone and Crockett Club to publish *From the Peace to the Fraser: Newly Discovered North American Hunting and Exploration Journals, 1900 to 1930*, by Prentiss N. Gray. After reading Gray's journals, we hope you will share in our enthusiasm.

———————

Theodore J. Holsten, Jr. is chairman of the Boone and Crockett Club's Editorial and Publications Committee and editor of this book. He has been a member of the Boone and Crockett Club since 1986 and is a columnist for the Boone and Crockett Club's national magazine, Fair Chase, The Official Publication of the Boone And Crockett Club. *Holsten collects and deals in rare books of hunting, guns, adventure, exploration, natural history and fishing.*

White Pass on the way to Seattle, Washington

Tear in pants shows Prentiss Gray's battle with chaparral in 1905

Prologue

Susan C. Reneau

From the Peace to the Fraser is more than a book about two rivers in Canada. Throughout Prentiss N. Gray's short, but action-packed life, dozens of travels throughout the world highlight his activities. Reading his journals tells much about the person and provides insight into the first editor of the Boone and Crockett Club's famous all-time records book, *Records of North American Big Game*.

Prentiss N. Gray was the man who began the tradition of publishing a records book about North American big game species and recording them in a publication for all to enjoy.

How thoughtful of Prentiss N. Gray to share his enjoyment of life with the rest of us who may not have the pleasure of exploring our world to the extent he did in the early 20th century. How many of us today think of future generations by recording our thoughts in such detail? What a tragedy that more modern-day adventurers, hunters and explorers don't take the time, as Prentiss did, to record their observations. My hope is by reading this book, more late 20th century hunters and adventurers will keep journals of their travels to share with their children, grandchildren and future generations.

Production of this book would not have been possible without the steadfast efforts of Prentiss Gray's son, Sherman, to preserve each and every journal his father ever wrote. Sherman Gray, who has been a Boone and Crockett Club member since 1967, not only respects the history of his family but has spent countless hours monitoring the artifacts and books that belong to the Club on display or in storage at Theodore Roosevelt's home in Oyster Bay, New York, now called the Sagamore Hill National Historic Site.

He worked arduously to locate written records of these treasures that include rifles used by Theodore Roosevelt and his sons, bronze medallions of the Boone and Crockett Club symbol, books from the collection of George Bird Grinnell, trophy heads collected by Theodore Roosevelt and furniture belonging to the Roosevelt family. I was privileged to assist Sherm in his efforts to catalog the Boone and Crockett Club's Sagamore Hill collection. Throughout the process, Sherman has been a driving force to insure that those artifacts given to the Club by Archibald B. Roosevelt, eighth president of the Boone and Crockett Club and son of Theodore, would remain in the Club's ownership.

Sherman admits it was his father who instilled this sense of respect for the past and encouraged his children to record their adventures of life in writing. Uncovered in this process of research for this book, the editors discovered that Sherman and his sister Barbara had also kept leather-bound, one-of-a-kind journals of their hunting and hiking adventures with their father and mother. Sherman loaned his original 1930 journal to the editors - a journal he wrote at age 12 during his travels to Alaska with his father only five years before Prentiss' death.

Sherman records in his leather-bound journal on August 15 and 16, 1930, that he had to sleep beside the exhaust pipe of a small boat, "The Discoverer," and the next day caught twelve lively trout in a stream full of salmon. His boyish joy unleashes details of hunts after Dall's sheep, bear and moose with his father and sister. The photographs in his red leather and cloth-bound journal were from his father's vast collection of illustrations that grace the Prentiss N. Gray books. My attraction to Gray's black and white photographs, that reflect the vastness and beauty of our North American landscapes and wildlife, cannot be underestimated.

My thoughts of cool Alaskan nights and steep Alaskan cliffs carried me away from the hum-drum daily schedule of activity as I read Sherman's and Prentiss' accounts of their 1930 trip. Reading all the journals contained in this unique book will continually entertain the reader as they experience the wilds of Alaska, Montana, Northern California, Wyoming, the Great Salt Lake of Utah, British Columbia, Alberta, Newfoundland and the Yukon Territories.

Prentiss N. Gray, called Prent by his family and friends, created twenty-one leather-bound volumes, measuring 11 1/4 by 10 inches in cranberry, navy blue and forest green leather. They contain his personal reflections of hunts and explorations throughout North America, Europe, Central America and Africa. Throughout each journal Prentiss included his spectacular black and white photographs to illustrate each volume's text. His first journal begins in 1900 in Northern California and is reproduced in this book as the first chapter. His final journal was compiled in 1935, the year of his death.

Ten of the thirteen North American journals Gray wrote and illustrated are included, with minor editing, in this unique book. The remaining eight, one-of-a-kind and never-before-published journals, are left for readers to appreciate in the future. Sherm Gray said his father never expected his personal hunting and adventure journals to become the basis for a book, but Sherm thinks his father would be pleased. How we wish Prentiss could be here to share in our delight at reading his words and viewing his photographs.

From the Peace to the Fraser: Newly Discovered North American Hunting and Exploration Journals, 1900 to 1930, will be a book to carry you away to a time and place preserved eternally by Prentiss N. Gray. His journals are a significant contribution to 20th century conservation efforts and wildlife biology history.

———————

Susan C. Reneau is the co-editor of this book and the co-editor of the Boone and Crockett Club's book, Records of North American Big Game, 10th Edition, *that was published in 1993. She is the author of the book,* Colorado's Biggest Bucks and Bulls, *a deer and elk hunting book, and* The Adventures of Moccasin Joe: The True Life Story of Sgt. George S. Howard, 1872 to 1877, *a western and military history book published in 1994.*

Sherman Gray, 12, fishing for trout in Alaska in 1930

The Life and Times of Prentiss N. Gray

SHERMAN GRAY

Prentiss Nathaniel Gray was born in Oakland, California, on July 2, 1884. He was the youngest of his family, with two older sisters, Mabel and Elizabeth. His father and mother, George Dickman Gray and Susan Hichborn Thayer Gray were one of a large group of Gray families and their relatives who had come to California from 1849 onward following the lure and excitement of the Gold Rush. As they prospered through the years, they moved from San Francisco across the bay to Oakland where the climate was thought to be better and gradually clustered in a group of houses, "The Gray Compound," at Tenth Street and Telegraph.

Prentiss Gray belonged, in fact, to the first generation of his family to be born in the West. His father was born in New York in 1844 and had graduated from Amherst College in 1865. His forebears, starting five generations earlier with a John Gray, had come to the American Colonies from Londonderry in 1718. The Gray family had then spent the next 100 years eking out a meager living in farming, quarrying and cooperage in Worcester and Pelham, Massachusetts, just a few miles to the east of Amherst. In those days, the Grays, like their neighbors, produced five to eight children in each generation and had representative members of the family in the Presbyterian Church, the American Revolution, and as an additional demonstration of spirit, in Shay's Rebellion against the State of Massachusetts.

George Dickman Gray, in Oakland, through an inheritance and his business ability in the shipping and lumber business, was wealthy enough to be characterized as a "capitalist" and a "millionaire" by the local, rather gossipy newspapers. He was considered to be fairly advanced in social customs because he saw to it that both his daughters got college degrees. In his old age, he demonstrated his talent for exploration by purchasing a 1907 Stevens Duryea automobile and taking a trip by the coast route from San Francisco to Los Angeles, visiting all twenty-one Catholic missions established by the early Spaniards. Because this took place some years before good roads and bridges were built, the trip required repairing numerous flat tires and fording most of the streams which ran from the mountains to the ocean.

Prentiss Gray graduated from Oakland High School in 1902 and immediately enrolled in the University of California in Berkeley, less than a mile up Telegraph Avenue from his home. He did very well academically and, in due course, was elected to the debating team and several honor societies. As left guard of the varsity football team, he became the subject of a campus uproar when, having concealed his condition from his coach and trainer, he played over half the 1904 "Big Game" against Stanford with two broken ribs and a badly infected foot. Blood poisoning was much more serious then than it is now and he came close to having his foot amputated. As business manager of the "Blue and Gold," the class yearbook, he distinguished himself by earning enough revenue to offset the debts of his and the previous class.

In the final months of his senior year, as captain of the University Militia, he was sent on guard duty to San Francisco following that city's earthquake and fire in April of 1906. That assignment produced the experience of defending himself from a drunken, chair-wielding, caretaker left to guard a Van Ness Avenue mansion at the very edge of the fire. On another occasion, when confronting a disgruntled and surprised looter, he luckily moved his head just enough to allow a bullet fired at him to graze through his hair rather than his brain. Unable to campaign on guard duty, he was nevertheless elected the president of Associated Students in the last few weeks before graduation over several active candidates left back at the campus. It was rumored in the local newspapers that the "co-ed vote" had supplied the winning margin.

At an early age, Prent Gray had been fascinated with deer hunting and had taken every opportunity to enjoy this sport. In 1904 he saw the chance to hunt bigger game and with Al Coogan, a fraternity brother from the University, carried out a hunting trip up the Stikine River, Alaska, to the Cassiar Mountains in British Columbia. Because his sisters shared his love of the outdoors, they somehow put him under an obligation to keep a diary and bring home every detail of the trip for his family to enjoy.

Young ladies, in those days, did not have the freedom to go haring off on a summer vacation hunting trip, so a detailed record for them to peruse later was the next best thing. In this case, Prent Gray kept his part of the bargain even to detailing where he spent every dollar of the $359.15 cost of the trip. From then on, the custom was established. Every night on every trip for the rest of his life, no matter what the weather or his physical condition, Prent wrote up his diary and, at the conclusion of each trip, he packed off a well-illustrated account of what had happened to his sisters and to the rest of his family. Each passing year produced more ambitious trips and a growing occupation with photography. On each hunting expedition, the difficulty and excitement of capturing wildlife on film became more important to him than the normal hunt with a rifle.

All this, however, was many years in the future and Prent Gray, at graduation from college, faced the choice of a career which stimulated his interest and suited his temperament. Although he did not find it immediately, he cheerfully started in his father's shipping business at the lowest level in the San Diego branch office. The California and Oregon Coast Steamship Company ran a fleet of ten to twelve lumber carriers, most named after members of the Gray family, which supplied lumber for the building boom in the post-fire ravaged San Francisco and the rest of California. Thus, it was a logical step that Prent Gray, in his spare time, arranged to build and sell a number of small houses in San Diego. He demonstrated this same initiative when he moved back to San Francisco as a manager for the shipping company and in his leisure time promoted a real estate development called Fairfax Manor in Marin County.

His marriage to Laura Sherman took place in Washington on May 27, 1908. His wife was the youngest daughter of Hoyt Sherman, a former official of the Union Pacific Railroad and then the senior partner in the law firm of Sherman and Wilson of Salt Lake City. She was a niece of General William Tecumseh Sherman, whose army captured Atlanta and Savannah in the Civil War and of Senator John Sherman of Ohio, the author of the Sherman Anti-Trust Act and a secretary of the Treasury for President Rutherford B. Hayes. The marriage took place in Washington because the bride's father was there to arrange the settlement of the John Sherman Estate. The honeymoon was an extended tour of the West Coast of Central America and a visit to the Panama Canal which had just been acquired by the American

Government. For the next six years, the Prent Gray family settled in Marin County with an active life in shipping and in real estate in Northern California. Their eldest child, Barbara Gray (Robinson) was born there in 1914. The author of his biography, Sherman Gray, was born in New York in 1918.

A chance meeting with an old college friend on a street car on the way to a University of California football game produced a dramatic change in Prent Gray's life in 1915 when he was recruited to help feed millions of starving Europeans during World War I. The War had already broken out and, in the opening campaign, the German armies had swept through Belgium around neutral Holland, and into Northern France only to bog down into a trench warfare stalemate extending from neutral Switzerland to the English Channel. All of Belgium and large parts of Northern France, some ten million people in all, were thus trapped behind German lines and cut off by the Allied Sea Blockade. They were seriously short of food because the occupying Germans in supplying their own troops seized whatever local food was available and made no provision for noncombatants.

At that point, Herbert Hoover, then a very successful mining engineer living in London, who had just finished a very efficient evacuation of some 120,000 American tourists trapped by the war on the Continent, was asked by the American Ambassador to Great Britain to organize some relief shipments of food to Belgium. A committee had formed in Belgium for this purpose and had obtained an understanding with the Germans not to requisition food imported through the Allied Blockade to the neutral port of Rotterdam for the Belgian and French civilians. Little realizing this was the first step in a life of public service which would lead him to the United States Presidency, Herbert Hoover organized a small group of his engineering friends together with most of the American Rhodes Scholars at Oxford to carry out this task. Neither he nor anyone involved in the beginning foresaw that the Commission for Relief in Belgium would need to find some $950 millions to pay for the food before the war ended and that this idea of relief for starving Europeans would be extended, geographically, across Europe to Russia and, in time, into the 1950s.

By 1915 the relief effort in Belgium was underway but groaning under the problems of finance, troubles with either the British Blockade or German submarines and lastly, suffering from the inefficiencies of a group of amateur if willing executives. Herbert Hoover, who had graduated from Stanford University in 1896, had sent recruiters to California - the man in the street car - for men with shipping experience and the search had uncovered Prent Gray. He was soon hired and by January 1916 was in Belgium as an American neutral behind German lines in charge of all the food supplies of Antwerp.

Gray's diary and letters to his family describe the next two years in intensely interesting detail. As the occupying power, the German Army had agreed not to use any of the food specially imported for the Belgians but it ruthlessly interfered with the local harvests, and, in controlling the civilian population, often disregarded the rules of war and treated the agreements with the Commission as "mere scraps of paper." Although outwardly neutral, Prent Gray's emotions were often torn by scenes of the Germans drafting Belgian men for forced labor, loading them into box cars for shipment to Germany and then beating back the women and children who had gathered to say goodbye to their husbands, sons and brothers.

Soon after arriving, Prent Gray decided to put himself on the diet that had been officially approved by the Belgian Government for those who were out of work on public charity. Breakfast consisted of a cup of tea without sugar and fifty grams of bread. Lunch was 150 grams of bread and three-quarters liter of soup. Dinner was a positive feast with 100 grams of bread, one-quarter liter of soup and half a can of corn. As the week's diet progressed, Prent Gray was able to supplement one lunch with 100 grams of potatoes and one dinner with seventy-five grams of rice. At the end of five days he found he had lost 6 1/2 pounds and, because his colleagues complained bitterly about his disposition, had to give the whole thing up. Mr. Hoover wryly planted this story in the British and American newspapers to gain support for the Commission.

The declaration of war by the United States against Germany in April 1917 dictated a change in the personnel of the Commission for Relief in Belgium. All the American executives except one were replaced by Dutch and Spanish neutrals and evacuated with the American ambassador. At Herbert Hoover's insistence, Prent Gray was designated to stay behind to conduct the final inventory and to balance the books. At that point the Gray family (His wife and three-year-old daughter had joined him in Brussels by sailing on the neutral Dutch ship, "Rotterdam.") were the only enemy aliens at large in Central Europe. In May 1917, when all the work was done, they were escorted through Southern Germany to Switzerland and freedom.

Many honors accompanied Prent Gray on this last trip. He was decorated by the exiled King Albert of Belgium with the Officier de l'Ordre de la Couronne and by the President of France with the Chevalier de la Legion d'Honneur. His family still has thirty-six lesser decorations and medals struck in honor of the relief effort and presented to him. In a self deprecating mention of these in his diary, he said "Every time you turn around in Belgium, someone hands you a medal."

By this time, Herbert Hoover had been designated head of the United States Food Administration in Washington and arranged that Gray join him as his head of the Marine Transport Division. He remained there until the war ended and then, in March 1919, Hoover again had him go to Europe to supervise the final liquidation of the Commission for Relief in Belgium.

Most of the surplus funds of this winding-up were used in rebuilding the four largest universities in Belgium, but at the time, some two million dollars was set aside and the income was used to finance a small group of Belgian graduate students studying in the United States. This effort continues to this day as the Belgian-American Educational Foundation which, some seventy-five years later, with net assets of twenty million dollars, now finances the education of forty-two Belgian students in the United States and twelve American students in Belgium each year.

In 1920, Prent Gray shifted his efforts from the United States government to the private sector and started an active export and import of grain business in New York. Within a few years, P. N. Gray & Co. had established branch offices in Antwerp, Hamburg, Warsaw, Vienna and Constantinople and was acting as buying agents for a number of Central European governments.

In 1922, Frank Tiarks, a director of the Bank of England and a managing partner of J. Henry Schroder & Co., a London merchant bank, visited New York for the purpose of starting a Schroder Bank there. It was rightly thought, in the post World War I world, that New York would emerge as the financial capital of the world and that Schroders, after 114 years in England, should expand to the United States. By chance, Tiarks consulted Herbert Schlubach, then a very successful investment banker in New York, who had served in the occupying German army in Belgium charged with dealing with the Commission for Relief in Belgium and who knew Prent Gray well. He recommended Gray and Tiarks hired him to organize the Schroder Banking Subsidiary; afterwards, explaining in a quixotic English way, that the best way to produce a successful banker was to start with a successful business executive and let him learn banking by experience.

In 1923 then, Prent Gray, with no banking background, organized, staffed, and launched J. Henry Schroder Banking Corporation in New York. This new banking corporation followed the traditional merchant banking pattern of underwriting securities, mostly foreign bond issues, and the financing of export-import trade with letters of credit, collections, acceptances, etc. From the beginning, Gray made a deliberate effort to staff the bank with mostly foreign born executives and demonstrated that their banking expertise often outshone the international departments of other larger New York banks.

In the financial boom of the 1920s, the most profitable banks were the underwriters of foreign bond issues whose position of each grouping were established by their distributive abilities, historical importance and connections to the borrower backed by an aggressive ability to negotiate. Schroders, in general, and Prent Gray, in particular, quickly developed the knack of obtaining a prominent position in each underwriting group despite their relative newness in the field. When he was told in early 1928 that Prent Gray was in Africa shooting lions, Ferdinand Eberstadt, the managing partner of Dillon, Read & Co., one of the oldest and most dignified of the traditional underwriting banks, was quoted as replying, "The Gray I know is not shooting them but is surely choking them to death with his bare hands." So much for the gentlemanly competition among bankers.

The Great Depression of the 1930s virtually closed the underwriting business down, and, at this point, Prent Gray was able to shift his bank successfully to the financing of foreign trade. His team of executives became so skillful in this field that, in the 1940s, within ten years after Prent Gray's death, the New York Schroder Bank was twice the size of its London parent.

There was no formal record found of this agreement, but it was generally understood with Frank Tiarks that, as soon as the New York bank had made its first one hundred thousand dollar profit that Prent Gray's vacation time was unlimited. The pattern of his hunting diaries bears this out when one sees that he at first went for relatively short trips to Eastern Canada. As the years passed, his trips got longer and more elaborate in the western United States and Canada, culminating in a full year's safari in Africa.

In the early 1930s, Prent Gray contributed a series of six to eight articles on hunting to "The Sportsman," a magazine devoted to all sports and edited in Boston by Christian Herter who later became Secretary of State for President Eisenhower.

This series culminated in a 33-page supplement of pictures and text to that magazine called *African Game-Lands*. The product of this expedition, notably a group of giant sable antelope, and a collection of 900 birds went to the Academy of Natural Sciences in Philadelphia.

Gray's wanderings with a pack train through the rugged country near the Peace River in Canada photographing sheep and goat, produced the discovery of a new low-altitude pass through the Canadian Rockies and a fellowship in the Royal Geographic Society in London which published the description of "Gray Pass."

In 1934, with the help of the Boone and Crockett Club and the Wilderness Club, Gray began transplanting antelope from Cody to Jackson Hole, Wyoming, where he owned a ranch. The first antelope herd there had been exterminated by the original settlers and the long, cold winters. Successful from the very start, there is to this day a sizeable, well-protected antelope herd there.

Prent Gray conceived the idea of a book listing big game trophies in 1929. He then persuaded the Editorial Committee of the Boone and Crockett Club to sponsor the project and to invite some thirteen other wildlife experts to write chapters on each species. At that time, Messrs. Rowland Ward, taxidermists in London, published a records book listing big-game heads from Africa and North America, but because of the distances and the expense, not many American heads appeared in this book unless they had been mounted in London. Then too, no single individual or trained group of measurers had examined all the listed heads to classify the freaks and fakes.

Manufacturing fake "record" heads from several sets of antlers or horns was a well developed art among American taxidermists and paid very large rewards. Lastly, at that time, there were no single measurements or group of measurements, or a scoring system, which ranked one head over another in massiveness and symmetry. Three years work on this produced a book of the Boone and Crockett Club, the first 1932 edition of the now famous *Records of North American Big Game* with Prentiss N. Gray as editor. The book was published by the Derrydale Press and was limited to 500 copies.

Over the next sixty-two years, the Boone and Crockett Club has continued the publication of this records book at intervals. The current edition of *Records of North American Big Game, 10th edition,* was published by the Club in October of 1993.

The final weeks in Prent Gray's life started in January 1935 when he conducted an inspection tour of the International Railways of Central America, of which he was chairman, in Guatemala, Honduras and Salvador. This completed, he flew to Florida to join R.R.M. Carpenter, a fellow member of the Boone and Crockett Club, for a jaguar hunt in the Everglades of Florida. He was enroute to the Carpenter's yacht, "Harmony," when the motorboat in which he was traveling caught fire and exploded. Both he and the guide who had been sent to pick him up in the boat were killed instantly, and their bodies were recovered by searching parties the next day.

In the 1930s, upon one's death, it was customary for boards of directors, clubs, etc., of which one was a member, to pass a resolution noting the sad event and conveying the sympathy of the group to the family of the deceased. The family of Prent Gray received a number of these resolutions and a significant one reads:

"RESOLVED: That the Board of Directors of the International Railways of Central America, having lost their Chairman, Prentiss N. Gray, by his untimely death on the 30th of January, 1935, leave on record their remembrance of his straightforward personality, his quick imagination, his loyalty, his gaiety, his leadership in the affairs of the Company through good times and bad.

"He became a Director of the Board in 1926. He was elected Chairman in 1931. He knew every foot of the Company's property; he put his heart and mind into the enterprise and worked for it with notable success. He had the admiration of his associates, and they were his friends."

The quality of gaiety was fairly hard to achieve in 1934, at the depth of the Great Depression, and the above resolution says a lot about the effect Gray had on his colleagues.

I was 16 years old at the time of my father's death and remember the event as an abrupt shattering of an idyllic sojourn at boarding school. Things were much more serious after that and the process of growing up was greatly accelerated.

The times that I treasured the most with my father were those which even now appeal to a 16-year-old boy; a pack trip across the Thorofare Plateau in Wyoming; a moose hunt on the Cascapedia River in Quebec; and, an extended hunting trip in Alaska described in the last chapter of this book.

It took me a long time to realize that, by age 16, without revealing his motives, Prent Gray had furnished me with the qualifications (three North American big game trophies) to join his favorite group, the Boone and Crockett Club. I was very proud to be able to do this 32 years later.

———————

Sherman Gray lives near New York City and became a member of the Boone and Crockett Club in 1967. Gray was first a banker for J. Henry Schroder Banking Corporation and later a vice president for Merrill Lynch, Pierce, Fenner & Smith Incorporated in New York for many years until his retirement in 1982. As a Boone and Crockett Club member, Gray was the treasurer for twenty years from 1971 to 1991 and is a member of the board of directors for the Boone and Crockett Foundation. He was active on the former Sagamore Hill Committee.

Tribute to
Prentiss Nathaniel Gray

On January 30, 1935, while enroute with a guide to join friends on a houseboat in Everglade waters of Southern Florida, Prentiss Gray was killed, apparently as a result of an explosion on the motorboat in which he was traveling. His guide died with him and both bodies were recovered a day later by searching parties.

Prentiss Gray was born and educated in California. He engaged in lumber, shipping and other business enterprises on the Pacific slope until 1916, when he became a member of the Commission for Relief in Belgium with Herbert Hoover. In 1917-18, he was chief of the Marine Transportation Division of the United States Food Administration; then went back to Europe as a director of the American Relief Administration. Since 1919, he had been in business in New York, first as an exporter and importer, then as president of the J. Henry Schroder Banking Corporation, but he had traveled extensively in all parts of the world.

His avocations for years were exploration, big game hunting, photography, and wildlife conservation. His achievements in each field were notable.

Mr. Gray wrote numerous articles on his scientific and hunting expeditions. He edited *Records of North American Big Game* in 1932, and, at the time of his death, he was engaged in preparing the second edition of this outstanding work which was to have appeared this autumn (1935). He was one of the editors of *Hunting Trails on Three Continents*, the seventh book of the Boone and Crockett Club.

Gray's expeditions to Africa and the American Rockies for the Academy of Natural Sciences of Philadelphia yielded valuable specimens for the Academy's museum as well as scientific data of exceptional importance. In 1934, Gray began the reintroduction of pronghorn antelope to the Jackson Hole region of Wyoming, in cooperation with the Boone and Crockett Club and the Wilderness Club. His initial work was successful and indicated that the project was feasible.

Many honors came to Prentiss Gray. He was decorated Officier de l'Ordre de la Couronne by the King of Belgium, and Chevalier de la Legion d'Honneur by the President of France in recognition of his high public service in relief work. Gray Pass in the Canadian Northwest Territories was named for him in commemoration of his work in surveying and mapping a remote section of the Peace River country.

———————

Horace Marden Albright (1890-1987) was acting director of the National Park Service from 1917 to 1919 shortly after the National Park Service was established in 1916. He was the acting director while the first director recovered from a serious illness. Albright became its second director from 1929 to 1933. Albright was a close friend and fellow member of the Boone and Crockett Club with Theodore Roosevelt, George Bird Grinnell and Prentiss N. Gray during the early 20th century at a time when many parks were being established in the United States. Albright is best known for organizing the National Park Service, setting policies and lobbying Congress for funds. He wrote the National Park Service creed which is used today. Horace M. Albright will be revered for his great contributions to a variety of causes, but perhaps he will be best remembered for his efforts to establish and protect the United States' national park system. Albright wrote this tribute to Prentiss N. Gray for the 1935 Boone and Crockett Club membership book.

Contents

Illustrations

ILLUSTRATIONS

FROM THE PEACE TO THE FRASER

Newly Discovered North American
Hunting and Exploration Journals

1900 to 1930

Covelo, California in 1900 - still an outpost

Columbia Blacktail Deer

1900

The first journal Prentiss N. Gray ever wrote was in 1900 and detailed his first deer hunt that was for Columbia blacktail deer. This journal also includes details about his successful California hunts in Southern Humboldt County in 1902 and in Sonoma County in 1912. He also comments about his introduction of deer to Golden Gate Park in San Francisco. He refers to the deer as, "Columbian black tailed deer," but the spelling for the species in current Boone and Crockett Club publications is, "Columbia blacktail deer," so that is the spelling used in this book.

The original journal has a cloth and leather hardcover binding of navy blue trimmed in gold ink. The printed marbled endsheets include colors of pale blue, cranberry and cream.

All of the original journals were trimmed with gold along the bindings of the books and measure 11 1/4 by 10 inches. Most of the original, and never-before-published, photographs of Gray's adventures in these ten journals are reproduced in this book. Every effort was made to reproduce the original journals as they were created by Prentiss N. Gray, including the spellings of geographic locations. The editors kept Gray's exact wording, wherever possible, to preserve his method of expression.

I made my first attempt to kill a deer in 1896, sitting up all night in a tree over a salt lick with a shotgun loaded to the muzzle with buckshot. I suffered a thousand nervous chills whenever a twig snapped or a leaf stirred in the wind. Before many hours, every muscle in my body ached from the effort to maintain my equilibrium on the limb of the tree. Never a sign of deer did I see and I was so disgusted with deer hunting, as I knew it, that it took several years to awaken my enthusiasm again.

Later I came to learn that waiting at a lick was not sport. However, in the '90s in the mountains of California, deer hunting was not practiced as a sport. It was a means only of procuring fresh meat to vary the monotony of a diet of smoked or salted pork on which the mountain farmers mostly lived.

During the next four years on summer outings, I often saw deer, mostly does and fawns, and the desire to kill a buck with a real spread of antlers gradually returned. Also, my school friends came back from their holidays with stories of still-hunting. These stories filled me with envy and banished the memory of that miserable night in a tree.

In July 1900, with Hiram Hall, I began my first real hunting trip in the Trinity Mountains of Northern California. Our outfitting place was Covelo, on the edge of the Round Valley Indian Reservation and reached by a 100-mile stage ride from the end of the railroad. Our ultimate destination was about twenty-five miles to the north along the North Fork of the Eel River, just on the border between Mendocino and Trinity Counties.

Covelo in 1900 was still an outpost - one of the last "cow towns" of California. In the center of Round Valley the little town sweltered in the summer sun. Its only street was generally deserted except for a row of horses at the hitching rail. In the deep shadow of the veranda of the largest building, you could discern a row of chairs tilted back against the wall and a row of sombreros tilted forward on the noses of the dozing occupants. This was Tule Bill's saloon - the center of the town's social life. Here the boys gathered when they came in off the range. If you sought Dr. Liftchild for medical reasons or to mend your windmill, you could depend upon it that he was occupying one of the chairs on this saloon's front porch. Justice Cummings was most likely in the next chair deftly rolling Bull Durham cigarettes with one hand. He only left this post on those rare occasions when Sheriff Redwine was sober enough to arrest someone.

The sheriff's job in Covelo was not a sinecure, as cattle rustling was not unknown and providing whiskey to the Indians for a dollar a pint was a crime only on the statute books or when the federal Indian agent came into town from the reservation. Consequently, there was always at least one drunken Indian per day who could be thrown in the hoosegow if the sheriff himself was sober enough to navigate.

There were several ways for the Indians to get whiskey. One was to put down a dollar on the bar and call for soda water. It was served at the end of the counter beneath which was a pile of pint bottles of whiskey laid out for this special purpose. The bartender watched these bottles carefully, but only to see that the hand that reached around the end of the bar did not take two bottles for one dollar.

COLUMBIA BLACKTAIL DEER

This was my first real camping trip and my first hunt; consequently, everything was novel and interesting. I knew nothing of the habits of deer and had not the slightest idea that the particular deer we were seeking were Columbia blacktail deer called *Odocoileus columbianus*.

For some time after we had made camp on the Eel River, I tramped vainly through the thickest chaparral, climbing ridges with my heart pounding vigorously for fear a look on the other side might disclose a buck and that I would suffer an attack of buck fever. All my kind friends had told me I was sure to have this malady on seeing my first deer within range. Buck fever is very real and after many years of hunting, I still feel sometimes a nervousness at the sight of game. In my early years I missed a good many shots as a result of it.

I recall shooting some years later in this same territory when a large buck broke cover in a canyon just below us. I waited a moment for my companion to fire but I saw him raise his gun, lower it and eject two shells. Finally I concluded that something was wrong with his rifle so I fired and killed the deer. As I turned to inquire what had happened, my friend's enthusiasm stopped my question. Although nothing but fully loaded shells could be found among the five he had finally ejected and his gun was as clean as the day it came from the factory, my companion was fully convinced in his excitement that he was firing rapidly and that the deer had fallen to his shot.

After five days of conscientious still-hunting on this trip without result, I awoke on the morning of my sixteenth birthday with a firm determination not to return to camp unless I came in carrying a buck. About 7 a.m., just as I began to be fearful that the morning hunt was over, I walked out into an opening high up on Lake Mountain. Below me stretched away ridge after ridge to the Great Bend of the Eel River, their tops glistening in the morning light and the ravines between them still in darkest shadow. It was a wonderful panorama of light and shade; the brown hillsides spotted with dark green live oaks and patches of lighter-colored chamise. I sat down, forgetful of my hunting, and drank it in. After a time my view unconsciously fixed on a dark spot in an opening 600 or 700 yards away and suddenly I jumped to the realization that it was a deer. I could not tell whether it was a buck or a doe, but I started precipitously toward the animal.

More fortunately than with wisdom I must have planned the approach correctly for I came out on a little ridge behind some scrub oak trees within ninety yards of

Dingle Plummer stands beside his buggy.

Scrub oak in Northern California

the deer. As I parted the branches, I saw it was a splendid four pointer and within easy range.

No shot was ever taken more deliberately and none more successfully for the buck dropped in his tracks. Up to this time I had been perfectly cool and collected but as soon as I saw the deer was down I was wild with joy. I dropped my gun, fairly flew across the intervening space and grabbed the deer by the antlers lest he still try to escape. I dressed him as quickly as possible and taking him clumsily on my back, tried to carry him back to camp, which was fully five miles away.

I had not then learned how to prepare a deer for packing. Later I was shown by one of the vaqueros a most convenient way, which was to skin out the four legs up to the knees and cut off the bones at this joint. Care should be exercised to leave the false hoof or dew claws on the skin so that the knots tied later will not slip. The skin of the right foreleg is tied across the belly of the deer to that of the left hind leg, and the left foreleg to the right hind leg. Then, if you slip your arms into these leg straps as into a coat, you will be surprised how well the deer rides on your back.

On this occasion I tried to carry the deer suspended from one shoulder, but a couple of hundred yards climb uphill cooled my ardor. I hung him in a tree and returned to camp for my horse. I have brought into camp since that day larger deer and finer heads but nothing could exceed my pride when, with the little forked horn strapped behind the saddle, I met my companion.

A few days before we started home from this trip I was riding back to camp one evening when I jumped an old doe with two fawns. They were funny little spotted fellows and the sum total of their education to date had been to get under the nearest bush and lie still. This they did but I had seen them and, dismounting, I grabbed the first one easily. The second took alarm and bolted so that it took quite a chase with one fawn under my arm to catch the second. Its legs were still wobbly but it could dodge quickly enough and flounder along just fast enough to stay out of my reach.

I finally caught it and carried both of them into camp, and that night put them in the tent while we slept in the open. The next morning we thought to tether them nearby but soon found there was no need to tie them as we could not drive them away from camp. They seemed to have acquired a dependence on us and a fondness for our supply of condensed milk, which we fed to them by pouring a quantity of it in a pan and allowing them to suck a finger immersed in the milk.

Prentiss N. Gray with his first buck - a blacktail

COLUMBIA BLACKTAIL DEER

We were totally ignorant of the law, newly passed in California, against taking fawns without a permit and when we started home we carried them with us quite openly into Covelo. We left Covelo on the stage for the head of the railroad and had gone thirty-five miles to Laytonville when we were overtaken by two deputy sheriffs from Covelo with warrants for our arrest. They had not arrested us in Covelo because they wished to earn the mileage and the travel allowance given them by the state.

We were hauled back to Covelo by Sheriff Redwine and were advised by the judge to toss up to see which one of us should plead guilty to owning both fawns as it was not necessary for each of us to be fined the minimum penalty. Fortunately, I won the toss so my companion had to take the opprobrium of violating the game laws. He was fined $30 but Justice Cummings was good enough to remit the fine and give us a permit to take the fawns to San Francisco.

For several years we kept these deer at our homes and they became the greatest pets. Mine developed a special fondness for the pink bills of the milk man and devoured every one he left. It loved to nip off all manner of bright flowers and we never had a blossom in the garden below the height to which this deer could reach by standing on its hind legs. It was always anxious to get into the house, and if someone left a door open it would steal quickly in, run up the stairs to mother's room where it generally found her knitting by the window. The first indication she had of its arrival was when it butted her on the elbow. There he would stay for an hour or more with his head on her lap waiting patiently for an occasional pat.

It finally met a tragic death when one day a strange dog got into the yard. In its endeavor to escape, the deer broke its leg trying to jump a six-foot fence.

Deer hunting in Northern California is carried on in several ways, according to the various kinds of country in which the deer live. The blacktail does not care for open country and is found exclusively in the heavily timbered mountains or the brush-covered foothills. As you go north into Oregon and Washington, the timber becomes more dense and in its somber shade the bushes on which the deer feed become scarcer. The giant ferns that form so much of the undergrowth in these mountain forests are not proper feed and the number of the deer grow fewer.

Moreover, the timber is so thick that 100 deer might be within range without your seeing them and your only shots are obtained by chance. The best hunting is farther south in the brushy hills of Southern Oregon and Northern California.

Here the evergreen brush or chaparral that covers most of the ridges is a favorite abode of the deer. Most of it grows so thick that a man can hardly penetrate it and once within its confines he finds it too dense to see through for more than a few feet in any direction. This tangled network begins too low for a man to crawl under it; it struggles upward often far above his head, forming the hardest obstacle that either man or dog has ever been called upon to go up against.

Botanists and tourists who overlook the vast stretches of California chaparral from the tops of ridges or traverse it on well-cut trails call this growth of brush the "Elfin Forest." Unquestionably, it is a botanist's paradise, as it contains more than 150 species of plants, but the hunter and cattle rancher are more prone to view chaparral as "Hell's Garden."

The word chaparral comes from chaparro, the Spanish name for live oak, which makes up about 15 percent of this forest cover; from chaparral comes chaps, the designation for the leather leg-covers worn by the vaqueros to protect themselves from the spikes and antlers of this tangle.

If you can view chaparral dispassionately you will find that the various shrubs that compose it have a good deal of individuality. You come to distinguish in passing through it the various dwarf trees, just as the Easterner notes the hickory, the oak, the spruce or the pine in his forests. You will thus pick out the chamise, buckthorn, chinquapin, scrub oak and manzanita and, remember, if you have not just finished a tussle with its thousand branches intertwined in an endeavor to strangle each other and you, that each of these shrubs has some attractive feature either in its wealth of blossoms or the protection that it affords the hillside against erosion.

About a third of all chaparral is chamise (*Adenostoma fasciculatum*), a shrub easily recognized by its small, almost needlelike, olive green leaves. It is not an early bloomer, but about June it whitens the mountain side with a profusion of white blossoms. Next in importance are numerous species of wild lilac or buckthorn (*Ceanothus cordulatus*). A thicket of buckthorn is positively aggressive in its hostility and belies the softness of the wealth of blooms. Chinquapin (*Castinopis chrysophyllus*) is much like a dwarf chestnut and its nut burrs are fully as prickly and hard to handle as those of its eastern relative.

It is a shock to the Easterner who first enters the chaparral to find acorns growing on bushes no higher than his head. But one of the principal shrubs of the chaparral is the scrub oak (*Quercus dumors*), which bears, not only great quantities of acorns but also numerous sharp points on its leaf edges that will penetrate the thickest cloth, and have called into being the chaps of our vaqueros. Probably the toughest, most crooked shrub of all is the manzanita (*Arctostaphylos*). Everything about it is striking; its waxen, pink and white bell-like flowers; red berries; smooth velvety red and greenish bark; the blows you receive when you try to bend the bone-like branches out of your way.

There is nothing elfin about the area covered by chaparral. Practically all the mountainous regions of Southern California and most of the ridges of the Coast Range and the lower Sierras in Northern California outside the actual forest region are covered with it. Throughout this range there are open spaces or sections where the heavy brush has been burned off and the new growth has not attained a greater height than three or four feet. Here it is possible to see the blacktail in all its glory.

During June and July the bucks lie up in this thick brush making their beds on the sheltered side of some particularly thick clump. As nothing can approach without considerable noise, they have ample time to slip away. This they will invariably do when disturbed, rather than break cover, especially in the summer months when their antlers are still in the velvet. I have often seen a crafty old buck, with antlers laid well back, slipping along under the brush for all the world like an old doe. Often they depend entirely on their cover for protection, allowing the hunter to approach within a few feet of their hiding place before moving. I have fired several times at deer across the canyon when only a few feet away from me another would break out of its hiding place with a crash, frightened by the shot.

Although this deer knows full well how to canter, when startled, he seems to enjoy a bouncing gait almost as if to tempt your fire by leaping high over the brush. All four hoofs strike the ground at the same time with a thump, only to spurn it again, sending the deer aloft on a ricochet that leaves you little cause to worry about the distance you will have to carry him back to camp after he is down from your shot.

He appears in ever-changing curves above the chaparral with twists from side to side interspersed just when you think you know where he will appear on the next jump. You have no time to aim, and shooting becomes a matter of instinct in pointing the gun. Nothing in all my experience has given the thrill that such shooting brings, and the hunter who has emptied his magazine at a buck in full flight without

Pack horses and men start from Blocksburg, California

result need feel no great shame at his inability to score on such a target.

Often the brush is so dense that men on foot can hardly get through it. The deer are likely to come out in fairly open country or where the brush is low. The blacktail is a difficult deer to drive. When left alone it will generally take an easy path, but when disturbed it will go anywhere over the roughest ground or through the thickest brush. Generally, in country such as can be driven with dogs in this way, there is a lack of water. On a hot day the dogs soon lose the scent, especially in the rough and brushy ground, and they do not pass water often enough to refresh themselves so that they soon lose interest in the chase.

Personally, I find little pleasure in this sort of hunting, as there is such an element of luck as to which direction the game will take. However, I admit that the baying of the dogs when they strike a hot trail gives a thrill. When the buck breaks cover, it takes good shooting to bring him down as he is generally traveling fast and you have only snap glimpses of him as he rises above the brush on his long jumps or dodges around rocks or over windfalls.

I greatly prefer to climb over the hills alone on the chance of finding a buck feeding out of the brush or on his way to water. It is ideal in the first hour after dawn to ride slowly through country on a cow pony in the hope of "kicking out a buck." There are slopes that catch the first rays of the morning light on which sometimes a deer will stand to warm himself in the sun before going off to lie down. There are plenty of rocky points from which you can survey a series of chaparral ridges where, in open spots, your eye may catch the glitter of the light on his reddish-gray coat. It takes a good eye to do even this, as a deer never stands out against the background as we see him in pictures. You generally see only a part of the body while his head is thrust into the brush, or possibly the wave of antlers or the flick of an ear. Sometimes it is only a patch of reddish-brown or gray that attracts your attention. It takes long training to see such an animal quickly enough to get a standing shot, as while this deer is stupid about making out the figure of a man at rest, he is amazingly quick to detect the slightest movement.

The blacktail is mainly a wanderer at night; they prefer a good moonlight night and during such times you will find plenty of tracks in the morning, but you will often travel far after daylight or just before sundown without seeing a hair or horn. As they have fed most of the night, filling their stomachs and getting all the exercise they require, they lie down before daylight and do not rise again until it is

The results of a good day's hunt for blacktail deer

entirely dark.

They also have a period of seclusion, generally during May, June and early July when their antlers are soft and they move about very little, and generally at night. As they are not forced to go to water since their feed at this time is tender and juicy, they remain in the densest thickets where you must almost step on them before they will go out. But toward the approach of the rutting season, which occurs along the Coast Range in the latter part of August, the deer begin to move about over a larger area and stay afoot longer in the daytime. They appear more in the open ground and the bucks are more careless, particularly when on the trail of a doe.

The most successful hunt I ever enjoyed was in southern Humboldt County in 1902. I staged south from Eureka sixty miles to the little village of Blocksburg. This was long before the railroad ruined this country for the hunter, or the paved highways and the automobile flooded it with tourists. Blocksburg at that time could hardly be dignified with the title of a village, for it contained only six houses, a saloon and a general store that supplied the sheep and cattle ranchers within a radius of fifty miles.

One of my three companions on this hunt was the owner of the general store in Blocksburg. He had arranged the trip with greatest care so that every comfort that could be packed over rough country on packhorses was provided.

For two days we packed farther back into the mountains and finally located our camp near the base of Lassic Peaks. As it was late August, the heat was intense on the ranges and one day while we were out the thermometer registered 114 degrees in the shade at camp. I feel confident it was nearer the boiling point in the sun on the ridges where we were hunting.

Meat was soon provided for the camp by killing three small bucks, but I was primarily interested in the big heads that were reported to have been killed in this territory. Therefore, I spent most of my time on the higher ridges where I expected to find the old bucks.

It was not till after our fourth day in camp that I had a chance to shoot. On this morning two of us left camp at 2 a.m., as it was some distance to the ridges where we wished to hunt and we wanted to be there by daylight. We hunted in vain until nearly 8 a.m., when our dog put out a splendid three pointer. My first shot appeared wild but later we found that it had nearly severed the buck's foreleg just below the knee. The second shot brought him down and we crossed the little canyon to the point where he lay. Just as we located the deer in the brush where he had fallen, we happened to look back and saw a splendid buck slipping out of the brush, close by the spot from which I had been shooting.

He was already moving off quickly and I fired just as he topped the crest of the ridge. We were not sure that he was hit, but we both thought that we had heard the bullet strike. My companion started back but before he reached the bottom of the canyon I heard him yell and I saw what appeared to be an enormous buck jumping the chamise just beyond him. I fired and the deer stumbled but kept going. We found the blood trail at once and in ten minutes the dog's bay changed to a series of short yelps and we knew that he had the deer at bay in the bottom of the gulch.

It was a slide and a scramble to get down there, as we were fearful that the dog, which was none too well-trained, would think we were not coming and leave the deer. We soon located the buck, who was rapidly weakening from a wound in the fore shoulder, but still able to keep the dog at a respectful distance by threatening with his antlers. Here was one of those occasional pictures that make hunting worthwhile. The splendid old buck had selected a spot in the creek bottom against a pile of rocks for his last stand. We watched him unseen from a clump of scrub oak a hundred yards away. The dog was threatening from first one side and then the other, but could find no opening past the antlers that were always presented to his attack. When the dog came too close the buck made short rushes at him but backed quickly to the rock so that the dog could not get behind him. After each rush and before the dog threatened again, the old buck's head would go up as he scanned the side hill for signs of our approach.

A final shot brought him down and we found that he was the largest deer I had ever killed, with a splendid head of five points. We packed him out of the gulch, past the point where we had last seen the second deer at which I had fired. Greatly to our joy, we found him dead just below the top of the hill, from a shot that had drilled him fore and aft. He was a fine three pointer, but a trifle smaller than the first deer.

I have never personally known of a deer charging a man, even when badly wounded and at bay, but I would hesitate a long time to tackle a big buck while it could still stay on its feet. I have seen them kill several dogs who ventured in too close and I have been myself pretty badly bruised in trying to catch a three-year-old buck inside an enclosure in which we trapped a number of deer.

One of the strangest sights I have ever seen was a man riding a wounded deer, which ended by the rider getting a bad fall. In 1912, Wallace Foster and I were hunting in Sonoma County. He had shot and knocked down a good-sized buck, but, as the brush was very thick, he called to me to go up to the deer while he kept the spot covered so that the deer could not slip away under cover. I toiled up through the heavy chamise and, unexpectedly, almost stepped on the wounded deer, which was lying in a clump of white thorn. The deer went out with a crash before I could get a shot. Foster joined me and we took up the trail, soon finding the deer lying in a game trail in a little open space. Its feet were gathered under it and its head was stretched away from us. As the hill was steep above and below the trail, Foster stepped straddle of the deer and reached forward to cut its throat. On the first touch of the knife it rose with a bound with Foster on its back. He stayed for only a few jumps, but I was so convulsed with laughter that I forgot to shoot after they parted company. We found the deer down again within a hundred yards and this time made sure of the quarry by another shot before we attempted to cut its throat.

For five years we lived twenty miles north of San Francisco at Fairfax and, although this was a fairly settled country and not far from a city of 500,000 people, there were numerous deer on the brushy hills. We had an apple orchard on the property and put up a light wire netting around about half an acre of it with a broad gate at one side. From the gate, for 300 yards, ran a straight road to the house. During the apple season, the deer would come into the enclosure for the apples that had fallen to the ground. Often at night, by speeding up the automobile along this straight road, we arrived to find one or more deer in the enclosure. Doubtless they were dazed by the headlights for we had time to jump from the car and shut the gate.

It generally took several of us to corner a deer and throw him and sometimes we were severely kicked and bruised in the process. We came to have a thorough respect for their hoofs and antlers. If we found that we had trapped an old deer, we opened the gate at once and let it escape, as we soon learned from experience that deer more than two years old were difficult to accustom to captivity. The young does that we caught soon became very tame and in a few days would eat apples from our hands. But generally the bucks, even spikes, had to be confined in a small

Hiking in the California underbrush

enclosure until they became accustomed to people at close range before we could let them out in the larger paddock.

A number of the deer that we caught were placed in the paddock in Golden Gate Park, San Francisco, and are as tame as domestic animals. It was surprising how quickly after their first fright they lost their fear of man. Within a few weeks, one yearling doe learned that each morning my wife wheeled the baby over to the deer paddock, bringing apples or sugar. From quite a distance this doe would detect the crunch of baby carriage wheels on the graveled walk and display the greatest excitement, running up and down inside the fence until the youngster arrived and passed over the tidbits.

The blacktail varies greatly in size and form and most figures given as to their weight are exaggerated. I am certain that few bucks will weigh more than 150 pounds dressed, and the average will be well below 120 pounds. The weight dressed of the largest I have killed was 176 pounds, but I have heard authentically of one that dressed 187 pounds. The antlers of the blacktail are a particularly poor index to the ages of the deer. The majority are forked antlers, even on old deer and the best heads, while generally symmetrical and well-shaped, seldom carry the number of points that would constitute a good head of a whitetail or mule deer.

This large percentage of forked antlers has led some old hunters into the error of announcing a new subspecies. You sometimes hear them speak of the "Pacific buck" or the "Pacific forked horn," but there seems to be little basis for the claim, as the classification is based mainly on the fact that the antlers are forked, while the deer is evidently five or more years old.

There are two distinct species of deer in California. The blacktail deer (*Odocoileus columbianus*) is the form found along the coast from Los Angeles County north to Alaska. But the deer of the Sierra region are primarily the mule deer (*Odocoileus hemionus*). The range of the mule deer is from Los Angeles southward into Lower California, eastward to the desert region, and northward through the Sierra Nevada Mountains. A special subspecies of the mule deer is reported in the northeastern portion of the state in Modoc and Lassen Counties and is called locally the Rocky Mountain mule deer. It is uncertain, however, whether this is really a subspecies or only a slight variation due to environment and feed.

Wrangell totem pole

The town of Wrangell in 1904

[18]

Stikine River

1904

The second journal Prentiss N. Gray wrote was in 1904 when he traveled along the Stikine River in Alaska. He spelled the river "Stickine," but the current geographic spelling is "Stikine" which is the spelling used in this chapter. The original journal has a cloth and leather hardcover binding of cranberry color and printed marbled endsheets with swirls of cranberry, gold and cream. The second journal becomes the second chapter of this book.

A trip down the Yukon to Nome in 1902 had whetted my appetite to see more of Alaska away from the beaten path of tourists. For twenty years the steamship companies had issued pamphlets picturing the scenic beauties of the Inside Passage. Splendid steamers thronged with tourists plied these waters every summer, but only the fringes of the country had been opened up. The towns could be counted on the fingers of one hand and except for the canneries of the Alaska Packers Association, a few mines, of which the largest was the Treadwell Mine at Douglas City, and here and there a sawmill cutting for local consumption, the thousand miles of coastline were unsettled. "Seward's Icebox" was still undeveloped and unspoiled for the sportsman.

Few of these tourists saw the land ten miles back from the shore, as the forests were damp and almost impenetrable and no roads existed. Snow-clad peaks, sapphire blue glaciers, cataracts leaping down the mountain side for the final plunge into the sea were to be seen from the steamer's deck. A thousand miles that rivaled the Yosemite Valley stretched from Seattle to the Lynn Canal and Sitka. So why bother to go inside? Not many heard the whisper:

"Something hidden. Go and find it. Go and
look behind the Ranges - - - -
Something lost behind the Ranges. Lost
and waiting for you. Go!"

Ice Mountain

Only a few heeded, but when, among them, George Carnac on August 17, 1896, picked out the first nugget from the gravel beds of the Klondike, all this was changed. Tourist travel vanished. Throughout 1897 and the spring of 1898, throngs of "cheechakos" swarmed north on any craft that could float. These travelers cared nothing for the charm of Wrangell Narrows or the emerald icebergs that had found freedom at last from the glaciers that were still cutting down rocks and changing the face of the land. They were interested only in what the gravel bars contained and the never-ending search for the Mother Lode.

Tales of hardship of the disappointed thousands that straggled out after the first rush had hardly lost their interest when the strikes were made at Nome and Tanana. The old stampede was repeated and something more of "inside" Alaska and the Northwest was known to the world. Each returning miner covered his disappointment by wondrous tales of the greatness of the country. Jack London, Rex Beach and Robert Service threw a glamour of romance about even the weather so that one almost could imagine enjoying 40 degrees below zero in "a snug shake-down in the snow."

Our trip in 1902 from Seattle up the Inside Passage, over the White Pass, down the Yukon, 2,185 miles past Dawson to St. Michaels and Nome showed much of this wonderful land. I heard tales of hunting, saw skins and horns of animals that made me long to get back from the traveled routes and see what the country had been before the "rush."

In the summer of 1904 I started Alaska-wards with my college roommate, Albert Coogan, without fixed purpose or destination. We were armed with steamship passes, a letter of introduction to the managers of the Alaska Packers Canneries and camping equipment. We sailed from Seattle on June 14th, on the steamer "Dolphin" and late in the afternoon of the 16th landed at Ketchikan, the first port in Southeast Alaska. It was not much of a town, just a group of wooden, unpainted buildings ranging along the shore behind a small dock, which, on account of the 28-foot difference in tide, stood up like a skyscraper at low water. The forest that threatens to crowd the little village into the sea reeks with moisture and unless you stayed closely to the rickety wooden walks you sank knee-deep in soft ooze.

The following morning it was raining hard so we repaired to the general store seeking information. Our first comment on the weather elicited this story from the storekeeper:

"When the first Sunday school was opened in Ketchikan, the teacher told the story of Noah. He explained how the flood came after forty days and forty nights of rain. That afternoon my eight year-old kid tells me that he didn't think much of this Sunday school business because they did not tell the truth.

"Why?" he said, "the teacher said the whole world was flooded after only forty days of rain and here it's been raining every day for two years steady and the river hasn't risen an inch."

Toward afternoon the rain slackened a little and we strolled up the stream a couple of miles to the falls. The pool was literally alive with salmon. We sat by the falls and watched hundreds of fish try to climb up through the rushing water. Most of them failed, at least on the first try, and fell back into the pool, which was already so crowded that fish were pushed out on the banks and their silvery backs glistened over the entire surface.

On June 18th we boarded the fish-tender "Novelty" to the Alaska Packer's Cannery at Loring where Mr. J. R. Hickman, the superintendent, took us in and entertained us most hospitably. We spent three days fishing and exploring the Naha River on which the first salmon hatchery in Alaska had been erected. It had been running for several years with splendid results. Best of all, we found Mr. Hickman to be a sportsman who had traveled extensively through the Northwest and on his suggestion we decided to try the Stikine River country. He pictured plenty of game, some new varieties, as only a few years before Andrew J. Stone had found a new sheep, now called the *Ovis stonei*. While there had been gold excitement in this district in 1868, the country had been visited infrequently since this rush.

We had a splendid canoe trip down the Naha River through Roosevelt Lagoon, Jordan Lake and Hickman Lake with just enough fast water between the lakes to keep our interest at high pitch. As the Naha approaches the sea, it takes on a quieter demeanor and few rivers can compare in beauty with the last five miles.

On June 21st we sailed from Ketchikan on the steamer "Derigo" and the following day put into Wrangell, which is located on Wrangell Island opposite the mouth of the Stikine River. From here we were to take a small steamer operated by the Hudson Bay Company to the head of navigation on the Stikine River at Telegraph Creek. This steamer made only two trips a year and we could obtain no definite assurance as to when she would start on her first trip. It all depended upon how much freight arrived from the south for the posts on the river. For eight days we possessed our souls in patience, explored and re-explored Wrangell's only street and played solitaire by the hour. We did a little fishing without spectacular results and with little sport.

On June 27th we started early for the Alaska Packers cannery and floundered over a mile of muddy trail, sinking often over our boot tops. After breakfast at the cannery we left on the fishing tender "Hattie Gage." Each day this boat visited the fishing camps, returning with hold and deck loaded with salmon. At our first stop, the fishermen were just drawing in a seine from which were tallied onto our boat 3,923 salmon averaging about ten pounds each.

We made the circuit of Wrangell Island and arrived back at the cannery late in the afternoon. We avoided steamer lanes by poking up narrow inlets that were not visited by the tourist steamers. In places the channel was not more than sixty yards wide and although rain threatened continually and the clouds hung low down the mountain sides, we found the scenery superb. Every few hundred yards a white cataract flashed among the dark green trees or fell precipitously directly into salt water from rocky heights. Through occasional rifts in the low-hanging clouds, we caught glimpses of snow-covered peaks that told of unsuspected altitudes far above the timberline.

Eagles were numerous and we acquired a strong dislike for our national bird after viewing his apparent preference for dead and rotting fish cast up on the shore. Occasionally we saw him drop to the water for a fish and rise screaming with a flopping salmon in his talons, pursued by several of his companions that were less industrious. We saw several deer picking their way through the forest but all appeared to be does or were out of range.

Shortly after our arrival in Wrangell we had purchased a fourteen-foot skiff that bore on its bow the name "George Simmons." We expected to come down the Stikine in this boat, not waiting for the September trip of the steamer. Though neither of us had had any swift water experience, we had no foreboding of the difficulties of this undertaking. Part of our waiting time had been passed in repairing and caulking this craft.

June 28th was the first clear day we had had since leaving Seattle and I must admit that it rained a little in the morning even on this day. We took advantage of the sunlight to get some pictures of Wrangell and its old totem poles and put a final coat of paint on the boat.

The winding Stikine River

Log cabins on Telegraph Creek

[24]

STIKINE RIVER

Finally, on June 30th, the Hudson Bay Company officials decided they had all the freight they could expect and shortly after noon the steamer "Mount Royal" pulled away from Wrangell dock. In appearance, she was not much of a boat but strongly powered to nose her way up the swift waters of the Stikine and Skeena Rivers for which trade she had been built.

The mouth of the river is wide and shallow and can only be entered at high tide on account of the sand bars. The lower reaches, even as far as the international border thirty-three miles from the mouth, feel the effect of the tide so that by 8:30 p.m., following up the crest of the flood, we had reached the Great Glacier forty miles from Wrangell.

Here we tied up for the night alongside a woodpile from which our fuel for the next day was taken aboard. Across the river from our landing place was the glacier stretching fully half a mile along the river and reaching up the valley beyond a point visited by any white man.

This "Ice Mountain," as it was locally called, ended in a moraine about a quarter of a mile from the river and carried on its surface as far up as we could see considerable earth and rock, so that it had a dirty, yellowish appearance. Directly across the river from the glacier was a hot spring whose steam could be seen for half a mile.

We were up the next morning and underway by 4 a.m.; we wanted to see every bit of scenery, as well as to look over the bad places we would have to run on our way down the river.

We were cutting through the Coast Range and on both sides of the river towered splendid mountains. We noticed that on the right bank the tops of the ranges were cut into rugged angular peaks. Great saw-toothed ridges seemed piled in confusion and above timberline white patches of snow separated the dark rocky peaks. In the shadowed canyons, blue fields of ice told of small glaciers. On the left hand the mountains had been rounded off by glacial action with broad fields of snow, capping everything above the dark green timber.

For a great part of the day we followed the tortuous course of the river over the Hudson Bay Flats where the valley widens and the silt of the upper courses has been deposited. Treacherous but not dangerous navigation, frequent groundings and vexatious delays in getting off was my sole impression of this part of the river. For three hours we wound back and forth across the valley in sight of Cone Mountain, near the base of which is Mud Glacier, a dirty colored glacier carrying tremendous quantities of debris from the hills.

Late in the afternoon we arrived at "The Canyon," which is also called "Cleutchman's Canyon" because the cleutch, or squaw, can steer the canoe through this piece of water, whereas it takes all the man's skill to handle the boat above this point. As a matter of fact, we found this the worst piece of water on the whole river on the way down but possibly this was because the river had later risen greatly because of melting snow and continuous rains. This box canyon is about 700 yards long at its widest part and fifty yards wide with perpendicular walls that rise straight above the water fully 100 feet. It reminded me greatly of Miles Canyon above White Horse where so many of the Yukon miners lost their lives in '97 and '98. It lacked the rapids at the foot, but made up for this by a swift bit of water above the canyon.

Here it took all the power the "Mount Royal" possessed to make any headway and even then we found it necessary to run out a line to a tree on the bank. This hawser was carried to the winch and helped materially to pull the steamer through. We tied up for the night just after passing the canyon at Kirk's Creek.

After supper I fished up this little brushy stream and in less than half an hour had pulled out three Dolly Varden trout measuring eighteen, twenty and twenty-three inches. It was not a great deal of sport as the stream was very brushy and I had great trouble casting. On the way back to the steamer I jumped a small black bear that made off rapidly through the underbrush. As I was armed with only a fishing pole I had no interest in this bear, but was mightily cheered by this sight of game.

July 2nd, my birthday, was to be our last on the "Mount Royal," as we expected to reach the head of navigation at Telegraph Creek before night. We cast off from the bank early and about noon tied up at Glenora to unload some freight for the trading post there. Glenora was a town of thirty log cabins in the days of the Cassiar gold rush but its sole inhabitant when we arrived was Mr. Tervo, who traps and trades with the Indians and acts as customs officer for the Canadian government. While they were unloading cargo we wandered back through the woods to hills above the river. The afternoon had turned out clear and warm; the woods were carpeted with brilliant flowers, and berries grew everywhere in profusion. We could hardly realize that we were not in California, but close to the Arctic Circle.

We left our skiff in the care of Mr. Tervo, as Telegraph Creek was only twelve miles away and the two worst places on the river lay between Glenora and Telegraph.

We decided that one river trip through the "Three Sisters" and the "Great Riffle" would be enough, and it was. However, the steamer made it without accident, although once our stern was swept within a few feet of one of the "Sisters" and I fully expected to see our paddle wheel smashed to bits.

Telegraph Creek, where we arrived at 8 p.m., we found to be a village of about 100 souls of which 90 percent were Indians. It contained cabins for five times this number as the result of the boom of 1868. It boasted two trading stores, one owned by the Hudson Bay Company and the other by Frank Calbreath, whom we had engaged to outfit us. On landing, we were offered our choice of all the vacant cabins and selected one that was soon made clean and comfortable.

We wanted to see something of the canyon of the Stikine above the head of navigation, of which we had heard stories on every hand. Therefore, on July 3rd, we started with only light packs on our backs to follow the north bank of the river. We followed the old trail running out to the Hudson Bay Company's post on the Liard River. After a twelve- mile walk we reached the Tahltan, a stream of considerable size that flows into the Stikine from the north. The trail had followed closely the edge of the Stikine but was several hundred feet above the water. For most of the distance the river has cut its bed through successive lava flows, leaving steep walls between which the turbulent stream boiled over rocks in a precipitous descent. Telegraph Creek is the head of navigation for anyone who does not want to get wet.

At the Tahltan, the lava flows - four in number with gravel beds between - are clearly discernible in the walls. The trail after crossing the river climbs up fully 1,500 feet onto a plateau. At this point the Tahltan and the Stikine come together at a very acute angle, leaving the high plateau shaped like a hairpin with a width of not more than a quarter of a mile, and a length of nearly four miles. We were told that in former years the Indians drove the caribou onto the plateau from which they could not escape down the precipitous cliffs that fell away to the river on all sides. Here their winter's supply of meat was killed in a single drive.

We found a trapper named Ira Day who had a cabin on this plateau and he agreed to put us up for the night. The next morning, July 4th, we pushed out six miles further on the Dease Lake trail as far as the Tuya River, another tributary of the Stikine. Just at the point where the trail drops over the edge is located an old road house called "Wilson's." It is fast falling to ruin but some of the furniture and especially the bar remains. What stories it could tell, this outpost of civilization, of

An Indian named Packer Johnny

Packing equipment up the mountain with guides

the eager enthusiasm and blasted hopes of the early gold seekers. While we were boiling a pot of tea an Indian with two packhorses arrived. He had been packing supplies to Dease Lake for a prospector, who for years had clung to the hope of finding pay dirt in this territory.

This Indian rejoiced in the name of "Packer Johnny," wore a straw hat, loud-checked vest and heavy gold-plated watch chain. It developed that he had been Andrew Stone's guide and we found later that he bore a splendid reputation as a hunter. He told us he had seen many caribou in the Haitaila Mountains and we tentatively decided we would have a "look- see." Together we returned to Ira Day's cabin where we had a supper of caribou and bear meat to celebrate the 4th of July.

The next morning we started for Telegraph Creek and covered the seventeen miles before noon. My feet were in bad shape; in fact, after our tramp I counted eleven separate blisters. My boots were doing the damage and I obtained a pair of moccasins from Day's cleutch and hoped these would solve the trouble. We put in most of the afternoon getting our outfit together, buying supplies and packing up. We found prices high at the store of Frank Calbreath, but when we considered the long haul and the dangers of navigation, we decided they were fair.

We were off early on the morning of the 6th, piloted by Packer Johnny with our equipment carried on a packhorse. We were traveling over the trail that was already familiar to us but we found new wonders in the deep canyons that we circled. At Ten Mile Creek we camped for lunch and were overtaken by eighteen Indians on their way to Tahltan to fish for salmon. All their household goods were packed by either the dogs or the women. The men carried nothing except a gun if they possessed one. In the afternoon we made four miles more, camping on the farther bank of the Tahltan. We were not tired but Packer Johnny had an eye on possible festivities among the fifty or sixty Indians camped here to fish.

As we passed through the camp, we left an order for some moccasins and I was astonished to see the cleutch who had undertaken to make them produce a small-sized sewing machine from under a pile of skins. The Singer Sewing Machine Company and the Winchester Arms Company are never far behind the whiskey people in reaching out into frontier country.

Packer Johnny appeared about 4 a.m. the next day, much the worse for wear. Native hootch must be powerful stuff judging from the headache he complained of. I threw away my boots as my feet were getting into very bad condition and tried

Preparations for a meal after a long day

the skin shoes. By noon when we arrived at Pleasant Camp my eleven blisters were doing nicely - most of them had broken. At this camp we loaded up with moose meat from the carcass of a young bull that Packer Johnny had killed on his way down.

Night found us at Mosquito Camp, thirty-one miles from Telegraph Creek, giving us seventeen miles for the day. This place fully lived up to its name for the little pests were as thick as the grass. Our backs, where we could not switch them off, were literally so covered with them that you could hardly see the color of the cloth and nothing but our head nets and gauntlets saved our being drained of every drop of blood in our bodies.

After supper, a Hudson Bay Company pack train of forty-one animals came into camp, bringing another army of mosquitoes. While we were all huddled in the smoke of a ring of smudges, one of the packers looked up and swore he saw three mosquitoes carrying off the hind quarter of a mule over the tops of the trees. We could not question his veracity because the next morning when we left they were short one animal in the roundup and we all agreed the mosquitoes were large enough and voracious enough to carry off an elephant.

The next day, July 8th, the country flattened out and we made splendid time covering twenty-one miles. The going was, however, hard on my feet and at noon I found another blister as big as a dollar. The timber on the flats was smaller but denser and everywhere swampy land increased the mosquitoes.

Late in the afternoon we reached the Tanzilla River, the last of the rivers that join from the north to make the Stikine. Here I essayed a swim but before I could get my clothes off and into the water the mosquitoes nearly carried me away in pieces. One cannot be clean and full-blooded in this country.

We turned up the Tanzilla River and all the next day followed its banks. After three hours walking, Packer Johnny showed us the Haitaila Mountains, our promised land. Their beautiful snow-capped summits promised freedom from mosquitoes and thrilled us with the thought that when we reached their farther side we should be on the Arctic Slope. These mountains are part of the Continental Divide and their drainage reaches the Arctic Ocean through the Liard River, which finds its way into the Mackenzie.

We kept along the main trail over the Continental Divide to the head of Dease Lake, which drains into the Liard River. Here we turned off and traveled for fifteen miles south along the eastern slope of the Haitaila Mountains, which are really a continuation of the Rocky Mountains. After we left the beaten trail, both we and Tilly, the horse, sank to our knees frequently in the swamps. The whole country had been burned over and the down timber made frequent work with the axe necessary before we could get through at all.

Toward afternoon we reached timberline and pitched our tent. Timberline is a misnomer. Really, it was only the highest point at which we could find even stunted trees from which we could get wood for our fire. It was a wind-swept, cold vista that lay before us but the scenery was magnificent. Below us, as far as we could see, stretched the tundra in a never-ending succession of rolling hills. To the north lay Dease Lake, surrounded by snow-capped mountains; to the west and south were nine smaller lakes nestling among the spurs of the Haitaila Mountains.

The next day we discovered a more comfortable camping spot about three miles away and moved our gear. Just as we arrived, we noticed Packer Johnny in earnest contemplation of a distant hillside. I studied the landscape carefully with my glasses but could make out nothing except scattered rocks on the tundra. At supper he announced that he had been watching a caribou and showed us where it was. At last we located it but even through our glasses we could not make out its movements as well as he could with his naked eye.

About 6 p.m. we struck out after the beast and as the wind was wrong for the only direction in which we could make the stalk, we each carried a load of wood with which to build fires on our route. When the fire was blazing, the Indian piled on some damp moss and, down the smoke thus created, we traveled in our approach.

After a good deal of creeping and crawling we reached a pile of rocks not forty yards from the unsuspecting beast. We both fired and the caribou came down with two holes behind the shoulder. It turned out to be a young cow, which even so early in the season had accumulated considerable fat and provided us with a plentiful supply of fresh meat for our stay.

On the way back to camp with a load of meat we heard a whistling and among a pile of rocks not far off sat a groundhog or marmot. As I had never seen one before, I shot it and was greatly surprised at its size and weight.

The next two days it snowed hard and we were confined to our blankets most of the time except during our meals that we cooked and ate standing around the fire. I tried a short hunt but did not venture far from camp. I found some ptarmigan which, on account of the storm, had a decided aversion to taking wing or even running over the soft snow. Although shooting a .30-30 rifle, I was able to knock off enough heads to fill the pot at camp. I saw also a few willow grouse and a drummer grouse had to be killed in order to get some peace in camp. The drummer had located a hollow log quite near our tent and made quite a din most all day. On the 15th, although it still continued to snow, we climbed up onto the ridge above us and studied the surrounding country through our glasses. After about an hour Johnny located a herd of animals some three miles away as they were crossing a snow field but was not sure whether they were sheep or caribou. We started the stalk at once but it was five hours later before we came up with them and found thirty-three caribou among which there were three good-sized stags.

We had covered some very rough country to get within range, often waist-deep in snowdrifts or crawling up precipitous, rocky slopes. The last quarter mile was through soft snow and our hands were very cold when we looked over the last little ridge and saw the animals scattered out within 100 yards and feeding quietly.

We each picked out a stag and both fell at the first shot. The herd appeared panic- stricken with fright and started to mill about so that it was impossible to get a clear shot at the third stag. In the endeavor to bring him down, Coogan shot a cow that got in the way of his bullet.

As soon as the caribou located the direction from which the rifle reports were coming, they started to circle us to get our scent at about 150 yards. This spread out the bunch and I was able to bring down the stag.

As it was the middle of July, the horns were still in the velvet and none of them had reached their full growth. As trophies they were poor, but while we had nothing to take home to prove our prowess except the hides, we had had all the joy of the successful chase. On our way back to camp we made a detour of four miles to the camp of Bob Reed who was prospecting the country. We told him of the four caribou on the hill and he was greatly pleased that his supply of meat was assured for a considerable time.

In this country there was no danger of the meat spoiling as the ground was frozen eighteen inches below the surface and when the meat was placed in a hole and covered over with a couple of feet of moss it soon froze hard. We, therefore, had the satisfaction of knowing that none of the meat was wasted. The next morning we awoke to find it still snowing hard and the guide counseled us to start back or it

Indian fishing camp at the Tahltan

might be some time before we could cross the fifteen miles of swamp that lay between us and the main trail. As it was, we mired the horse down to the rump four times and had to unpack and pull her out. We were lucky to get out at all during this spell of bad weather. When we reached the main Dease Lake trail we camped at once and spent four hours thoroughly drying out our clothes and equipment.

Our trip back to Telegraph Creek of eighty miles was accomplished in four days of steady hiking. We tarried a few hours at the Tahltan to watch the Indians catch salmon, which were at the height of their run. They used a pole about nine feet long with a three- hook grapple fastened with a thong on one end. They moved the butt end of the pole slowly about in the muddy water till they struck a fish working its way upstream; then they quickly reversed the pole and generally hooked the fish with the grapple.

The Indians were laying in their winter supply of dog feed and as soon as a fish was landed, a cleutch cleaned it and carried it off to the nearby frames where it was smoked and sun-dried.

We reached Telegraph Creek on July 16th and the next day walked the twelve miles to Glenora where we had left the boat. This completed our tramping and our log showed we had covered 188 miles in ten days actually on the trail, or an average of 18 8/10 miles per day, exclusive of ground covered in hunting. We were a bit footsore and the prospect of sitting still in a boat for a few days held unspeakable charms for us.

At Glenora, Mr. Tervo gave us a splendid meal, drew us diagrams of all the bad water on the lower Stikine and accompanied us five miles down the river to Shakes Creek to have a try for bear.

On landing here we scrambled over windfalls for four hours but not a sign could we see of a bear and finally we pushed off on our 160-mile trip to Wrangell with a good deal of trepidation as every one had assured us we were the first people to tackle the river without some swift-water experience, of which we were woefully lacking.

Our fears were not groundless, for in less than an hour we were whirled into the midst of Dutch Charlie's Riffle and before we knew it the boat was full of water. We were overboard trying to swim it down the center of the rapid and keep it clear of the jagged rocks that poked their heads above the foam.

The next fifteen minutes we shouted directions at each other across the boat but the roar of the water drowned our voices. Suddenly we shot out into the smooth pool below and soon swam the boat to a sandy beach where a fire dried out our clothes and blankets. Our sugar and salt were irretrievably lost but the flour bag was only caked a little on the outside and the beans and rice a little swollen.

The next day we had regained a little of our courage in the splendid sunshine and as we worked our way down the river we saw smoke issuing from the trapping "tilt" of Capt. Conover and Wilson at Clearwater Creek. We put in and received such a hearty welcome that we stayed the night and reveled in their reassuring talk about the three bad places remaining on the river.

The following morning we were off early to get it over with and half an hour later were piled up on a rock in the middle of the Devil's Elbow. Here the river makes a right- angle bend and the whole stream piles up against a steep cliff. The trick is to run this rapid on the inside edge of the curve but stay just in the swift water so as to avoid falling off into the back eddy.

We were fearful to get as near the cliff as this required, and in spite of all the advice we had received, the first thing we knew we were in the back eddy and being whirled around and around in spite of our best efforts at the oars. Finally, we were thrown out into the main stream and before we could get steerage way on the boat, were piled up broadside on a rock that capsized the boat and dumped us in the stream. Carelessly, we had not tied in the bag of provisions and cooking gear and these were lost. The rest of the stuff was secure and when we came out at the lower end of the rapids, we were able again to swim the boat ashore and right it.

Two miles below, the next bit of bad water was Grand Rapid Slough, which we got through safely although we came on it so quickly that we took the wrong channel and bumped badly a couple of times. There only remained the Grand Canyon. Although it is called Cleutchman Canyon because it is supposed to be the safest piece of bad water on the river, we found it actually the worst because the water was low. We shipped a little water at the riffle at the head of the canyon but the rest was soon over as the cliff-like walls sped past us at express train speed.

While it was only shortly after noon when we emerged, a little deserted cabin at the lower end of the canyon looked so inviting that we camped at once. Here we dried out and while all the food was gone and we went to bed supperless, we were content that all the bad places were behind us.

Early the next morning we heard a porcupine gnawing the underpinning of the cabin. We pictured him in an old rusty pot that we had found and crawled quickly out of our blankets. We soon dispatched him with a stick and later in the morning found a companion for him that assured us of two days supply of food. Truly, porcupines are named the "Prospector's Salvation."

It had rained hard all day and the next morning, with the continued downpour, the river had risen three feet and big driftwood was running in the swift current. The two following days it still poured and it was not until July 23rd, after four days at the cabin, that we pushed off, spurred on by our lack of grub. Besides the two porcupine we had killed only one duck that we ravenously ate almost bones and all.

The high water on the Hudson Bay flats had deposited many snags - great trees whose roots had caught in the rocky bottom and whose tops bobbed out of water rhythmically in the swirl of the current. To have run the boat onto one of these would have meant that the next moment we would have found ourselves and boat thrown upside down in the river, thrown over by the rising stick. The steersman was kept on the "qui vive" watching out for them and picking the main channel, which in the Flats proved most elusive. We camped for the night on a little island without any idea as to our position as we were only able to guess that we had covered about thirty five miles.

The next morning, after only a short row, we came in sight of the Great Glacier and were agreeably surprised to find we had made such good progress that we were only thirty-three miles from the mouth of the river. We landed on the terminal moraine and climbed up the face of the glacier. We found, however, that without nailed boots the going was so slippery as to be dangerous and the deep blue crevasses did not look inviting. We gave up our climb and were soon back at the river and pushed off again on our trip to Wrangell.

Two hours later we arrived at the international boundary and found an American survey team headed by Mr. Morse. We had dinner with them and after our fast of the past few days we devoured most of the food in camp. Never did canned peaches and corned beef look so good to human beings.

One of the surveyors wanted to go to Wrangell so we had an extra hand on the oars for the rest of the trip. We planned to camp at the mouth of the river for the night, crossing to the island in the morning when the outgoing tide served better; but the letters we knew were waiting for us and the prospect of more food made us push on and by shortly after 7 p.m. we pulled alongside the wharf at Wrangell.

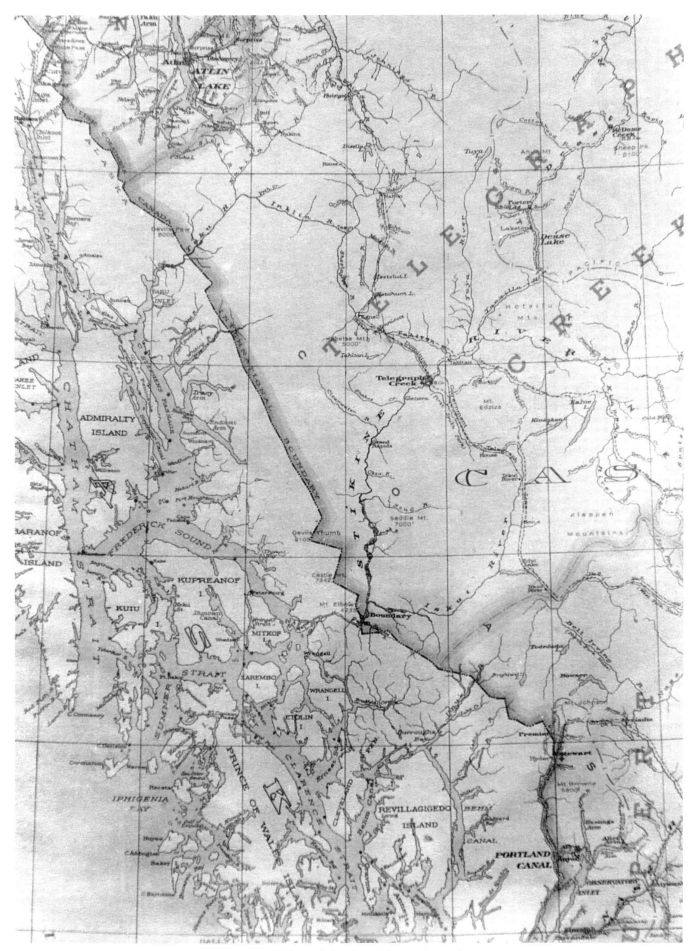

A map of Telegraph Creek and the trip in 1904.

STIKINE RIVER

We had travelled on the river actually only twenty-four hours, which figured out that we had covered the 160 miles at 6 2/3 miles per hour. After three interminable days wait at Wrangell we sailed on the "City of Seattle" for Skagway. The trip north was rainy and a low-lying fog hid the wonder of the scenery. This was of special regret to Coogan who had never seen the Lynn Canal. We hoped for clear weather on our return trip and were not disappointed.

We arrived at Skagway on July 29th and put up at the Fifth Avenue Hotel. We had hardly unpacked our bags when we heard violent weeping and in the hall near our door found a woman in tears huddled on the floor. She sobbed out a story to the effect that she was on her way to Fairbanks and someone had stolen $1,200 out of her trunk. Coogan was most sympathetic and wanted to call the police or take up a collection. When he suggested we start a fund with a substantial donation, I began to laugh. I had seen the game worked so often in the three previous years on the Alaska boats at Dawson and Nome that I thought it had died out with three-card monte and the pea-and-shell game.

Coogan was furious with me for my cold bloodedness but when he saw the woman pay her hotel account later in the day from a large roll of bills he decided he had misplaced his sympathy.

The next day we wandered out to the cemetery to see the grave of Jefferson Smith - Soapy Smith - who in the early days had been the terror of Skagway. Soapy had arrived with the early rush of miners but had found Skagway a more profitable field for his gambling operations than the gold creeks. He derived his name from a confidence game that long had been practiced in the frontier towns of the West. The operator mounted a platform in the street posing as a soap salesman. He soon collected a crowd by his antics and then with a great flourish he placed five and ten dollar bills inside the wrapper of a number of cakes of soap, which he apparently dropped onto the pile in front of him. Each one in the crowd was sure he knew which cakes of soap contained the prizes and when the cakes were auctioned, the operator gathered in his profit as he had previously palmed the five and ten dollar bills.

Smith was so successful in his gambling operations that he obtained control of the city administration, appointing his friends as deputy sheriffs. Thereafter his own "games" ran undisturbed and all others paid tribute to him. Complaints finally reached the U. S. government officials at Juneau and they dispatched Deputy Sheriff

"We push off on our 160-mile trip."

Cabin at Cleutchman's Canyon

Reid to arrest Smith. Soapy immediately sent back word that Reid would be killed as soon as he stepped onto the Skagway wharf. A few days later he sent his henchmen to meet the incoming steamer to carry out his threat.

Reid landed but no one dared open hostilities. Soapy heard of it and hurried to the dock. As he approached the representative of the law, he started firing and when the smoke cleared away both Reid and Smith were dead. The grave of Reid is marked by a monument inscribed, "He gave his life for the honor of Skagway." Back of the cemetery Reid Falls tumbles down the rocks - a most lasting memorial to this hero of frontier days.

Our last day in Skagway we decided to spend tramping over the old White Pass trail of 1897. We wanted to see how hard a trip this was so as to better judge the hardships of the early "sourdoughs."

We started off at 8 a.m. loaded only with our cameras and after reaching White Pass City about ten miles out, climbed up a narrow gorge known as Dead Horse Gulch. The numerous whitened skeletons among the rocks bore silent testimony to the loss of pack animals along the trail. We could picture the despair with which the gold seeker saw his horse go down. It meant that an extra 150 to 200 pounds had to be carried on his back over the pass. Abandoned stoves and camp gear of every description proved that many loads had been lightened in this gulch and that much of the equipment sold to ignorant cheechakos by the outfitters of Seattle had been found unnecessary.

Most of the little bridges across the stream had been washed away in the spring for the past four years, and we found it necessary to leave the main trail for a detour around the face of a cliff. We had climbed up about 200 feet when I missed my footing on a steep place and slid about twenty feet. I caught my fingers on a ledge just at the edge of a straight drop of more than 100 feet. Here I hung for what seemed an age, not daring to move. The camera on my back felt like a ton weight supplying just the necessary load to overbalance me. Coogan fastened together his camera strap and his belt and by working his way down carefully, lowered the end within my reach. It was a ticklish moment while we wondered if the straps were strong enough before I hauled myself up to the ledge where I had a finger hold. We sat quietly for a few minutes to regain our nerve and thereafter kept pretty close to the floor of the gulch, even though we had to wade knee-deep through the stream in several places.

"Soapy" Smith's Grave

We reached the summit of White Pass at 1:30 p.m., five and a half hours out of Skagway. We had lunch at a section house of the railroad and started on the return trip, which we covered in four and a half hours. The trail was seventeen miles long, which made the day's trip thirty-four miles, the best day's walking we had done on our entire trip.

The next day, August 1st, we boarded the "S.S. Jefferson" for Seattle. We were favored by splendid weather, and gave ourselves over to lazy enjoyment of the ever-changing panorama of sea and mountains, of snow-crowned peaks and densely wooded slopes of luxuriant vegetation at the water's edge. For a thousand miles the steamer threads its way among the islands, through channels where the waters run deep and often swiftly on the changes of the tide. Sheltered from the swells of the Pacific by the many islands, the sea was as quiet as a lake, and even in crossing Dixon's entrance and Queen Charlotte Sound, where for a few hours the vessel was exposed to the open sea, we fortunately found the same calm prevailed.

We arrived at Seattle August 5th, and the following morning sailed for San Francisco on the "City of Pueblo," where we landed at daylight, August 9th.

Laura Sherman Gray

Prentiss Nathaniel Gray

The bungalow at Grand Lake

Paper mill at Grand Falls

[44]

Newfoundland

1922

Gray's third and fourth journals were written about his 1911 and 1920 trips to Central America, Panama and Austria, and are not in this book. The fifth journal was written in 1922 about his trip to Newfoundland and becomes the third chapter of this book. The original Newfoundland journal is bound with brownish cranberry cloth and leather with printed marbled endsheets of brown, tan and cream color.

On the morning of September 1st the steamer "Kyle" drove into Port aux Basques at full speed in spite of the narrow, tortuous channel that in places leads close to the rocks. It was hard-a-starboard, then hard-a-port until a hundred yards from the dock the anchor rattled out to swing us around and we backed into our berth at the railroad wharf. The overnight run from North Sydney had been smooth as a pond, so Laura and I left the ship with healthy appetites at 6 a.m. However, we were destined to undergo a lengthy customs examination and purchase our shooting licenses before we could obtain breakfast on board the narrow-gauge train that stood waiting.

We had heard mostly pessimistic reports about this railroad but our inspection disclosed a train of two sleeping cars, spotlessly clean, an excellent diner where the food was ridiculously cheap in comparison with New York prices, two-day coaches and two baggage cars - quite a long train for the diminutive locomotive. Our speed during the next ten hours averaged less than eighteen miles per hour and there was considerable jolting and rocking but the ever-changing view from the car window fully compensated for the rough roadbed. Altogether we were agreeably disappointed as not once did we leave the rails as we had been led to believe was this train's invariable habit at least once each trip.

The country around Port aux Basques is a bleak, barren waste with not a tree in sight. It is "the country God gave Cain." The houses of the villagers cling to the rocky walls and cod drying frames are perched on every semi-level spot. It is fortunately true that exposed coastlines the world over are not to be taken as indicative of the true character of the country behind them. And so here it proved, for before many miles the aspect changed. First scrubby trees and alder brush added a touch of green to the brown marshes, then a dense growth of spruce, "var" and birch covered the gently rolling hills.

At Curling, on the Bay of Islands, the road skirts a bluff that falls precipitously to the ocean. Below us the narrow arm of the sea lay shimmering in glorious sunlight. To make the picture complete and to add a thrill, a whale spouted. Here and there dories "jigging" for cod dotted the water and offshore a short distance lay at anchor a fleet of "bankers," as the fishing schooners that go out to the Banks of Newfoundland are called. There was a coldness in color of the water; a hardness in the grey lichen-covered rocks; the air had lost its languor. Here the North begins.

At Humbermouth the railroad leaves the coast and winds up the narrow gorge of the Humber River. This is one of Newfoundland's best salmon streams and its dark pools at the foot of white rapids held out a tempting invitation.

We were only two hours late in reaching Grand Lake where Mr. J.H. Whitaker took us to his house, the Bungalow, and whetted our appetites for the hunt by giving us our first dinner of caribou meat.

We put in most of the next two days repacking our plunder into eighty-pound loads that looked much too heavy to me but which Whitaker assured me the men could handle. We made a short trip to a hill at the northwest corner of the lake to gather blueberries, which grow in profusion on the high ground. We were not the only berry hunters for eighteen Canada geese, our first sight of game, flew within gunshot protesting with loud honks against our invasion of their favorite feeding ground. After circling the hill they decided to leave us in possession and flew off to a nearby swamp.

We received, too, our baptism of fire from the black flies that swarmed about our heads and nipped any piece of exposed skin to our infinite distress. Frequent and generous outpourings of citronella only seemed to increase their voraciousness. We returned to the Bungalow considerably disturbed but fortunately at no other place during our whole trip did we find the pest so bad. On the open marshes we occasionally had to put on our head nets when there was no wind, but we later learned that Grand Lake enjoyed throughout the island the reputation as the blue ribbon place for black flies.

NEWFOUNDLAND

We left the Bungalow on the afternoon of September 3rd by rail. The road reaches its highest elevation (about 1,500 feet), at the Topsails. This must be a stormy place in winter for on both sides of the track for many miles were snow fences eighteen to twenty feet high. In spite of this protection, every year there are periods of several weeks when the train cannot get through because of the snow drifts.

Close to midnight we got down from the train at Grand Falls, where our guides were waiting for us. Here the Harmsworth interests have a very large paper mill turning out 150 tons of paper a day - enough for all of Lord Northcliffe's publications. Surrounding this mill a typical lumbering town of 5,000 people has grown. We wanted to look over this plant so on the morning of the 4th I started the four guides off to pack part of the outfit out seven or eight miles while we remained in town. We had a most interesting afternoon going through the mills, from the power plant at the Falls of the Exploits River to the shipping room of the mill.

We had engaged four guides, Francis King, William Cormier, James MacDonald and Andrew Young. All were from the St. George's Bay region and made their living in the spring and summer in codfishing and "going to the ice" for seal. In the fall and winter they guided and trapped. Hardy, sturdy men, they were capable of carrying an eighty-pound pack all day, on which they used a special harness that I had never seen before. This was a broad breast strap that slipped down across the chest just below the shoulders. Above was a head strap, which, after the load was adjusted to their backs, carried most of the weight.

Francis King was the head of the party by virtue of his long experience in guiding "sports" - a term that annoyed us greatly but which they always used in referring to foreign sportsmen. King was of French descent; tall, angular and, despite his forty-nine years, as agile as a bobcat.

He was never still and when excited about something, which he was most of time, his hands waved with the speed of an electric fan. It took little to excite Francis - a fox track or a beaver house was sufficient provocation and likewise stirred all the wells of optimism in his nature. Every time we approached a beaver pond Francis would point to the house and assure me that it contained "the three little 'uns from this year, the three young 'uns of last year, and the two old 'uns."

This is all the house could contain providing a full litter was whelped each of the last two years and none had been killed or driven away. It seems to be generally

Francis King, one of four guides

William Cormier stirs the pan

[48]

believed by the trappers in Newfoundland that the beaver does not have as large a litter as on the mainland, where the average is four and numbers sometimes as high as eight. I could find no one who had seen a litter of more than four and all agreed that the average did not exceed three. To Francis it was always a certainty that the full number were there. This optimism almost cost me the chance of getting my caribou head as each stag we saw would be surpassed by the next one and I was cautioned not to shoot.

I have never seen a better woodsman than Francis, but like most Newfoundland guides, he was a poor hunter. Caribou have been so plentiful and so easy to approach that no special care was necessary in stalking them and if a stag became alarmed and made off there was always another to be had just around the hill. This has bred a carelessness in the Newfoundlander that was astonishing. We did not make a single perfect stalk and the fact that we approached within gunshot at all on two occasions was due partly to luck and partly to my positive refusal to approach directly downwind.

MacDonald was a Scotchman, a quiet, taciturn man with an analytical way of looking at you that made you feel your gravest question was trivial. He was about thirty-five years old and had spent most of his life "to the ice" or in the woods. Evidently this life had its rewards for he had acquired a farm at Heatherton, a Scotch settlement of thirteen families where they all spoke Gaelic. His quiet way of doing things for our comfort - building seats and tables, adding extra spruce boughs to those already gathered by the other men for our beds, soon made us very fond of him.

Mac had "some learning" and he came to be the authority about camp as to the weather and distances. He was the only one of the guides who understood how to read a map and so helped me considerably in correcting and properly locating on the map the lakes and brooks that we crossed. While he finally lost some of his reserve with us, his cautious Scotch nature always came to the fore when imparting a story or a bit of information. "Folks in Bay d'Espoir allow it's true," he would say in telling us a story, "but I can't altogether find myself believing."

But there were other elements in his character besides this wariness of making positive statements that had earned for Jim MacDonald a reputation for honesty so that William could say: "A man ye and the Missus can trust all the time. He will never be fooling ye, Jim MacDonald."

William was the bosom friend and lifelong companion of Francis. They had shot their first caribou together at the age of thirteen and ever since had lived as neighbors. William was engaged as cook but it is doubtful if he had ever acted in this capacity for a party before.

He explained the first day out: "I am clean and I can cook simple grub such as we eats, but maybe ye may not be liking my cooking as I ain't much hand at cooking for gentlefolks."

We forgot how heavy were his biscuits and how watery his baked beans when we realized that he spent most of his waking hours trying to make "The Missus" more comfortable and in earnestly wishing that the "Skipper" would get a head.

He was as French as Francis, with a fierce black mustache that belied his pale, almost watery blue eyes.

He explained: "I never had no learning but my wife has lots. Everybody to home found it funny when she married me, she is kind of a lady and can read any book." But we did not find it funny when we learned his kindheartedness and true gentlemanly spirit.

Andrew's only claim to fame was that he had married Francis' daughter. He was a strong, husky lad of twenty-four years but every muscle of his body was paralyzed with laziness or stupidity, we could not determine which. In any case, he had always the lightest pack and chopped the least wood. Francis was busy doing double shift to cover Andrew's shortcomings and the other two men hated to stand silently by and see this.

One day William exploded with, "Sometimes, Missus, I get so vexed at him I could let a screech out of me."

Andrew had been to the war. He enlisted at eighteen "for a kind of picnic" but he was all done with fighting as the "grub was no good." He could not remember whether he had landed on the other side in England or France and while he was quite sure he had been in one town in Belgium for eighteen months he could not recollect the name of it.

We left Grand Falls early on the 5th. All the men carried packs of more than sixty pounds and I undertook a thirty-pound knapsack and the three guns that weighed at least twenty pounds more. We had miserable going most of the way through windfalls and burnt timber.

The country had been burned over seven years before and was now a tangled mass of alder thickets interlaced with fallen trees. After the first two miles there was not a sign of a trail and I was curious to know why MacDonald, who had trapped in this section for eight winters, had not cut a trail over which he could have more easily packed in his winter supplies. MacDonald explained that he feared he would be followed and his traps robbed by men from Grand Falls who were too lazy or unskilled to put out a line of traps of their own. Here and there throughout the woods we found marshes (pronounced "mash" in Newfoundland), which were a great relief to our legs, tired by stepping over windfalls. The marshes, however, were soft and at every step we sank to our ankles and occasionally went in knee-deep. We were very glad to reach one of MacDonald's trapping huts at 4 p.m. and although we only had covered 7 1/2 miles we called it a day. Laura was pretty well done in and probably it was too long and hard a hike for her first day.

We only had rested an hour in camp before Francis and MacDonald were off with their axes to cut the windfalls out of our trail for tomorrow. These men each had packed 140 pounds over this trail in the past two days and had energy to spare to cut the trail ahead. I began to marvel at the Newfoundlander. After about two hours MacDonald returned with a bad cut in his knee. His axe had slipped on a dead pine and cut a two-inch gash deep to the bone over his knee cap. We soon had it dressed and MacDonald made light of it.

The next morning we broke camp at 9 a.m. in foggy weather and after a short piece through downed timber we were out on the marshes. Because of MacDonald's knee and Laura's stiff leg, we decided to move only four miles but it was 1:30 p.m. before we had covered this distance. The going was soft on the marshes and in the fringes of timber between them we encountered many windfalls that made progress exceedingly slow.

The afternoon was busily employed getting up a semblance of a permanent camp while two of the men went back to pack up another load. On their return shortly after 7 p.m., we ate supper by the light of a wonderful full moon that shone through the rifts in the clouds and dissipated the gathering darkness. The clamor and struggle of New York seemed on a distant planet as we sat there in the silence of the Newfoundland wood with only the crackle of the fire and the murmur of the men's conversation in their tent to recall the fact that we were in a physical world.

As MacDonald's knee was still badly swollen, we decided to remain in this camp a couple of days. We were beginning to see caribou tracks and the men

Andrew Young carries wood and an ax

Guides rest on marsh with camera equipment

assured me we might find a stag at any time.

With Francis the following morning, I started to hunt a big marsh that lay to the north of us. After an hour's tramp over boggy tundra we saw two caribou feeding west in the center of the marsh. One was a cow and the other a three-year-old stag with a small head. I was anxious to shoot as we needed meat in camp but Francis insisted we would see plenty of caribou nearer our permanent camp to which we could pack the meat easier. After watching the two caribou for a half hour, I suggested we see how close we could come to them before they saw us. We walked straight toward them on perfectly open ground and had approached to within 150 yards before the cow saw us. Her snort galvanized the stag's attention and for fully five minutes they stood motionless, watching us. Then, at a hesitating trot with a stop every few steps to see what we were doing, they started to circle to leeward to catch our wind.

They did not appear particularly frightened and some freakish slant of the wind carried our taint over or away from them. The cow kept rising on her hind legs or jumping with all four feet off the ground to sniff the air higher up but evidently their fears were not confirmed for they began to feed again before they had traveled a half mile.

We started our last pack at about 9 a.m. on September 9th. We had only four and a half miles to cover to reach our permanent camp but it was slow work as the first mile was straight uphill through fallen timber. The balance of the distance was through open marsh country, wet and soggy under foot. We passed up through one big marsh that was fully two miles long, dotted with ponds and here and there a "droke" of stunted timber. While we were "biling the kettle" at noon, somebody saw a duck swimming in a nearby pond. After an elaborate stalk and a great waste of ammunition, I succeeded in bagging it. This, with a rabbit that Andrew had found in his snare this same morning, was our first bit of meat and we welcomed it as a relief from the diet of biscuits, oatmeal and beans. At about 2:30 p.m. we reached the end of this marsh and camped on higher ground on the edge of the woods. Francis and Andrew started back shortly for the rest of the stuff and the rest of us busied ourselves in making a comfortable camp.

We made our camp on the little hill between two great marshes. Our tents were pitched just inside the wood so as to be on dry ground but by moving a few steps to the edge of the swamp a beautiful panorama to the south and west was spread out before us. In the foreground the dun-colored marsh stretched away for two miles, splashed with the gray-green drokes; over beyond, the blue hills south of the Exploits River; to the westward, Hodges Hill stood up, a barren knob.

The next morning I started with Francis and MacDonald to hunt the big marsh that runs to the northwest of us beyond Hodges Hill, which enjoys the name of "Forevermore Marsh." We covered fully twelve miles of heavy going, sinking every few minutes up to our knees in the bog. We did not see a single caribou but had a little practice with the .22 rifle on a flock of ptarmigan. Out of the flock of nine we bagged eight, which was not due to good shooting but to the stupidity of the birds, which ran along the ground only a few yards after each shot and were easily followed till all were killed but one. We reached camp at 6 p.m. well tired out. During the day, I heard the heat, the sunshine, the lateness of the season, the flies and a dozen more things blamed for our failure to see caribou. Tracks we found aplenty and some were of good-sized stags so we felt hopeful that sufficient perseverance would bring our reward.

The next three days were a repetition. Long hours of "slogging" over marshes, varied only by still-hunts in the dense woods where it was almost impossible to move without stepping on a dry branch whose sharp crackle you were positive could be heard in Grand Falls. We had some hours of fog when we could not see fifty feet ahead and more hours when the black flies swarmed about our heads till we sought the cool of the woods or found a height where a breeze carried them away.

I could well understand why the caribou would not venture out on the open marshes in this hot weather and preferred the dense woods where, by merely moving about under low-lying branches, they could be used as efficient fly brushes against the few of these pests that were found in the shade.

We saw a few Canada geese during these days but found them so wary that it was impossible to approach within range of the small rifle. We were obliged to confine our hunting to ptarmigan, which at least furnished food but little sport.

Late in the afternoon of the 13th we returned to camp hot, tired and discouraged after a long day on the marshes. I had just cooled off with a swim in a nearby pond and was trying to photograph a friendly Canada jay when I heard Laura running up the trail to the camp calling at the top of her lungs, "Bring a gun. I don't know what it is but you ought to see it."

I grabbed a gun and camera and just at the edge of the wood, not forty feet from where our trail emerged onto the swamp, I saw a caribou cow feeding peacefully. She had approached down a lead that we had tramped over in the morning. She had crossed the trail entering our camp that we had used continuously all day and yet she showed no alarm at our scent.

I stood behind a tree and took a moving picture of her but the clicking of the camera seemed not to disturb her. She took only a mouthful or two of moss when she found it necessary to shake her head violently and trot on a few feet to escape the flies that swarmed about her. Doubtless this so distracted her that she had failed to catch our scent when she crossed our well-trampled trail. For twenty minutes she wandered over the marsh within a hundred yards of us and finally passed on into the woods. Just as we turned back to camp and supper, William spied another caribou across the marsh, which the glasses showed to be a young stag. It took us but little time to make the approach and at 118 yards, after two very poor shots, he fell to the third, which struck him in the ham and passed lengthwise through him.

I was at a loss to account for the two first shots going astray until I asked Francis and MacDonald how far it was. They guessed 225 and 200 yards and I myself should have said more than 200 yards. When we measured the distance I realized that I had been taking in too much of the front sight. Whether it was the marsh or the deceptive light at 6:30 p.m. I cannot say.

The stag turned out to be a small one, not over four years old with only fifteen points. However, the meat was a welcome addition to our larder as we were all getting tired of a near-vegetarian diet. Somehow birds and rabbits do not satisfy the craving for meat and even these had been scarce. Two rabbits and eight ptarmigan for six people for eight days could hardly be called a surfeit. Still, we had done well on an otherwise vegetarian diet and had tramped many miles. It did not take long before the men had the stag cut up and had carried the hindquarters back to camp. Later we put the forequarters in the lake to keep so that none of the meat might be lost.

The day following promised to be as hot as its predecessors, so we decided to work around camp and hunt only in the evening. We were busily engaged stretching the young stag's skin on a frame when a crash in the brush announced a visitor. We jumped for the guns but before we could get even a glimpse of the animal it had made good its flight. The tracks were those of a fair-sized stag that had approached

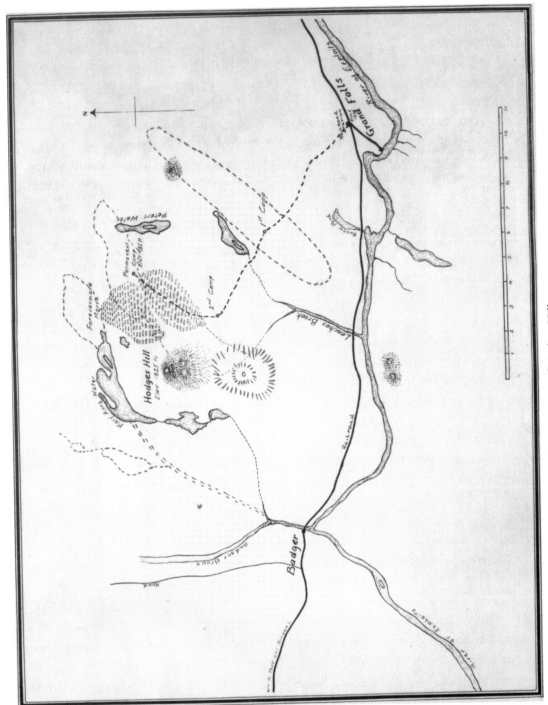

Gray's survey map of Hodges Hill country

within twenty yards of camp before it took our scent. As we traveled a short distance along its retreating track, it seemed impossible that an animal of any size, especially one with antlers, could pass through the dense growth. After the first crash or two it moved away without a sound.

Never before have I deliberately hoped and prayed for bad weather but as each succeeding day brought clear skies and hot sunshine it began to look as if our chances of getting a stag were small. As we had walked every foot of the open country and realized the futility of hunting the dense woods where we could not see thirty feet ahead, we decided to turn our attention to mapping until the weather changed.

I wanted to reach the top of Hodges Hill, both to locate its correct position on the map and to view the surrounding country. The side toward us appeared steep and heavily timbered so we followed a small brook around the southern end of the Hill as the approach looked easier from the western side. Part way up, the brook grew shallow with many riffles. We could see some good-sized trout in the pools and we tried chasing them into the shallows. A half-hour's splashing and grabbing amid shouts of laughter as we slipped on the stones and took a ducking gained us thirty trout from six to ten inches long. Though thoroughly wet, we enjoyed this fishing as well as taking them with rod and flies.

Almost at the top, at an elevation of 675 feet, we found two beautiful little lakes nestling between the southern and northern knobs of the hill. They were little gems hidden away among the trees and while we were enjoying this surprise we saw a beaver swimming in our direction. He came within twenty yards of us and seemed unafraid but curious as to the three unfamiliar objects perched on the bank.

We finally made the top at 3:30 p.m. and what a view was spread out before us. In the clear air we could see at least fifty miles in each direction. From the Topsails to salt water at Norris Arm, from the ranges south of the Exploits River to north of Twin Lakes - Newfoundland lay at our feet, a panorama of lakes, woods and marshes.

When we arrived on the rocky, barren top, I laughingly said, "Mac, I wish you would run down to one of those lakes in the marsh and get me a drink of water."

In two minutes he appeared with a big mug of cool, clear, water from a spring that he had found right on the very summit among the tumbled rocks. It was most welcome and washed down our lunch of bread and cheese.

We spent an hour taking various observations to locate the hill and the surrounding lakes. From the top of the hill we could see the tower at the paper mill at Grand Falls and also, westward along the railroad, the town of Badger. With these two points as a base, we laid off angles to the various lakes. We checked our observations further with the bearing of the Main Topsail and Millertown Junction.

Subsequent calculations showed that Hodges Hill was misplaced on the government map. We located it three and one quarter miles to the north of its plotted position and we found that the lakes as shown on the existing surveys were entirely incorrect, both as to form and size. We were able to plot in two new lakes of considerable size in addition to the two ponds near the summit of Hodges Hill. One very large lake which the government survey showed to be eleven miles long, we found to have a length of less than three miles and one six-mile lake claimed by the official surveyors did not exist at all.

Our altitude observations may not have been as accurately made but we carried a compensated aneroid barometer and checked it by half-hourly readings against one in camp. From camp to Grand Lake, I had the barometer carried back and forth four times taking readings at each end of the trip. These checked out quite close. For the altitude of Grand Falls, we accepted the government figure that is undoubtedly correct as it checks with the Reid Newfoundland Railroad Co.'s and the Anglo Newfoundland Co.'s altitude. From these, we made out the elevation of Hodges Hill to be 1,825 feet instead of 2,200, as given by the government.

We came straight down the eastern slope through some heavy brush and timber over very hard going till we reached Forevermore Marsh. It took us a full three hours actual walking to reach camp, so we figured that camp was close to five miles from the summit.

At last, during the night of September 17th, a hard storm came up. The wind hauled into the northeast and was soon blowing a gale, driving before it sheets of rain that seemed to gather momentum as they swept across the marsh.

Even our roaring camp fire, which the men kept piled high with birch logs, was short comfort in the storm. However, we all had prayed for rain and cold and here it was so that none of us admitted that it was anything but what we wanted. We anxiously watched the barometer to see if we could find promise of clearing skies for the next day as the caribou would cling to the shelter of the woods while the gale kept up, just as they had done for a week to escape the heat and flies on the barrens. Only a cold, clear day after this rain would bring them out in the open.

NEWFOUNDLAND

After dinner we were seated around a roaring fire with a side camp stretched over our heads to keep off the rain drip from the trees when we found we were in the land we had always searched in vain for - a land where the people still believed in fairies. Laura was telling the story of Barrie's play, "Mary Rose." When she finished, MacDonald asked if it was true. Laura fortunately answered, "I do not think so."

"But I know a true story," said MacDonald. "It happened on the Labrador and the man who it happened to is an honest man. Six Bay St. George men were fishing on the Labrador and one Sunday afternoon this man lies down in front of the camp in a sunny place and goes to sleep. When supper is ready they calls him but they can't find him nowhere. All that week he is gone but the next Sunday at the same time, in the same place, handy to the camp, there he is lying fast asleep."

"When he wakes up he tells them he has been back to Bay St. George, that the fairies took him over on a piece of birch rind and that he had been to a funeral and a wedding - just who everybody was there and who was the corpse. There was a good fairy in those who took him on the birch rind and she told him not to eat nothing or he would not get back, so he was most starved."

"When they got done fishing after three months and they came back home, they found that just what the man said as to who was the corpse and who got married was right but not a bit of writing had any of them had from home. So it must of been the fairies what took him."

William, not to be outdone, told of how "poor father" (he and all the other men always referred to his deceased parent as "poor father"), had on several occasions found the horses' manes braided "such as none of us could come to fix them."

Francis, who was a Catholic, knew positively of a Methodist minister who was traversing a lonely road near Bay d'Espoir when the fairies attacked him and took off all his clothes. I suppose even a Methodist minister once in a lifetime is entitled to some bad luck, but it is fortunate it happened in Newfoundland because a New York congregation would probably never accept such an explanation.

What a joy it was for us to hark back thirty years to our youthful days and in the light of the campfire with the stars shining though the tops of the trees to believe again in the little people of the woods and glades.

The next morning all our hopes of the weather were realized for the sun was shining brightly out of a clear, cold sky. Francis and I were early out on the marsh

Forevermore Marsh - perfect wildlife habitat

Laura Gray reads in camp.

as everyone in camp foretold that such a day was all that was necessary to bring the caribou out of the dense woods in droves. As soon as we left camp, the effect of yesterday's downpour was evident. Every caribou lead was turned into a rivulet; every brook was over its banks; every pond full to the brim; and the whole marsh, even on the high places, oozed water and quivered for several yards ahead under our footsteps.

The going was hard as we sank over our boot tops every few steps but we laboriously made our way down Forevermore Marsh. About noon we reached the brook where we had caught the "trouts" two days before but, while the fish were still apparent in great numbers, the shallow places in the brook had all disappeared in the greater volume of water that flowed past.

While we were eating our lunch we spied a flock of ptarmigan and soon knocked over six with the .22 rifle. This was the only game we saw for we circumnavigated the marsh without seeing a caribou or even a fresh sign. I say circumnavigated advisedly, for we actually waded nine-tenths of the twelve miles that we traveled this day. Not to see even cows or small stags under these ideal conditions was a sad disappointment as it proved that the caribou were so scarce that finding a good head was extremely unlikely.

In spite of the lack of game we had a wonderful day. The clear blue sky; the touch of fall in the air; the great lonely stretches of brown marsh dotted here and there with ponds whose only mission was to flash back the brilliant sunlight; the fringe of grey, moss-draped trees in the distance; the white moss-covered hillside of the barrens - velvet to the feet; this was the picture I shall remember of this country.

But I could not bring myself to quit this territory without one more try. I wanted to hunt the small marshes through the woods so we started early the next day to the eastward and although the going was terrible after the heavy rain, by noon we reached Peters Waters, about four miles from camp. From the summit of Hodges Hill we had noted that this country was densely wooded with small marshes scattered here and there. It was, however, very difficult to find these little marshes in the thick tangle of the woods and a good part of our time was spent trying to break through dense underbrush.

The only game we saw was a red fox gingerly picking his way across a marsh, trying to keep his feet dry. He disappeared into a patch of woods before we could get close enough to shoot. We reached camp late in the evening, tired and wet and thoroughly discouraged because we had not seen even a fresh sign of caribou.

Doubtless there were caribou in this territory last fall and even this spring and summer. We have seen old tracks, and shed antlers, aplenty, but only four caribou and two of these we saw virtually from the camp door. From our camp we could "spy" over at least five-square-miles of marsh and hardly an hour of the day had passed but someone in camp had gone over every foot of the country with the glasses. The only conclusion possible was that something had moved the caribou out of this territory and we imagined that this was either the big forest fire south and east of Grand Falls this summer or the blasting to the northward by some men clearing out a brook in which to drive logs this fall.

There seemed to be no lack of feed. The ground was well-covered with caribou moss on which the caribou feed largely in spring and fall and the trees were festooned with "maldow," which, when the snows are too deep to dig down through, gave them at least sufficient nourishing food to sustain life. The ponds were full of lily pads that some claim form an item in the caribou diet and the dense underbrush of the woods should have provided ample browse. Yet the caribou were not here. In fact the lack of all animal life surprised me. During our seventeen-day stay in this section we had seen only four caribou, twenty-one ptarmigan, eighteen geese in three flocks, six black ducks, seventeen northern divers, one beaver, two rabbits, one fox, two loons, a few Canada jays and not more than a dozen small birds. However, millions of black flies and mosquitoes had, on warm days, supplied all the animation necessary to the landscape.

With the utmost regret at leaving our comfortable camp, we started our outward pack on the morning of the 20th. We hated to acknowledge defeat but the country to the north, west and east, as viewed from Hodges Hill, appeared heavily timbered for thirty or more miles with only widely scattered small marshes or barrens. To the south beyond the Exploits River was out of the question as the lumbering operations of Grand Falls were in this direction and the woods were full of men. We decided, therefore, to shift our base back to Grand Lake where, with a bit of climbing, we could get up onto the high barrens.

Our outward trip was made without difficulty in two days as we did not have to double pack, and a hot bath and clean clothes were most welcome at Grand Falls.

Our first night's sleep in a real bed was not a great success. Possibly it was the unaccustomed softness of a box mattress or possibly our fear that we would not awake in time to take the train that was due at 3:40 a.m. Finally, as we were doing nothing more than looking at the watch every ten minutes, we got up and dressed. The train, late as usual, came along shortly after 5 a.m. and we crawled into the playhouse sleeping car and went to bed again. At 10 a.m. we arrived at the Bungalow at Grand Lake and were welcomed by the Whitakers, who had prepared a dory that would take us down the Lake.

Repacking and sorting our stuff occupied several hours and by the time we were ready, a southwest wind was kicking up a considerable swell on the lake. At 2 p.m., however, we decided to try to cross to the lee shore. This proved successful, but not without shipping some water and drenching ourselves with spray. However, there it was better and we pulled on till 5 p.m., when we reached Whetstone Point. Here it was blowing a gale and as we could not round this point, we were forced to camp for the night until the wind should blow itself out.

I was up half a dozen times during the night to see if it had calmed down. I was fearful that we would be wind bound within sight of our goal. Every day was precious, as the season was fast drawing to a close. A serious holdup would ruin our chance of getting into caribou country. Unfortunately, we were on the wrong side of the lake, for back of us, almost to the western coast, stretched only forest, in which it is impossible to hunt, while across the lake from the tops of the first ridge, the great barrens on which we hoped to find the caribou stretched eastward for forty miles.

When I crawled out at 5 a.m. for another look at the weather, it was apparent that the wind was hauling into the northwest, so I called the men and we made all haste to break camp and stow the dory. It was not, however, until 6:30 a.m. that we finished our breakfast and pushed off clear of Whetstone Point. By this time it was almost dead calm and a heavy fog had settled down.

At 9:30 a.m. we arrived at Barbers Cove and thought to go ashore to rig up a sail as a gentle, favorable breeze promised. Just as we were about to land, a stag stepped out of the brush and viewed us with great curiosity. We quickly looked over his antlers but as they were small, we decided that his fate was to be photographed. As the weather was still thick I had taken out none of the cameras and even the bustle of getting them out of the packs did not disturb him for he kept on advancing toward us till he was not more than twenty-five yards away. There he stood for fully two minutes, eyeing us gravely and wondering what all the clicking

Laura Gray, right, in camp with a guide

was about as I shot him three times with the camera. Then he trotted quickly off into the brush.

We rigged our sail and thereafter, with its help and the oars, made slightly better time, arriving at the Narrows at 1:30 p.m., thirty miles from the Bungalow.

Grand Lake is the largest body of water on the Island. It stretches northeast and southwest for fifty-eight miles with an average width of three miles. Whitaker's house, the Bungalow, is at the northeast end of the lake and from here, twenty-five miles down the lake, is Glover Island. This island is itself twenty-five miles long and about three miles wide, rising at its southern end to a height of fully 600 feet above the lake. All the shores and the island are heavily timbered with fir and spruce with scatterings of birch, juniper and scrub maple. This growth of timber makes the development of a lumbering or pulp-wood industry inevitable and already there are surveying parties working on the lake. It is rumored that next year will see a big power plant erected to draw water from this lake and that the axe of the lumberman will desolate the shores.

Once ashore at the Narrows, with the dory secured in the Narrows River, we proceeded to repack, leaving in a cache all our surplus stuff. I discovered that the men considered their blankets as surplus and were leaving them behind. They proposed to set up a side camp or fly, and with a fire before it, assured me they would be warm and comfortable.

We took the trail at 4 p.m. straight up the mountain to the eastward of the Narrows and in the first four miles rose 1,375 feet above the level of the lake. The trail leads through some splendid woods where the fir and spruce stand straight and clear with very little underbrush. Everything is carpeted with low ferns and vivid green moss and it seems as if a windfall is hardly down before the moss begins to cover it. I was greatly surprised to see juniper eighteen inches in diameter and forty feet high as I had always considered this a scrubby, stunted tree growing generally on the edge of marshes.

We pitched camp at timberline four and one-half miles from the lake and Francis and I climbed on up to Maxim Young's lookout on the top of the ridge to view the country and see what sign we could find of caribou.

Sixteen hundred feet below us lay Grand Lake, reddened in the light of the setting sun, its shores clearly defined by the dark green forest that came down to the water's edge. To the east and south of us stretched the barrens as far as we could see. Blue Hill rose sharply out of the plateau and just south of it in the fading light we could make out the gash in the hills through which South River finds its way into Grand Lake. This was to be our hunting ground and I was interested in appraising it from the point of view of the miles that we were bound to tramp over it. It is certainly a country of magnificent distances and the "footing" appears not to be as swampy nor the woods as numerous or as dense as the country we had left at Hodges Hill. Although the next day was Sunday, we left camp at 9 a.m. and after five hours of hard walking in which we covered only six miles, arrived at an old trapping camp that Francis had built several years ago on the slopes of Blue Hill. We began to see fresh signs of caribou soon after leaving our first camp and in the territory approaching Blue Hill we found the tracks of numerous large stags.

After lunch we were soon on the ridges of Blue Hill but we searched till almost dark without seeing a caribou. Francis located a white spot about two miles away as a caribou lying down on the edge of a droke, but a long and successful stalk proved it to be a weather- beaten old tree. We were almost back to camp when we saw a small, two-year-old stag get up from behind a rock, 150 yards distant, and view us with suspicion. We stopped in our tracks and with great deliberation he approached to within forty yards. As the evening was too far advanced, we could not photograph him and were content to admire his stately disregard of our presence after he had satisfied himself we were nothing to fear. He soon fed away from us over the crest of the hill and we made our way back to camp.

We were up on the barren early the next morning and our first survey of the country to the north showed four scattered caribou at least a mile away so that we could not tell whether there was a head among them. However, this determined our hunting ground for the day and we struck off at once with a much better feeling than we have had at any time on the trip. Before we reached our position to leeward of them, we almost bumped into an old cow who paid not the slightest attention to us, so busy was she fighting flies. I was afraid to try to photograph her for fear she might take fright and disturb the caribou to windward of us.

After we were up on the height to leeward of where we had seen the four caribou, we could locate none of them. After a great deal of searching, Francis saw two white spots on a little marsh fully a mile further on but MacDonald swore they were rocks. We worked, however, in this direction and as we cut down the distance it became apparent they were two caribou lying down in a position that afforded little cover for a stalk.

Francis and I tried the approach, leaving MacDonald to watch for other caribou. When about 300 yards away one of these caribou, an old cow, saw us, she promptly stood up for a better look. We froze immobile and it was fully fifteen minutes before she began to feed again. This allowed each of us alternately to crawl back to shelter while the other watched her every move carefully with the glasses. After we reached cover and were planning another way of approach, MacDonald appeared with the announcement that there was a big stag just over the hill from where these two caribou were feeding. We had not seen the second of these caribou from near at hand as he was lying down in a little patch of junipers on the edge of the marsh.

Yet we dared not go to windward of them to look for the big caribou MacDonald reported as they would take fright and run over the hill, probably taking the other caribou with them.

We decided to have at least a look at this second caribou and tried a stalk up a little gully. This was successful and our friend the cow did not see us till we were within sixty yards. Her snort put the stag on his feet in a second and as he trotted onto the little piece of marsh we saw to our surprise that he had a real head. I fired but, to my horror, he still stood on his feet. The second shot went true behind the shoulder and he was dead as he fell.

We did not then go nearer but ran over the hill after the frightened cow to see if we could catch a glimpse of the big stag MacDonald had seen before she alarmed the stag. It was, however, in vain, for he had departed. However, while we were searching every little gully with our glasses, Francis, looking back along our tracks, threw his hat in the air with a whoop.

"There's the big head, look dere," he said.

Sure enough, half a mile east of us, slowly working his way along with four cows was a splendid stag. It was a Radclyffe Dugmore picture. The old stag, marshalling his four cows ahead of him, had his head lowered as if the weight of his antlers bore it down. He was not eating as he walked as were the cows but appeared only to be gazing stupidly at the ground just under his nose. He was alert, however, for when one of the cows strayed off behind a little hummock he threw his head up and was after her like a shot. With a vicious hook he drove her back to the others.

We were off on the run in a big circle to head them off without giving them our scent. We must have traveled a full mile through the "tucks" or scrubby spruce about two-feet high, over boggy places, in which I floundered knee deep. All in vain, for their walk, which appears slow but is indeed fully five miles an hour, carried the caribou ahead of us at the point where we expected to meet them. We were faced with the problem of paralleling them to windward, and our only choice was to run down a little brook in the hopes that the wind would not carry our scent up onto the higher ground where the caribou were walking.

We ran hard down this gully for half a mile until I felt I could not travel another foot. MacDonald urged me on and soon Francis poked his head over a little knoll and announced the stag was "right handy." He certainly was, for not more than fifty yards separated us, but one of the cows had seen Francis' head and when I

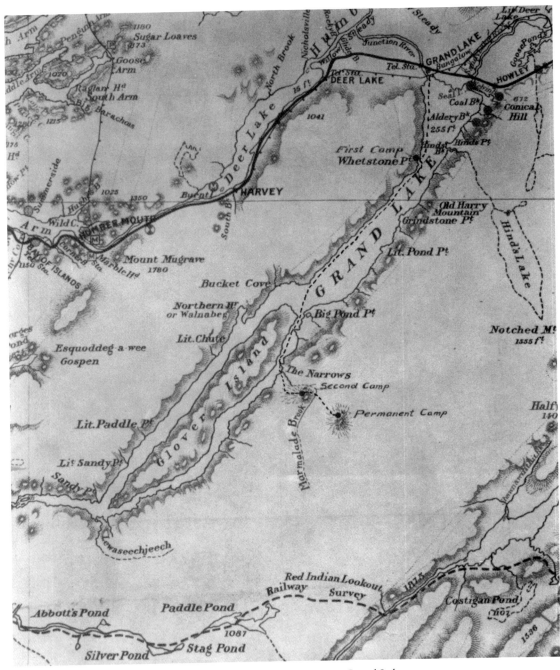

Gray's map of second expedition to Grand Lake

looked over they were milling around the stag ready for flight.

I had a standing shot, however, but for some reason the gun miss fired and the click of the hammer started them off. By the time I had thrown in a new shell they were in full flight and in the hurry, or perhaps because of my pounding heart, I overshot the stag.

They made off while Francis swore and waved his arms. Finally, I stopped his gesticulations long enough to explain that I wanted him to stand still so I could fire again using his shoulder as a rest as the "tucks" were too high to see over when kneeling down. By this time they were just entering a little wood 265 yards away. I raised my sight to 300 yards and let drive. The answering thud as the bullet struck the stag's hind leg and his kick were frankly a surprise, though a most welcome sight. As the caribou came out the other side of the woods, we thought the stag was not with them and we started in high hopes to search the wood. Here was sign of blood but it had begun to rain hard and as we followed it, the sign became dimmer and dimmer, washed away by the driving downpour. Finally it was gone altogether and we were forced reluctantly to turn back.

Dejectedly, we decided to go down and see how large the first stag was. We had only just arrived and were congratulating ourselves that he carried a symmetrical head with twenty-six points, when MacDonald cried out, "There's the beast."

Sure enough, our big fellow was up on the crest of the hill, slowly picking his way along, dragging one leg.

We were off again at even a faster pace. The rain was pouring down and the fog was drifting in. Finally, after half a mile uphill run, we reached the top of the hill but no stag was in sight. The fog was so thick we could not see a hundred yards and we felt beaten again. However, we kept on along the crest and finally Francis saw a shadowy shape making along a little ridge. We started once more on a parallel ridge to get ahead of him. Try as hard as we could, we only just kept abreast of the stag and the fog was too thick to shoot at what appeared only as a ghost, although he was not actually more than a hundred yards from us.

Finally, he stopped a moment and we gained the head of the gully where the two ridges joined, just a minute ahead of him. As he came over the ridge we first saw the tops of his antlers and noted that each carried at least four points. Then his whole head came into view and I could see by his open mouth and his generally dejected appearance that he was spent and doing his level best to escape. Doubtless he had seen or scented us in the fog and was traveling as fast as his remaining strength allowed. I raised the gun and to my disgust found that the rain had clouded the lens of the telescope sight and I could see nothing through it. I tried to wipe it but found I could not get it clear. The stag was coming directly toward us not more than forty yards away so I unfastened the telescope and decided to try with just the ordinary sight, which I had never used on this gun. The shot went true and he fell with a broken back.

He was a big stag but the head that had appeared so large in the foggy light had only twenty-seven points. It was well-shaped, however, and the chase was an exciting close to the season's hunt. I had killed my limit and although we were dead tired and the rain was coming down in torrents, we put back to camp with light hearts. However, long before we made out the smoke where William was baking bread, we realized we had had nothing to eat since 6:30 that morning and it was now close to 5 p.m. We were also very cold and wet to the skin. All this had been forgotten in the excitement of the day as we had been pretty busy with the ten caribou that we had seen since morning.

When we arrived in camp, I sent William and Andrew posthaste off "to the shore" as these fisherfolk always call the main base of supplies, to fetch the large moving picture camera. I did not bring in the big camera as I expected we would have to travel a much greater distance before we found a head, and the extra sixty-pound weight would hamper our movements.

We awoke the following morning to find the ground white and snow aplenty falling. The men were sheltered in a log cabin that Francis had built as a trapping base some years before. Although a bear had torn off a part of the roof and the tin stove was a mass of rust, they had a fire going and we found the cabin much more comfortable than my tent, which was sagging down with the accumulating snow.

The cabin was only eight-by-eight feet and four feet high at the eaves - rather small quarters for five men, especially as the center was occupied by our makeshift stove set on a big rock that was too hot to get very close to and the space under the hole in the roof had to be avoided on account of the rain and snow. The height made no difference as none of us stood up for longer than necessary on account of the smoke, which seemed to dodge the hole in the roof and hung like a pall about three feet above the floor.

The hours dragged, although occasionally someone looked out and reported hopeful signs of clearing. The conversation during these two days of confinement to the cabin centered on caribou and "furing." We had heard at the Bungalow that a war threatened between England and Turkey but the men had no interest in the subject and I steadfastly put everything out of my mind that had to do with the outside world. I wanted a complete rest and I made myself believe that a war in the Near East was too far distant to even think about. Newfoundland and its caribou were all that mattered.

The books of Selous and Millais and the photographs of Radclyffe Dugmore had inspired my trip to Newfoundland. I imagined that great herds of caribou still roamed the island and that big heads were to be had by hard work and industrious hunting. But after four weeks we had seen only sixteen caribou, which was less than Millais had seen on his poorest day.

Continuously I had sought the answer from the people of the country and their explanation had invariably been that the timbering operations around Red Indian Lake were responsible. This lake, paralleled by Victoria Lake, lies southeast of the "Reserve," across which the great migrations formerly took place. The government has assiduously policed the "Reserve" with game wardens, but after passing through this sanctuary where no one is allowed to shoot or even camp, the caribou encountered the timber camps, cutting for the pulp mills at Grand Falls. These camps lie directly in the line of the migrations between the "Reserve" and the high barrens where the caribou winter. During the past ten winters, 3,000 men have taken a ghastly toll of the herds as the animals worked their way south. A six-month's supply of meat for these men has been killed and I heard many stories of reckless slaughter and a great waste of carcasses.

Mr. Whitaker, who lives on the edge of the "Reserve," told me that for the past four years there has been no migration. I take this as a comparative statement meaning that only a small percentage of the old herds have passed and that most of these have crossed the railroad right of way unobserved at night.

Certain it is that each year more and more caribou are wintering in the same section where they feed during the summer and spring. They are only moving great distances when they are driven on in search of food by the "glitter" that sometimes locks the country in its icy hold. Certainly the caribou are becoming more wary and are not exposing themselves in the open country. They are learning they are safe by day in the dense woods and that neither black flies nor men can disturb

Caribou cow almost enters camp.

A small caribou stag steps from the woods.

them on the marshes at night.

While I appreciate that we were hunting at a time when the heat kept the caribou under cover, it was astonishing that in the variety of country traversed and the variety of weather experienced we did not see more caribou or at least more fresh tracks. The inevitable conclusion is that the caribou have been greatly diminished in numbers.

Still, I am convinced that a part of our failure to see caribou was due to the guides themselves who will have to adapt to the changed conditions and learn to hunt with greater care. Their present slipshod methods of approach are startling to one who had hunted in countries where game is scarce.

William and Andrew reached camp with the cameras at 1 p.m. from Grand Lake. They were cold and soaked to the skin and I felt mean for sending them on this tramp in such weather. However, after a cup of hot tea and when their clothes were warm, they seemed as cheerful as could be. I protested that they get into dry clothes but they assured me they always dried their clothes on themselves. Why they are not all crippled up with rheumatism is a mystery!

The afternoon passed somehow, in our hope that the next day would be fine and that the snow would start the caribou traveling and give us a chance to get some photographs. But we were doomed to disappointment for more than a foot of snow fell during the night and the storm was still driving when we awoke. It looked as if our chances were slim and, what was more serious, the snow made the traveling very heavy and a continuance might mean that we would have to make snowshoes for all before we could get out to the lake. With only two day's food left we decided that we could no longer sit around the fire looking at each other through a smoke haze. Any sort of action was better so at noon we started to bring in the two heads shot on the 25th. We had left them out the 26th and 27th hoping that the weather would clear and allow us to get some pictures of the caribou as they lay. We felt that it was a risk to leave them any longer and in spite of the storm we started, knowing full well that it would be "dirty going" on the soft snow.

When we were clear of the woods in which our camp was situated, we found traveling fully up to our expectations. There was at least fifteen inches of snow on the barren. Every bush was covered; every brook was bridged over; every rock was leveled by the light, feathery snow. We stumbled over the bushes and rocks and fell into every hole on the route, until at the end of an hour we reached the first stag.

Gray's tent began to sag with weight of snow.

So far, exercise had kept us warm, although we were wet to the skin, but when we stopped, first to photograph and then to skin out the stag, we nearly froze. After this job was over we went on to the other stag on the top of the hill, a mile further on. This was even worse as the wind had a clear sweep at us on the height, driving the snow almost horizontally in cutting blasts. However, the job was finally done and we headed for camp. Our trail had been entirely covered and as we could not see more than a few feet ahead on account of the blizzard I wondered how we were going to make camp, but the unerring sense of Francis took us straight. When we arrived after 6 p.m. there was a steaming kettle of tea and soon afterwards a hearty dinner that we ate before changing our wet clothes.

We broke camp at 10 a.m. the next morning as it was still snowing and the last of our flour had been eaten the night before. We had an additional quantity at the Lakeshore but as the weather showed no sign of improvement it seemed useless to pack in additional supplies.

The going was a repetition of the previous day, stumbling through the "tucks," drenched in the woods by showers of snow from every branch we touched in passing. The men fell repeatedly, tripping over hidden snags or stepping into holes. It seemed as if someone was down most of the time and as they could not get up with their heavy packs without assistance, there was considerable delay. I was carrying only thirty pounds and the two rifles but I fell flat thirty-seven times in the 6 1/2 hours that we were on the trail during which time we covered only 9 1/2 miles.

We finally dropped down the hill to Grand Lake and found no snow below the 600-foot level. We arrived at the shore a wet and tired crew but the indefatigable William soon had supper ready and after this we found energy enough to bring the "dory" around from its moorings in the Narrows River.

We were away long before daylight the next morning for fear the wind, which seems invariably to blow from some direction on this lake, would prove unfavorable. When the breeze came with the rising of the sun it was on the quarter so we hoisted the side camp as a sail. By 1 p.m. with four hands rowing and the sail pulling for all it was worth, we landed at Whetstone Point, twenty-one miles from our camp at the narrows.

During lunch it began to rain and sleet and we hastened to get underway again. I had found sitting still in the stern sailing the boat for seven hours, very cold work, but we hoped that the train to Port aux Basques would be late and that we might still catch it so we pushed on. We arrived at the Bungalow about 4 p.m. through a choppy sea. We were a bit wet and cold and found we had missed the train by only two hours. However, we were not down cast at the prospect of a two-day wait at the comfortable Bungalow as it gave us a chance to finish cleaning the heads and skins and Mrs. Whitaker's delicious cooking was an acceptable change from our simple camp food.

We bade farewell to Newfoundland on the night of October 2nd and our last sight of this fascinating country was from the deck of the steamer "Kyle" as she picked her way seaward through the tortuous channel at Port aux Basques. The forbidding coastline softened in the moonlight but the deep, steel-blue waters that now swirled about the rocks carried a hint of their power when driven before a storm - a hint of the ever-changing moods - of the softness and the fury of this strange land.

Seven hours of rowing a boat to reach the bungalow

"We arrived on the shore a hungry crew."

NEWFOUNDLAND

Prentiss N. Gray -
PERSONAL EQUIPMENT

1 Pair woolen mittens
4 Pair woolen sox
3 Pair cotton sox
3 Suits underwear
2 Suits pajamas
2 Cotton shirts
1 Woolen shirt
1 Sweater
1 Filson suit

1 Extra trousers
1 Fleece lined canvas coat
1 Pair woolen puttees
12 Handkerchiefs
2 Pairs boots
1 Pair moccasins
1 Belt
1 Hat
2 Pair shoelaces

Laura Sherman Gray -
PERSONAL EQUIPMENT

1 Pair woolen gloves
4 Pair woolen sox
2 Pair cotton stockings
5 Suits underwear
2 Pair pajamas
2 Woolen shirts
2 Cotton shirts
1 Sweater
1 Riding suit
2 Extra trousers

1 Mackinaw
1 Pair leggins
12 Handkerchiefs
2 Pair boots
1 Pair moccasins
1 Black tights
2 Belts
1 Hat
1 Pair easy shoes
2 Cotton bloomers

GUNS - CAMERAS - SUNDRIES

1 Tarpaulin
2 Perfection Capes
2 Binoculars
2 Compasses
1 Extra Eye Glasses

2 Rifles
2 Telescopic sights
80 - 6.5 mm Rifle ammunition
120-8mm Rifle ammunition
1 .22 Rifle

FROM THE PEACE TO THE FRASER

400 .22 Ammunition
1 Pathe movie
1 Pathe tripod
1000-foot Pathe films
1 Sept movie
1 Sept movie tripod
800 ft. Sept movie films
1 Graflex
8 films
1 Goertz
12 Goertz films
2 Harvey meter
1 Telescopic lens
2 Rifle cleaning rods
1 Fishing rod

1 Reel
1 Fly Book
1 Camera changing bag
1 Rifle cleaning cloth
1 lbs. Tea
2 Sleeping bags
2 Pneumatic mattresses
2 Pneumatic pillows
1 Silk tent
3 Needles and sail thread
2 Drifoot oil
3 Packages pipe cleaners
300 Cigarettes
1 Cigar Lighter
50 Cigars
2 lbs. Pipe tobacco

GENERAL EQUIPMENT

1 Sewing kit
1 Medical kit
2 Mirrors
2 Match boxes
2 Knives
2 Tubes vaseline
1 Can "3 in 1" oil
2 Mosquito head nets
1 Box hobnails
1 Toilet articles kit
6 Cakes soap
3 Towels
6 Packages wax matches

200 ft. 1/4" cotton rope
2 Balls heavy twine
3 Needles for above
1 Sewing Palm
2 3-inch nails
2 Packages toilet paper
2 Candle lanterns
2 Flashlight, 2 extra batteries
1 Thermos bottle
10 Cans Oxo
2 Knapsax
1 Pack playing cards

NEWFOUNDLAND

COOKING AND CAMP EQUIPMENT FOR SIX PEOPLE

2 Tents 8 x 8 with Flies
1 Dutch Oven
1 Large Tea Kettle
1 Small Tea Kettle
2 Frying Pans
3 Stew pans nested
7 Knives
7 Forks
7 Teaspoons
7 Large spoons
7 Mugs
7 Plates
2 Axes
2 Mixing pans
1 Basin

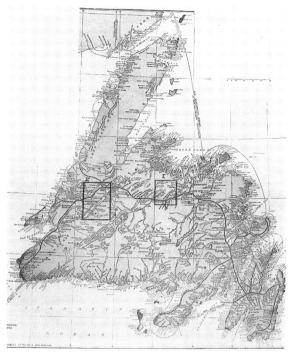

Newfoundland map shows the Gray's
first and second hunt areas.

GRUB LIST FOR SIX PEOPLE FOR TWENTY-FIVE DAYS

30 lbs. Bacon
118 lbs. Flour
5-1/2 lbs. Tea
24 lbs. Sugar
3 lbs. Candles
7 lbs. Baking Powder
21 cans Milk
9 lbs. Jam
12 lbs. Butter
1/4 lbs. Pepper
15 lbs. Dried Fruit
8 lbs. Lard

5 lbs. Tobacco
10 lbs. Hard Bread
10 lbs. Rice
10 lbs. Beans
5 lbs. Cheese
3 doz. Boxes Matches
10 lbs. Rolled Oats
5 lbs. Corn Meal
5 lbs. Salt
2 lbs. Soap
8 lbs. Fat Backs
6 cans Baked Beans

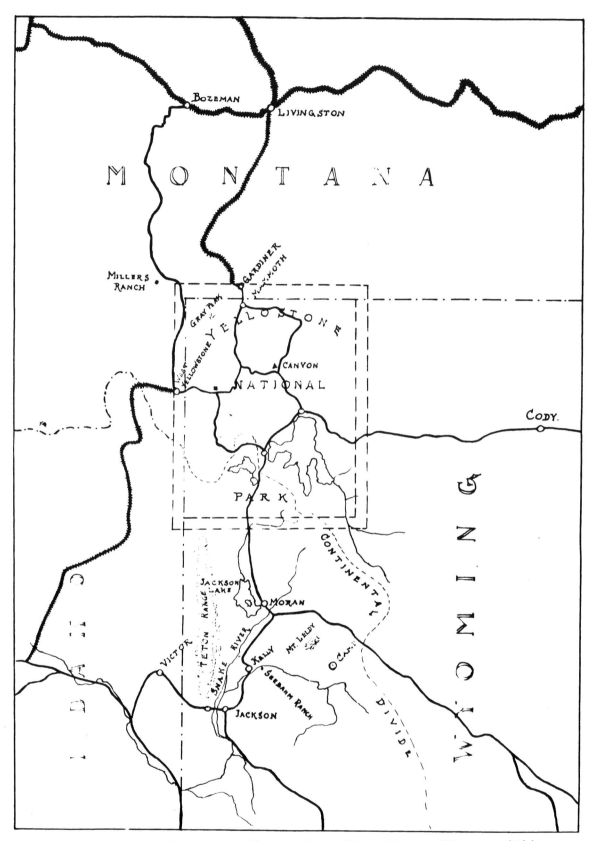

Prent Gray's map shows boundaries of Yellowstone National Park in Montana, Wyoming and Idaho

Wyoming

1925

Journals written in the summers of 1924 and 1925 detail his trips to Gaspe Peninsula, Canada, and are not included in this book, but the eighth journal Gray wrote in September of 1925 about the Elkhorn Ranch of Wyoming is the fourth chapter of this book. Gray searches for elk in Yellowstone National Park with George Bird Grinnell and reports his findings. The journal of his trip to the Elkhorn Ranch is bound in kelly green cloth and leather with printed marbled endsheets of cranberry, kelly green and pale green.

We first realized we were in the mountains when, from the observation platform of the train, we saw a sign reading, "Reas Pass, 6,934 feet Continental Divide."

The slopes of the Rocky Mountains are so gradual that when crossing the continent by rail you hardly grasp the fact that you are climbing. Even the sight of the lofty Wasatch Mountains around Salt Lake City had not impressed upon us the 5,000-foot elevation of the city, nor had the drives up the nearby canyons suggested the typical West. But the printed statement, "Continental Divide," drove home the fact that we were sitting on the top of the United States, and a real "He" breakfast at West Yellowstone of cantaloupe, oatmeal, bacon and eggs, coffee and stacks of hot cakes proclaimed that the real West was at hand.

We climbed down from the train with a few score other tourists, all of whom were bound for Yellowstone Park. The season was practically over as it was September 1st and most of these people acted as if they were afraid the park gates would close before they could get inside. They bolted their breakfast, collected their baggage in little heaps as near the stages as possible, feverishly bought post cards of scenes they hoped to see and boarded the auto coaches in a scramble, only to sit two hours in the boiling sun before starting.

We were not destined for the park but for Elkhorn Ranch on the Gallatin River

Valley of the Gallatin

northwest of the park, and Ernest Miller, our guide and mentor, was waiting for us with a Studebaker car and a Ford truck.

In a very short time our duffle was loaded and we heaved a sigh of deep relief to get away from the tourist mob interested only in doing Yellowstone in four and a half days. Four and a half months would be too little and one of the rangers told me he had been there five years and had only just begun to feel that he knew his corner of the park, its moods, varying every season and every day; its inhabitants of moose, elk, deer, bear and antelope; and its ever-changing coat of brilliant shrubs and flowers.

Thirty-six miles through forests of jack pines and some spruce took us to the ranch. The road parallels the western boundary of the park and for the first ten miles crosses a sandy mesa where the forest grows so densely there is no possibility of seeing either game or the wonderful mountains that fringe the edge of the plateau.

Then the road climbs out of the valley of the Madison River, crossing on rickety bridges one of its tributary streams, Grayling Creek, nineteen times in eight miles, until it reaches the divide and drops dizzily down into the basin of the Gallatin River. Here we got our first views of the gigantic mountain masses that lay about us. Down the valley, Black Butte, in the northwestern corner of the park, towered a splendid boundary post.

It was more than a three-hour drive in the car and lunch at the Elkhorn Ranch was most welcome, as we had already acquired mountain appetites. We had decided on a day's rest at the ranch to repack our gear, try out our rifles and readjust our lungs to the altitude, so that we did not start our pack trip until September 3rd.

We saw something, however, of the surrounding country. Meanwhile, George Bird Grinnell arrived from Washington to look over a proposed new winter range for the elk herd and Miller took us about with him, pointing out the advantages of the open hills on Taylor Fork and the Shedhorn Ridge as winter feeding ground.

Early the morning of the 3rd we began our trip in earnest but it was noon before we were all packed and away. We had started the pack train off at daylight as we proposed to meet them twelve miles ahead at the end of the road. We were taking our duffle in the car to this point so that we might save the horses as much as possible.

At the confluence of Fan Creek and the Gallatin we left the car and threw our first "diamond." It had been many years since I had thrown a diamond hitch, not

Ernest Miller points to his Elkhorn Ranch.

since my hunting days in California, and I found that a Montana diamond is put on quite differently from the one I had used in California. Therefore, I stood back and contented myself with bringing up the loads as a new "dude" should do.

For now we were "dudes;" Laura was, in fact, a "dudine." Since the West became infested with tourists, anyone who goes camping with a paid guide or a rented outfit is a "dude." In Alaska we had been "cheechakos;" in Newfoundland, "sports;" in Austria, "Grunhorner." I believe it hurt most to be called a "dude." The term does not, however, imply contempt, it merely distinguishes the stranger from the natives, called "roughnecks." Still it gave us great satisfaction when we later overheard the horse wrangler tell the cook, "Hell, these people ain't no dudes, they're regular."

Our pack train consisted of five riding horses, two pack horses, six pack mules and a bell mare and all except the bell mare were carrying loads. We followed an easy trail up Fan Creek, climbing slowly till we reached an elevation of 9,050 feet. From this point we dropped down to the headwaters of the Gallatin and made camp for the night.

Miller, Grinnell and I took a short further ride to locate elk but it was not until dark that we found a cow feeding quietly in a meadow. In spite of the failing light we tried to photograph her but were interrupted by a shrill bugle of a bull not far distant. We ran over the hill and there below us were three cows and a splendid six-point bull. It was the first time I had heard a bull bugle and I had expected something like the "roaring" of the red deer stags in Austria or possibly like the "call" of a bull moose. It bore no similarity to either. It was more akin to the braying of a donkey, only it carried through it a shrill whistling note.

We were greatly cheered by this sight of game and returned to camp jubilant at our chance of getting some moving pictures of elk, which was the principal object of the trip. It shows how great a factor luck plays in the picture-taking game. This was the only chance I had of getting an elk picture on the entire trip until our last evening twenty-four days later when I took a bull elk in the Yellowstone under similar light conditions, knowing in advance there was not sufficient light for a proper exposure.

The next morning, after we had waved good-bye to Grinnell, who was returning to the ranch, Miller and I started on our first camera hunt. We loaded the moving picture cameras, tripod and lens case on a white horse named "Wampus" and took our way up to the ridge toward Faun Pass.

Riding horseback up cliffs in Wyoming in 1925

About 11 a.m. we located a bunch of twenty elk in which there was a big bull. However, they discovered us simultaneously, although we were half a mile away, and displayed signs of uneasiness. As it had started to rain, we picketed the horses in the thick timber and ate our lunch to give the elk time to quiet down. After an hour we took up their trail, packing the cameras on our backs. Each of us was carrying fully seventy pounds in unwieldy form. Miller with the tripod over his shoulder and a suitcase containing the telephoto lenses in his hand, looked like a bootlegger or a traveling salesman carrying his samples. Our elk had evidently been more frightened than we figured, for we followed their track more than two miles over rough country before we heard the bull bugle again. These two miles seemed fifty to me, for at that altitude (over 9,000 feet), the least exertion made me pant vigorously. A seventy-pound pack traveling up steep hills is hard work even at sea level, especially after a year at a desk in New York.

Finally, we could hear the bull whistling only a few hundred yards ahead of us and, although the band was evidently traveling, we were urged to greater effort by their nearness. Soon the sound seemed to be repeated several times from the same place and we judged that they had settled down in a thick clump of lodgepole pines. We crept forward and almost stepped on a small bull that was hanging about on the outskirts of the herd trying to steal one of the cows. In this case he served the old bull well, for the youngster went off with a crash, warning the band and taking them all with him.

We now realized it was useless to track them further and started back for the horses. On the way we spied an old cow and hoped she was the outpost of another band. We made a careful stalk but found she was alone and her position in the thick timber did not allow enough light to photograph.

We took the horses up to Faun Pass (altitude 9,200 feet) and at 6 p.m. located the band of elk we had been pursuing all day feeding in a little gully at the foot of Gray Peak. Through our glasses we could see the bull was a magnificent animal with seven points. He was lying down in the center of his herd, bugling at times and keeping a watchful eye on his cows, contentedly feeding about him.

We had two choices of approach, both bad. One had cover but was upwind - the other was a barren hillside with only such protection as we could get by crawling on our stomachs through the grass. As the wind was fitful and not strong, we chose the former and made a splendid approach. We finally reached a point where we

Mule deer rest in the snow drifts

could set up the camera with the old bull, not fifty yards away and his cows still quietly feeding. Suddenly, one of the cows caught a taint in the air and trotted up the hill followed by the whole herd with the bull in the rear.

We missed the picture on film but I shall long retain in memory the sight of this splendid specimen of the largest of our deer, surrounded by his family as he stood in Faun Pass pawing the earth and throwing back his magnificent head to bugle. In the still evening air his exhalations turned to mist and the sound reverberated against the rocky slopes above. It reminded me of an evening in the Johannestal high up in the Alps when we heard the red deer roaring, making the box-like canyon echo with the wild sounds.

We were loathe to leave, but it was already getting dark and before we finished our ride home we were trying to guide our horses through the densest of forests where abundant downed timber made the way difficult even in broad daylight. To add to our troubles, it was now raining torrents.

The downpour kept up throughout the night and breakfast was a wet affair. We were further discouraged by the report of the horse wrangler that Miller's saddle horse and the camera pack horse, Wampus, although hobbled, could not be found.

We decided to move camp but it was a tedious job packing horses in the pouring rain and it was not until 2 p.m. that we started the pack train over the trail through Faun Pass. We dropped down on the eastern side of Gray Peak, making camp on Faun Creek. We had seen one small band of elk enroute and just before we reached our camping place two splendid bulls had come out into an opening near the trail and for several minutes had stood watching us with undisguised curiosity. Unfortunately, it was too late to photograph.

On our arrival at the camping spot we had selected, it took a terrible chase to round up the mules to unpack them and several new brands of profanity were discovered among our several wranglers. Just as we finished supper, Frank Dewing, another cowboy from the ranch, rode into camp with some extra horses and the news that additional supplies and more horses would arrive the next day from the ranch with Harold Elkins in charge.

September 6th was Sunday and we awoke to view a steady downpour of rain. However, by 9 a.m. it had cleared enough to justify Miller, Laura and me in starting after a herd of thirty to forty elk, which during breakfast we had noticed feeding quietly on the hillsides above us and not over a mile distant.

Grand Teton rises above a lake.

WYOMING

After a hard, slippery ride, we reached their vicinity at an elevation of 10,150 feet, but just as we were beginning to unlimber the cameras it came on to hail mightily and we sought the shelter of a clump of jack pines for a couple of hours. Meanwhile, this band moved off and we did not locate them again during the day.

While we were trying to find them during the afternoon, Miller reported a splendid six-point bull lying down just on the edge of the timber and not more than 200 yards away. We slipped down toward him and finally started to set up the cameras behind a fringe of pines. The glasses showed the bull was still sleeping and everything looked very promising.

Suddenly, another bull bugled in the woods nearby and instantly our elk was on his feet. He must have imagined that some outsider was trying to run off with his cows, which, unknown to us, were lying down in the nearby woods, for our quarry started on the run at top speed. That ended our chance and we folded up our camera and started home. A warm fire and supper were most welcome, as we had had no lunch and most of the day it had been snowing or hailing at the higher altitude.

The next morning we were in the saddle early and before we had been out an hour we heard a bull bugle in the thick timber just below us. We hurried down and after locating him, quickly set up the camera at the end of an opening through which we figured he must pass. Just as we finished we saw his horns glistening through the trees at the lower end of the opening and I reached forward for the camera crank and corrected the focus. For 100 yards I followed him in the finder but never did he come into full view. He slipped from one clump of firs to another and each moment we expected that a patch of tan that we could see through the leaves would materialize into a whole elk that we could photograph. He never suspected we were about and nothing but hard luck kept us from getting a splendid picture. When he left, Miller and I just looked at each other, and without a word packed up our things and returned to camp. Neither of us had a word in our vocabulary to express our disgust, although Miller had wrangled mules and I had once driven a bull team in a California logging camp - both good schools for what we wanted to say.

When we reached camp we rounded up the stock. I fear in packing the mules, all of which had to be blindfolded before we could put a pack on them, we blew off our suppressed feelings. Finally at 4 p.m., the job was done and we started for

[91]

September camp on Slate Creek

Laura Sherman Gray powders her nose among wildflowers.

Indian Creek seven miles away.

Just as we were pulling out, Harold Elkins rode in with eight more horses and Frank appeared with the two that had strayed from our first camp. Our train now consisted of twenty-two head of stock, of which eight were mules. We made camp about 6 p.m. at an old corral in a valley at the foot of Electric Peak. We had been greatly cheered enroute by seeing numerous elk and one bull moose. One band of elk comprised more than 100 head.

At the morning roundup two horses were again missing and as we sat at breakfast discussing whether they could have taken the back trail, Laura spoke up, "There's one of them now." We all looked up and saw a splendid bull moose 300 yards away on the ridge-crest, rubbing his horns against a fir tree.

It did not take three of us more than a moment to grab the cameras and start after him and, although the light was bad, we obtained 100 feet of film before he disappeared in the willows in the creek bottom. After we finished with him we felt our luck had returned and tried for a herd of elk on the ridge above us. It was no use, however, as they moved off feeding as fast as we could approach. The direction of the wind prevented our getting ahead of them.

Finally we gave it up and started on our twenty-mile ride to Norris Junction. It was raining hard by this time and not until 8 p.m. did we reach the cheering fire of the ranger's cabin at Norris where Mr. Ord kindly offered us the hospitality of his kitchen and, after we had cooked supper, drove us in his car to the Canyon Hotel.

We were very dubious whether they would let in such tramps but we stormed the place and were soon glorying in the luxury of a hot bath and a real bed. We did not get up till late and when Miller arrived with the cameras at 11 a.m., we took a few pictures of the Yellowstone Canyon and then started after bear, which are quite numerous hereabouts.

Laura was to wait for Mrs. Miller, who was arriving in the car with the children, as she was to go on with them to the Lake Hotel while we were bringing up the pack train.

About 4 p.m. we located an old she brown bear high up on the ridge. She was busily tearing an old log to pieces for grubs when we came on her and, as she was directly below us over a steep cliff twenty feet high, we were able to approach quite close before setting up the camera. For the next two hours we followed this bear over the hillside, taking several hundred feet of film. Finally she showed considerable

Camping near Middle Leidy

irritation and started for the camera, whose whirring seemed to annoy her. She came straight for us and I was about to seek the nearest tree and abandon the camera to her when she changed her mind and turned downhill. I stepped off the distance after she had gone and it was just seven steps away. One more and I should have been up a tree. When the light failed at 6 p.m., we gave it up and started on our sixteen-mile ride to Lake Hotel where we arrived at 11 p.m.

The next morning we loaded all the duffle, saddles and gear in a Ford truck and eight of us - Mr. and Mrs. Miller, the two children, Mademoiselle Stella Ettinger, Laura and I - climbed aboard the Studebaker car and started for Moran in Jackson Hole. We arrived there at 6:30 p.m. with the sun sinking in a blaze of crimson behind the Tetons. It was one of the most glorious sights I have ever seen, but it is useless to try to describe sunsets - it never has been done.

The next day, September 4th, was the first really clear day we had had on this trip and, after we started Mrs. Miller and the children back to the ranch in the car and the truck for Kelley, Laura and I loafed. All day we lay under the trees on the edge of Jackson Lake and filled our souls with the Tetons. One could not absorb so much beauty even in a week of such glorious sunshine days.

After this day of leisure, we were away early. The pack train was light as all the duffle had gone ahead on the truck so we made good time on our way southward. All day our route lay almost parallel to the Teton Range. While it did not rain in our immediate neighborhood until late afternoon, dark foreboding clouds began to gather early about the top of the Grand Teton and Mount Moran. About noon these black masses were torn apart by streaks of vivid lightning as a terrific thunderstorm played about the summits. Deafening peals of thunder reverberated through the valley - the power of the gods was displayed before us.

It was a long, hard ride across the sagebrush-covered floor of Jackson Hole to the little "cow town" of Kelley and before we reached our journey's end it was pouring rain. Saddle weary, wet and cold, we welcomed the fire at the Seebahm Ranch and a cup of hot tea. An hour after our arrival, Edward Tiarks drove into the ranch from Idaho Falls so that our party was now complete.

The next morning we packed thirteen horses and mules and, riding seven with two extra horses light, we started on our way for the hunting country. We proposed to make our base camp on Slate Creek, which flows into the Gros Ventre River at the foot of Mt. Leidy twenty miles from the Seebahm Ranch. Our route took us

Frank Dewing - the horse wrangler

over the slide, which on last June 22nd descended into the Gros Ventre Valley, damming the river and forming a lake seven miles long.

It is estimated that seventy-five to eighty million cubic yards of dirt, rock and trees slid off the mountainside into the narrow canyon at the mouth of the valley. Certainly an inconceivably tangled mass of debris is piled up in the narrow gorge 300 feet high. Above yawns a great open wound on the mountain nearly a mile long and 600 yards wide. Behind this dam has formed a beautiful, peaceful mountain lake whose placid surface reflecting the towering peaks tells nothing of the homes and hopes of the settlers hidden beneath. Several prosperous ranches were engulfed and some of the ranchers escaped on horseback, riding for their lives just ahead of the onrushing mass of the slide.

We talked with one man, named Hough, who told us of his ride and his narrow escape. With his wife and family he had just time enough to mount and ride headlong down the valley only a few feet ahead of the avalanche. Everything they possessed, except the clothes they stood in and the horses that carried them, was lost. His ranch now lies 300 feet under the surface of the water. For twenty-one days not a drop of water flowed down the Gros Ventre River below the slide and the farmers on the lower reaches enjoyed excellent fishing, dipping the stranded trout out of the few remaining pools. Finally, however, when the lake had filled, the water worked its way through the dam near the top and the river has again taken up its normal flow.

The road into this fertile valley now ends abruptly at the foot of the slide and a trail has been cut around the dam. The old road can only be used beyond the head of the lake where it emerges again from the water.

Just at the upper end of the lake, tall red sandstone cliffs rise abruptly a thousand feet, sculptured into fantastic shapes like the walls of the Grand Canyon of Arizona. Their brilliant red was splashed with light green of the quaking aspens that nestled in the gulches on their lower slopes. Here and there a tree had been touched by the frost and had taken on a yellow hue.

At the foot of these cliffs ran the river sluggishly as it approached the lake. Its deepened pools were a rich emerald shade and reflected in their depths was Sheep Mountain which, already snow covered, towered above us.

The storm that had been brewing all afternoon broke as we passed Crystal Creek and let down upon us a torrent of rain. We were glad to turn up Slate Creek

Prentiss N. Gray rides into camp.

and a last pull of three miles brought us to an old corral where we proposed to make our permanent camp. Before dark we were fairly shipshape, and just as we sat down to supper, Fred Feutz, our hunting guide, appeared. He had ridden across country from his ranch on Spread Creek trying to locate game.

The next day was a lazy one. We were waiting for the hunting season to open and we occupied ourselves cleaning guns, greasing our boots and watching the hills through the glasses for elk. We were considerably cheered by the sight of several bands high up on the slopes of Mt. Leidy and the interest in these elk three to five miles away was so great that it was difficult to get any work done around camp.

Our tents were pitched in an open valley (7,200-foot elevation), as we expected snow before we left and had therefore avoided the heavy, damp woods. All about us the low hills, covered sparsely with woods of fir and jack pine, rose gradually, culminating to the north in three peaks of Mt. Leidy.

September 15th: In many parts of the West, hunters were crawling out of their blankets early on this morning. It was the opening of the season for some kind of big game. We were up before daylight but Frank, the horse wrangler, could not locate the horses because of the dense rain clouds that had settled down over everything.

It was not until 6:30 a.m. that we heard the bell of the bay mare that told us that at least the riding stock had been located and were headed toward camp. Although we started at once, it was not before 8:30 a.m. that we climbed above the clouds and found the sun shining in all its glory on the tops of the ridges. Sheep Mountain and Mt. Leidy lifted their heads above a billowing white blanket that enshrouded all the valleys.

We only just had emerged into the sunlight when we heard a bull bugle and Tiarks and Fred started at once to try to locate him. Miller and I worked around the side of East Leidy in order not to disturb their stalk.

We had gone only a short distance when we heard sounds that suggested a bull walking in the thick woods. We made a careful and successful stalk that developed a rascally pine squirrel in a tree dropping nuts which, in the quiet of the forest, made a prodigious noise as they fell. A snowshoe rabbit, which jumped up almost under my foot, startled me out of a year's growth but, aside from this, we saw no game during the forenoon.

Through the middle of the day we hunted in the thick timber and put up two

Whitetail deer graze in Yellowstone.

spike bulls but their lack of "heads" did not tempt our fire. Toward 4 p.m. we found ourselves almost on the summit of East Leidy. As we scanned the country below us we made out a cow moose running through an opening. In examining what had startled her, we saw Tiarks and Fred winding their weary way toward the horses and over Fred's shoulder we could see a red fresh liver. We knew then that Edward had killed and started down the hill at once to intercept them and hear the good news.

We were delighted to learn that he had, after a long and careful stalk, come within range of a good bull feeding on a hillside among a bunch of cows. Three shots from the 6.5 Mannlicher, each of which went home, had settled the affair. We were all greatly pleased at his good fortune and straight shooting. They went on to camp and Miller and I continued our evening's hunt toward Middle Leidy, where Fred reported a bull bugling.

We soon located him and spent the next two hours trying to approach. Once we were within forty feet of him but two old cows were between us and, suspecting danger, started him off through the dense woods. Again we saw his horns and the top of this head just over a little ridge, but it was only for a moment and then he was gone. Meanwhile, the light faded and finally reluctantly we had to admit we could not see the sight on the gun and started for camp where we arrived at 9 p.m. It is a long day from 4 a.m. till 9 p.m.

We were all so anxious to see Edward Tiark's bull that we were away early and by sunup were high on the slopes of Middle Leidy. Close to the top we found the animal and sat about admiring the head, which was a bit irregular but with a heavy beam and good spread. We found that sometime in the life of the bull his right foreleg had been broken and although this had healed entirely, it may have accounted for the five points on one horn while the other carried the regular six.

The men soon had the carcass quartered and after something of a struggle with the pack animals we packed the meat, horns and scalp on the two pack mules we had brought along. Tiarks returned to camp with the outfit while Fred and I started off to locate another bull. We hunted hard but seemed destined to find only spike bulls (eight) and cows (three) and finally at dark we made our way off the rocky slopes of the mountains and returned to camp.

Tiarks left the following morning as he was anxious to reach Vernal, Utah, for a lion hunt, and he was pressed for time to get his car through the passes of the

Elk on the ridge and mule deer in the brush - prime habitat in Wyoming

Rockies and back to New York before snow fell.

Fred and I decided to abandon the slopes of Leidy and try to locate a big bull high up on the mountains to the south of Slate Creek. So far, we had not seen many cows and as the rutting season was already in full swing, there were few big bulls. The country we proposed to hunt was not as precipitous as the slopes of Mount Leidy but it was more heavily wooded with jack pines, spruce and firs, with here and there dense clumps of quaking aspen, which were rapidly turning to a brilliant yellow as the frost touched them.

Halfway up the slope we jumped a band of elk and as the cows strung off across a small opening, hope beat high in our hearts that bringing up the end of the procession would be a big bull. Ten cows we counted and as each appeared I raised my gun expecting to see a big set of horns. Our disgust was unbounded when a small four-point bull with a head not much bigger than a mule deer came trotting along at the end. We let him go to grow another year.

We toiled up the hill another thousand feet in elevation when we heard a bull bugle. From the coarseness of his voice we felt sure we had at last found what we were looking for and worked our way cautiously into the timber where this elk was "tuning up." We approached within fifty yards and could distinctly hear him pawing the earth and could vaguely catch a shadow of moving animals here and there through the trees. But we could not tell which was the bull we sought nor what kind of a head he carried. We sidled a little to the right and almost stepped on an old cow that had been sleeping peacefully in a mass of huckleberry bushes. She was on her feet in an instant and in her frantic efforts to get away took the whole herd with her. We ran as fast as we could through the timber hoping to find an opening, but all we saw was a spike bull and a little later three cows a long way off on the crest of the ridge.

We toiled farther up the ridge. Fred's profanity was improving with each new disappointment. Several times during the last few days he had led me into a particularly rough country covered with downed timber, assuring me this was "real bull country where only big old devils lie." Each time we had put up either a spike bull or a few cows until finally I began to tease him about it. After such an experience on our way up the mountain, he sat down and with considerable vehemence exclaimed, "These ___ ___ elk ain't got no principles."

As we worked our way along the very crest of the ridge about noon, we heard an

Pack mules and horses carry equipment to make camp

elk bugle just below us on the slope running down to Ditch Creek. Instantly our hopes rose and we slid down the rocky side hill to a clump of timber, which offered convenient cover. Soon the shrill whistle came again and, moving stealthily only a short distance, we made out through the glasses a calf elk peacefully sleeping in a dense thicket only seventy yards away. We should have missed it entirely but for the glasses, through which we could see much better into the deep shadows.

As we watched, a spike bull appeared followed by an old cow and just behind them we caught the glint of the sunlight on a set of horns. Slowly we made out parts of the bull and came to the conclusion that he had a warrantable head. I sat down and waited for perhaps ten minutes while the little group below us browsed about. I was hoping the bull would stand out clearly so I could place my shot, but he did not and finally I had to decide which patch of tan showing through the foliage I would shoot at.

I fired and nothing happened except that the bull walked ahead a few feet, startled by the noise. I fired again and still he did not drop - only the underbrush swallowed him up. We ran the short distance but could find no blood sign and after two hours of searching, finally decided I had overshot both times. I have often missed quick shots, but such shooting from a sitting position with all the time in the world to aim carefully was incomprehensible.

This, I thought, was the last straw of a day of disappointments and I confess I had little heart in the hunting for the next few hours. I just trailed along behind until Fred told me that early in the morning he had seen through his glasses two bulls a long way off enter the timber to lie down and he proposed we should try for them late in the afternoon. Toward 5 p.m. we were approaching the opening where these bulls had last been seen when we heard a shot directly ahead of us and no more than a quarter of a mile away. We knew at once our chance had been forestalled by some other hunter, probably a native hunting for meat. Fred was so mad he did not even speak but simultaneously we turned on our heels and started for our horses.

We were a gloomy party as we rode down the hill toward camp. Suddenly I saw Fred pull up his horse with a jerk and, looking ahead, I saw a splendid spread of horns, and beneath was a head looking at us over a small mountain ash. I jumped from my horse and tried to pull the Springfield from the scabbard. As generally happens when you are in a hurry, it stuck and my efforts to disengage it only excited the horse until I found myself being dragged along the side hill hanging to the stock

Laura Sherman Gray, center, makes plans to hunt elk. Guides think she is the Goddess Diana.

of the gun.

Finally it came free and I turned to see only a patch of light tan on the bull's rump as it disappeared among the pines. We ran to head him off but it was too late and, greatly out of breath, we returned to our horses. Just as I was pushing my gun back into the scabbard, we heard the bull bugle. Out came the gun again and we were off on the run.

Fortunately, the whistle was repeated frequently and we were able to direct our course almost straight toward him. Suddenly in the midst of a dense pine wood Fred grabbed my arm and pointed to a dark shadow just ahead between two trees. I strained my eyes to find the white bead of my front sight as the light was fading fast, and pulled the trigger.

With the report, the old bull reared up and fell over backwards. We knew he was finished and the yell Fred let out must have speeded his departing spirit for he was stone dead when we reached him, although the distance was only twenty-two yards. As we came up to him, I looked at my watch and saw that it was 6:45 p.m. and the light had so far gone that I could not see the front sight at all. We were just in the nick of time.

This bull carried a very even six-point head. It was not all I had hoped for, not a set of horns to send to a museum, but an average head, and I was content. While Fred opened the animal I sat down on a log and reviewed the incidents of the day - its succession of rising hopes and abysmal disappointments. I was tired, so tired I could "hear the angels sing." I did not feel the intense satisfaction I had experienced in getting a good hundred feet of moving picture film of game. I had only a set of horns to take home, which would never tell from their place on the living room wall what the noble animal looked like or in what surroundings he had lived. I felt no regret for my shot. I had unquestionably brought a merciful end to this bull's life, which in the course of at most a few years would have been ended tragically by a predatory animal or by the intense suffering of famine when the snow lay deep over the land. In the gathering darkness I realized only that hunting with a camera, and especially a moving picture camera, was many times more difficult than hunting with a high-power rifle. More difficult but eminently more satisfactory because when successful you brought home a trophy of life, a study of habits and of surroundings that awakened more recollections of the trip than a mounted thing of hair and horns.

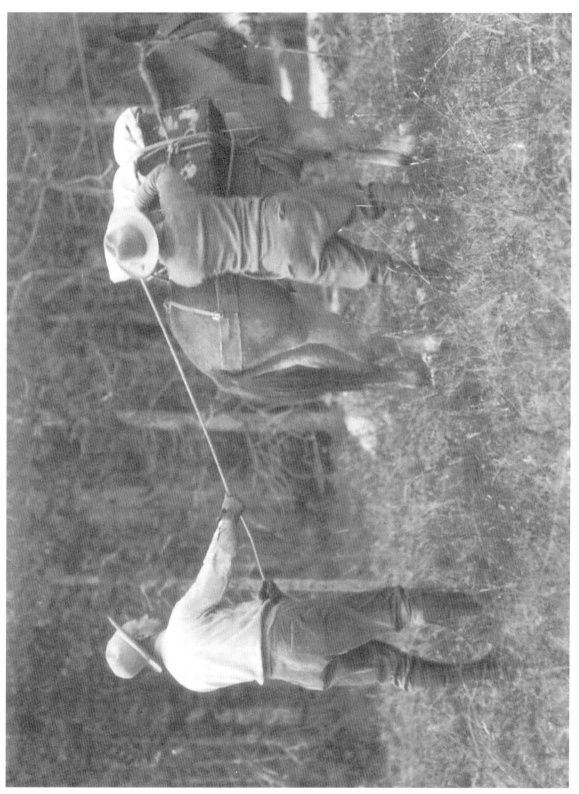

A horse receives its pack – "throwing a diamond hitch."

The strain was over. We had killed all the law allowed us and we had only to look forward to lazy days in camp until we felt inclined to try again with the cameras for the game we had had difficulty in hunting even with the rifle. We packed in our elk but before we started homeward a torrent of rain descended and we made camp very wet and very cold. We found a visitor awaiting us who proved to be Game Warden Bill Emery, but as our licenses were entirely in order he could find no fault with us. However, he liked our food and company so well he stayed three days.

It was still raining on the following morning but toward noon it cleared and with a pack horse carrying the cameras we started for Bear Paw, a narrow valley where Harold Elkins claimed he had always been able to locate a bull or two. We climbed to an elevation of about 9,500 feet and saw through the glasses some elk a long way off but nothing that seemed to offer an easy chance for Laura to get a head or for camera work.

It came on to snow viciously so we sought lower levels and straggled into camp again drenched and nearly frozen. Frank had, however, been hard at work all afternoon and on our arrival brought forth a dinner that was a marvel: hot biscuits, elk steak and a pudding. It made all previous kitchen efforts pale into oblivion.

Our last day in the Slate Creek camp broke clear and cold. Ice in the water bucket and two inches of snow on the ground told us that winter was not far away, but the sun was warm and its first rays touched the fresh snow blanket on the peaks around us with a rosy hand. It was a glorious fall day such as only the mountain West can produce.

Laura had half an idea that she wanted to kill an elk although she quietly told me aside, "You will have to stand behind me and shame me into pulling the trigger. Maybe you will have to even swear a little." Before the guides she was Diana herself. So to do the thing properly we all decided to take her on the hunt.

We worked to the northeast and around East Leidy and had not been out an hour before we located a bull feeding in an opening in the thick timber. However, the growth was so thick and the air so still that a lengthy conference decided that an approach within easy range could not be made. The decision was a great relief to Laura.

 Up we rode through wonderful park-like openings in the forest until we were close to the top of East Leidy. A succession of ridges stretched to the south to snow-covered Sheep Mountain and the jagged Tetons raised their majestic heads to the

Pronghorn watch photographer from a ridge.

west. By common consent we dismounted and forgot all about elk, as we stretched out in the rank grass. Here we dozed and slept for an hour until our lassitude was interrupted by a bull's whistle not far away.

Fred was instantly on his feet and I felt morally obligated to follow his example. It took some urging to get Laura started but finally the three of us set out to investigate this fellow. Soon we located two cows and knew the old bull and the rest of his herd were in the timber close by. We crept forward and came on a spike bull, but try as we would we could not locate the old bull, who was probably lying down in some particularly dense cover. The herd of fourteen that we gradually made out were now all around us and it was only a question of minutes before one would get our wind. Laura by now was thrilled by the excitement and as anxious as Fred and myself to locate the bull. Suddenly, the inevitable happened. A cow caught a whiff of us and away she went, startling the others. By this time we had come to damn all cows. With the let down in our nerves came the doubtful joy of a sudden snowstorm with a cold, biting wind, so we started for camp with Miller.

More damp snow fell during the night, which made packing our wet equipment difficult. However, we were away by 11 a.m. on our twenty-mile ride to the Seebahm Ranch at Kelley. I have never seen a more slippery trail. It was a sea of mud and you had no idea at what moment your horse would slip out from under you. It rained and snowed alternately all day and with packs on the horses constantly slipping as the lash ropes stretched, we were in a fair peck of trouble. Harold Elkins expressed what we all thought when we were trying to catch Maud, a recalcitrant mule, whose pack for the third time had turned completely under her.

"Old man Weather has sure dished us up a lot of misery," Elkins said.

The trail around the slide in the Gros Ventre Valley was a perfect toboggan; it additionally had been churned up by the passage over it during the morning of about 1,000 head of cattle.

We met the herd in the lower valley - all white face Herefords, as sleek and fat as possible after their summer on the rich feed of the high ranges. They were being moved to the lower winter range and, from the amount of bellowing, they did not care for the process.

This cold day in the saddle only accentuated the joy of a warm fire, a wonderful dinner and a tight cabin at Seebahm's. We crawled into our blankets full of regret that the hunting part of our trip was behind us.

The Grand Tetons of Wyoming

WYOMING

September 22nd was a date to be remembered on this trip. It was brilliantly clear all day. However, the car that was coming for us from the Miller Ranch could not get through on account of the storm of the previous day and so we had the morning to photograph the Tetons and repair our outfit. Finally the car arrived and we were away just before noon on the trip back through Yellowstone Park to Miller's Ranch, 197 miles away.

We negotiated the first five miles fairly well over a road feet deep in only such mud as Wyoming can produce. Then the bottom dropped out of the road and into this abyss sank our car. Four hours of prying, cursing and pouring sagebrush and pine saplings into the hole finally started us on our way again. We found, however, that the only safe thing to do was to take soundings of each mud hole as we approached and, if it showed no bottom, to build a corduroy road over it or go around. We were all the rest of the day getting to Moran, twenty-four miles from the Seebahm Ranch, and then we found the car so used up that we had to requisition the garage and a mechanic to labor most of the night.

As if the weather had done its worst, the next day was also clear and bright. We were on the road before the frost had thawed out of the ground and so made excellent time to the south entrance of Yellowstone Park, after which we knew the roads would be hard-surfaced and passable.

We were held up by a black bear between West Thumb and Old Faithful. This bear had earned the name of Jesse James because he had learned to sit patiently on the middle of the road blocking the way for cars in the hopes the occupants would coax him from his position by throwing food for him to the side of the road.

We had no food with us so we tried to intrigue him by taking his moving picture. It had no interest for him - he would not move until a team of horses appeared hitched to a lumber wagon. He started for the woods at once, scared to death. It is strange how the bears in the park are now terrified by a team and show not the slightest fear of autos, while a few years ago they would not have not paid any attention to horse-drawn vehicles and would have fled at the sight of a car.

After taking a movie of Old Faithful in action, we hurried on through the Norris Geyser Basin to Mammoth and thence to Gardiner, where we spent the night.

The Red Gods were kind to us on our last day in the woods. It was clear and warm. We were away from Gardiner early and rapidly covered the eighteen miles to

[113]

Old Faithful Geyser erupts in 1925.

Tower Falls. Here we left the main road headed for the buffalo ranch but before we had gone far we located a bunch of six antelope and thought it would be easy to stalk them. For the next six hours we chased these keen-sighted animals over most of the state of Wyoming. Every time we came within 300 to 400 yards of them they would locate us in spite of our best efforts at concealment. They stopped just long enough for us to set up the camera and then as I was about to turn the crank they would leave for parts more distant.

We soon found it useless to use anything but the big lens - the twenty-four inch - and as it was impossible to rig this up each time, we tried to carry camera, lens and tripod all together. This weighed more than eighty pounds and made a most unwieldy load. Miller did most of the carrying and after one attempt I was quite willing to let him do it.

After each fright the little group of antelope would run about half a mile and then quietly go to feeding as if nothing had happened. We came trudging after trying to find some cover but generally crawling on our stomachs the last 200 yards dragging the camera.

Luck finally played into our hands, for out of the blue appeared a solitary buck who walked up to within 100 yards of us, so interested was he in joining the little band we were pursuing. We got seventy-five feet of film of him before he decided to leave. Our six hours' efforts netted us only 125 feet of film all told but fortunately it was perfect light and most of this was good.

At 4 p.m. we got back to the car and soon drove to the Forester's station where Ranger Bowman very kindly set out several loaves of bread, jars of jam and a pot of tea. We made short work of these and half an hour later started our return trip to the ranch 104 miles away.

Just after we passed Mammoth, a big bull elk walked down to within fifty yards of the road, but before we could unlimber the camera he was off. A little further on a cow moose and calf watched us from the timber but it was becoming too dark to photograph. Another elk crossed the road just ahead of us and a splendid mule deer with a spread of horns like a hat rack stood on the road's edge as we drove by. The game certainly had come down off the high ranges and since the closing of the park on September 20th, they had invaded parts of the park that during the summer had been infested with tourists.

We drove into the ranch at 11 p.m., full of grief that it was all over.

Prentiss N. Gray stands ready for the hunt.

The Canadian Rockies

1926

Following Gray's 1925 trip to the Elkhorn Ranch of Wyoming, he documents his travels to the Canadian Rockies in September of 1926 that become the fifth chapter of this book. This is the ninth journal Gray wrote. The original journal is a thick cranberry red volume bound in cloth and leather with printed marbled endsheets of pink, blue, pale green and cream. This journal, along with the journal of his trip along the Peace and Fraser Rivers, are the largest of his North American writings.

We were up and had breakfasted on September 20, 1926, before the train passed the eastern boundary of Jasper Park. We had learned from train companions that the Rockies rose out of the prairie suddenly and the timetable told us we would soon be within the 4,400 square miles of Canada's largest national reserve. Suddenly, up the valley of the Athabasca we saw a vista of jagged peaks, snow-capped and towering, till their tops were lost in the leaden sky.

A few miles more and we were mightily heartened by the sight of an old mule deer doe standing off in the brush and gazing in apathy at our fast express. For the next hour we sat with noses flattened against the car windows discovering more deer or exclaiming in wonder at the succession of magnificent mountains that unfolded before us.

We rolled into Jasper and found Jake Otto, our outfitter, extending us a hearty greeting in spite of the mountain of cameras and baggage that followed us off the train. His words were a welcome but his eyes were wide with astonishment as the porter brought out more and more to add to our pile of duffle. Finally, when Whitney Shepardson allowed that he would go up ahead and get the camera trunk and the other duffle bags from the baggage car, Otto nearly fainted.

As the fault was mine, I'll confess at once that we were loaded with two moving picture cameras, five still cameras, three guns, four tripods and a lens case, 7,000 feet of moving picture film and fifty dozen still films, besides bedding rolls and a

The grand Canadian Rockies near Jasper Park

duffle bag of clothes apiece.

Col. S. Maynard Rogers, superintendent of Jasper Park, was also at the train to meet us and very graciously offered to turn the park over to us for any purpose but shooting. He brought us maps, sealed our guns and offered us the services of his rangers if we wanted to take any game pictures.

These formalities over, we moved all our gear to the front porch of Otto's bungalow and soon made his little house look like a general merchandise warehouse. Until noon we balanced packs and at his earnest hint discarded a few things that seemed superfluous as we looked at the precipitous mountains over which we must travel.

We lunched at Jasper Lodge, stopping just a moment enroute to see an old black bear and two cubs work their way off into the thick timber above the road. This was to be our last fancy meal for a month so we ate all the staple food on the menu plus all the trimmings we could persuade the waitress to bring. Our last civilized cigar, smoked in front of the enormous open fireplace of the lodge, was somewhat disturbed by the sight through the window of softly falling snowflakes. The equinoctial storm had begun and the indications were that we were liable to have a cold, wet start.

The pack train of twelve horses and six riding horses had been moved out twenty-eight miles the day before, so we left by auto after lunch for Devona where we were to ferry across the Athabasca River and join our outfit. Along the road we saw deer, large flocks of mallards that were trying to make up their minds to start south, and a bunch of sheep (*Ovis canadensis*) consisting of one fair-sized ram, one small ram, three ewes and a lamb. It was our first sight of them and they were decidedly feeding out of range. We approached within fifty yards of them.

We crossed the Athabasca River in a punt and there met the boys. Bruce Otto and Aleck MacDougall were the two guides; Abe Reimer, the horse wrangler; and Joe Healy, a Blackfoot Indian and the cook. They had been waiting some hours for us and evidently Bruce Otto and the cook had been "lifting their elbows" rather often. However, whether the result of liquor or not, Bruce said when he saw my camera pack saddle exactly what we had been betting he would say ever since we left home.

"J.C., what in hell is that contraption?" flowed out the minute he laid eyes on it.

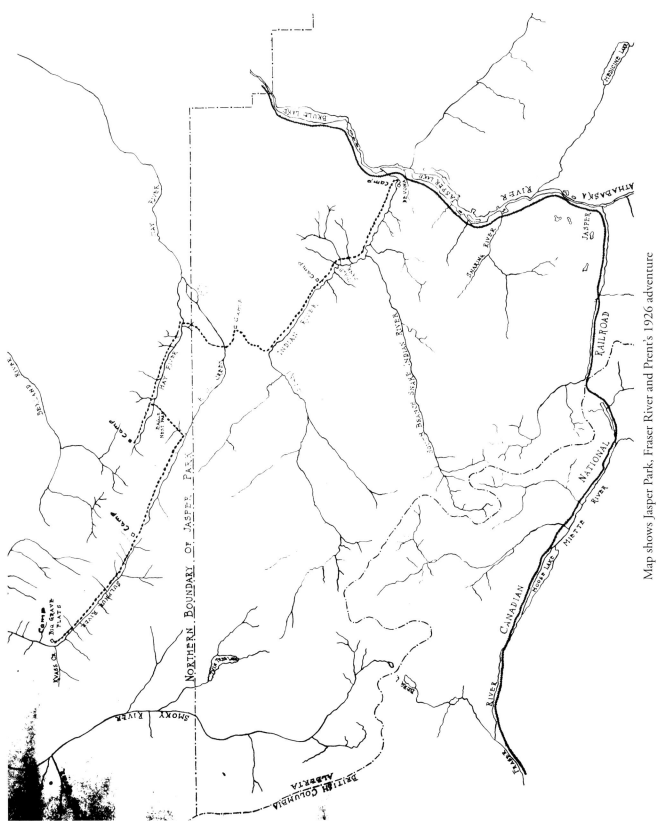

Map shows Jasper Park, Fraser River and Prent's 1926 adventure

THE CANADIAN ROCKIES

We made camp in a fall of snow. Joe gave us a really good dinner and sought to impress us by trying us out in French, which he had learned at school at St. Boniface. After a pipe we shook down our Kenwood sleeping bags and prepared for the night. But the storm had grown heavier, the wind whistled through the tall spruces and, sheltered though we were, the snow swirled around us, drifted under the tent and it was cold. We snuggled down into our sleeping bags and tried to sleep. It was no go and at midnight we sat up and smoked. Again at 2 a.m. and at 5:30 a.m. we tried to summon sleep by a cigarette. Finally we dozed off and neither of us awoke till after 8 a.m. It is ever thus the first night in camp but this time the warning of the extreme cold was not to be ignored. We had disproved the efficacy of the westerner's cure for a cold: "Just lie there and shiver yourself into a sweat." We determined to get more bedding.

When we awoke we found there were five inches of snow down and still more in the air. We stayed in camp all day and let it snow. We could not travel in the soft stuff, and what was more, our head guide, Bruce Otto, had disappeared. He came into camp about noon looking much the worse for wear and reporting that the storm out on the flats and away from our sheltered campsite was a tail twister.

During a lull in the storm Shep and I pursued some mule deer whose trail we struck near camp. We came up to three and approached within thirty yards but they were in the timber, and my slicker announced our coming afar off by scraping on every branch and flapping in the breeze in a flamboyant yellow way that the mule deer thought offensive. We gave it up and returned to camp to take a few movies of the tents sagging under the loads of snow.

After lunch a council of war decided that we needed eiderdown sleeping bags to avoid freezing to death, so we tramped through the storm a mile to the Canadian National Railway and found a section crew who had a rigging with which we could tap the telephone wires. It consisted of a thirty-foot pole, or rod, with two hooks on the end connected to lead wires that ran to the instrument. After a deal of balancing this rod against the wind, with the snow driving down his neck and into his eyes, Shep connected up to two wires that appeared conveniently together. I took the phone and caught hell from the train dispatcher for interfering with his particular line. Finally, after much persuasion and a vivid explanation of how cold we had been last night, he hooked us up with Jasper and we ordered two eiderdown bags to come down by the night freight.

[121]

Pack horse with Gray's camera - "that contraption"

On our return to camp, Bruce Otto was so afraid the things would not come that he wanted to go into town on the way freight and bring them back himself. So he started off bearing our hopes he would appear in the morning with the bags.

About 4 p.m. three cowboys rode into camp with twenty-six head of horses; it was another Otto Brothers outfit leaving in a few days with a party of four sportsmen. We seemed to be treading on each other's tails but there was said to be a lot of country up north and possibly we could keep off the tin can route.

The next morning we were up by 6 a.m. after a much better night and, with anxious eyes skyward, started our packing. It had ceased snowing steadily but occasional flakes drifted down. We packed and the boys got up the horses and saddled the bunch. Then we ate breakfast and waited for Bruce. About 10 a.m. he ambled in and told us we were crazy to start as there must be two to three feet of snow on the ridge and we would cripple the horses and be entirely unable to find horse feed. Whether he was honest in his convictions or sleepy and tired after a wild night in town we could not tell, but as we knew nothing of the country and they were his horses, we could do nothing but acquiesce and spend the day in camp.

About 11 a.m. the sun came out gloriously and the sky cleared almost entirely of clouds. It was the sort of clear-off we had prayed for and at once we began taking camp pictures, snaps of Canada jays, etc. After an early lunch, Aleck, Shep and I started for some rocky cliffs on the other side of the Athabasca, which we crossed in the punt in a stream running thick with slush ice. We first saw two does who allowed us to approach within 200 feet but, as this was too great a range for the camera, we did not get a picture. As we drew near the bluffs we saw a ewe sticking her head over the top. Soon a lamb appeared and in his gambols fell into a pothole full of snow just under the crest of the cliff. It was so deep that he disappeared entirely in the soft snow but by valiant struggles he floundered to the edge and crawled out.

We made our way slowly up the cliffs that rose about 250 feet above us. It was not dangerous but it was our first taste of real climbing and first blood was drawn when I slipped and cut my hand on a sharp rock edge, which slashed like a knife. As we approached the top we saw a ewe watching us closely and showing only her head from behind a rock. We stopped, and to get a better view of us, she stepped out to the edge, which gave us a couple of shots with the camera. When we reached the crest we found a two-year-old ram and seven ewes and lambs scattered over the bench before us. We made several exposures before they worked off.

Just as we were about to leave, Aleck discovered that five sheep had taken refuge on a narrow shelf just under the edge of the cliff. I worked up to within forty feet of them and it looked as if we had them cornered and could get a lot of pictures, but I had only time to run off fifteen feet of film with the Eyemo, or fifteen seconds, before they made up their minds to go down the face of the cliff. This had appeared an impossible feat as it was smooth and absolutely sheer up and down. When they went over we thought they certainly had been killed, but they appeared on the slope at the bottom and trotted leisurely away as if it were an everyday affair.

We moved on to another set of bluffs and soon made out a bunch of eight sheep that we photographed as they worked off across the snow on the bench above. Fifty yards off from this bunch lay a coyote, evidently hoping that a lamb would stray his way. He saw us almost as soon as the sheep but, while they were more trusting, he departed at once. We did not try a close approach and took only a general view with the six-inch telephoto on the Eyemo camera.

On the way home we jumped three does and a fawn and two bucks. The bucks would not let us approach at all, but one of the does and her fawn were a little more obliging and we took a long-range snap in poor light.

A little farther on we saw the water in a small pond disturbed and watched carefully to see what caused it. Below the surface we made out a beaver swimming. He broke water not fifty feet from us and, as soon as he saw us, dove with a loud slap of his tail. He soon came to the surface, however, and as we remained motionless, he swam about on the surface for some time within thirty yards of us.

We made camp just before 6 p.m., a bit weary from tramping the first day through snow, but this was a good starter for the days to come as we had covered about eight miles.

It was snowing the next morning and looked like a nasty day but we did not give Bruce a chance to postpone our start again and vigorously gathered our gear together in pack loads, hoping the horses would be brought in soon. However, luck was against us and, while the boys brought in the main bunch before 9 a.m., one horse of our eighteen was missing and was not rounded up till nearly 10:30 a.m. As luck would have it, it was Frank whose destiny was to carry my camera on "that contraption" of a pack. When finally Abe showed up with the truant, all hands started packing and at just 11 a.m. we hit the trail.

We crossed the Snake Indian River just above its junction with the Athabasca and worked up onto the sidehill where the trail paralleled the river 800 to 1,000 feet above it.

It snowed hard for the first two hours on the trail and, in fact, up until we made camp we had flurries. It was hard traveling for the horses as the footing was uncertain under the feathery blanket of twelve inches that hid all rocks and small downed timber. This, added to the slipping of the horses' feet as they collected little mounds of snow on each hoof, made the going difficult.

About 3 p.m. the sky began to clear. Gradually the magnificent ranges and isolated peaks began to emerge from the cloud banks and to stand out snow-clad against the blue background. We realized we were on a low ridge in an amphitheater of towering peaks. The clumps of jack pines through which we rode were heavily laden on every branch with mounds of feathery snow. Their trunks were spotted with tiny balls of white where flakes driven by the wind had found lodgement on the rough bark. As the sun played upon these masses of crystal they glistened like the splendid Christmas trees we plan each year in our fancies and never accomplish in reality.

We had two accidents on the trail. The pack on one of the horses turned and he proceeded to kick it off. There was lots of excitement for a moment when a sack of flour flew one way and the bake-oven another. In the effort he threw himself, snagged his leg and broke the pack saddle into splinters. Shortly afterwards Shep fell over a rock and tore the ligaments in his ankle and knee.

After fifteen miles we were glad when Otto pulled up at the campsite he had selected. It was not a bad location but that had nothing to do with his choice. The only factor that was allowed to cut any figure was horse feed so that our eighteen head should not wander too far during the night. How Bruce could see what feed there was under a foot of snow is a mystery to me, but as soon as the horses were unpacked and turned loose they began pawing and soon were uncovering a sufficient amount of rich grass to keep them busy all night.

We put up our tent, set the stove and shook out our beds on a covering of pine boughs. The sun sank below the mountains to the west leaving a rim of light atop the long spruce-clad ridge. We heard the horses' bells ringing as the weary animals nosed through the snow for grass; Aleck's axe rang out and indistinct talk drifted to

Five inches of snow in camp

us from the guides' tepee. We were tired as we sat smoking by the tent stove, but we were glad we were alive and in the north woods again.

Day broke auspiciously; the sky was slightly overcast but it was not snowing. The horses were soon found and in camp by 7 a.m.; still we were not able to get away before 9:30 a.m. Of course it is a job to break camp and pack twelve horses and one is always very glad when he gets to a semi-permanent camp and does not have to spend two or three hours breaking camp every day after he has spent at least the same time making it.

Finally the horses were strung out along the trail and we started on our way. We followed along the valley of the Snake Indian River, which is flanked on the west by a magnificent range of snow-capped mountains. Most of the time our trail kept up on the bench 500 feet above the river and on the east bank so that we could look across the valley at these wonderful peaks.

As Shep and I were riding at the rear of the pack train we saw little game, but one coyote sat on top of a cut bank and watched from a distance of 100 yards while we all straggled past him.

At noon the sun came out weakly and I took advantage of it to snap a few pictures of the superb vistas. While I was busy with the cameras my saddle horse moved off. I tried to catch him but he only went the faster. Finally the little metal tripod tied to my saddle began to flop and this scared him so he lit out at a furious pace, bucking as hard as he could go. My lunch, then the tripod and finally the saddle bags containing the Eyemo and sundry lenses flew to the four winds. I gathered up stuff through the tundra for a half mile. The horse caught up with the pack train and Abe rode back fearing I had taken a fall.

We pitched camp early about two miles up Willow Creek. It was too late to get over the pass into the next valley and, as it had been a hard day on the horses, we were glad of the extra hour or so in camp to clean and straighten our gear.

A glorious morning greeted us and put a more cheerful look on the eighteen inches of snow that hid the trail. It was well we started in a happy frame of mind, for the first six miles up Willow Creek were through muskeg and downed timber and it was slow work picking our way. After three hours we came out on a good trail that runs from Entrance to Grand Cache. We struck this trail close to Rock Lake and followed it for seven miles till we turned up Hay River.

Up to this time we had seen some magnificent single peaks and one short range

[127]

Roche Myette along Davona Creek near a campsite - prime mountain goat habitat

that towered, snow-capped, above timberline. But as we turned into the Hay River Valley we climbed close to timberline and on both sides of the valley stretched a magnificent range of jagged peaks.

We stopped once to set up the Akeley camera and while Shep and I were working at it, Aleck spied two moose. They were a long way off but were quite clear to us even without glasses. We watched them feed along the edge of timber for twenty minutes until we had to pull out to catch up with the pack train.

About 5:30 p.m. we saw the pack train bunch up in a clearing and, when we came up, found Bruce's saddle horse tied to a tree and the wrangler busy catching the packhorses and making them fast. The ground was examined to find first the best place for the cook tent; second, the best place for the dudes' tent. Then two pack covers were laid on the snow near these selected spots and the packs were unloaded and neatly arranged in rows on the canvas. The cook had meanwhile been busy with the dishpan, clearing snow off the ground on his tent site. Our duty was to do likewise - using the frying pan - for our tent.

The cook and one guide put up the cook tent while we dudes erected our own. Setting up the stove, storing away dunnage bags, rifles, cameras, and lastly cutting and spreading out over the damp ground a covering of spruce boughs to keep the bedding out of the wet was the work of an hour. By this time the horse wrangler appeared with an armful of wood and a welcome fire was soon roaring in the stove. Perhaps you have time to strip off your wet socks and boots and set them up before the fire to dry or perhaps you idly sit by and smoke, but not much gets done, for the cook has been very busy and his, "Come and get it," meets a ready response.

After supper there are always many odd jobs: changing films, drying boots, cleaning the guns and rearranging the packs. Possibly you drift over to the men's tepee to chat about plans for tomorrow, but darkness is bedtime and soon after 8 p.m. you crawl into the eiderdowns and smoke your last cigarette looking out the tent door across Hay River where the moonlight has turned the snow peaks to sheer silver.

We were away on our first hunt at 8:45 on the morning of September 26th toward the pass at the headwaters of Hay River. We topped the pass after about an hour's walk and here left the trail, cutting across country toward a large basin at the head of the Little Berland River. When we left the trail we immediately got into snow two feet deep. It was crusted slightly but not enough to carry our weight so that we broke through knee-deep at every step. It was tremendously heavy going and after a mile of it Shep's crippled leg gave out and he decided not to risk further injury but to return to camp. He left us at 11:30 a.m. and we struggled on for another hour and a half, getting into some very deep snow in the heavy timber on the north slope. Here it was waist-deep and very soft and feathery, so that we ploughed our way along rather than walked. We finally emerged on a bench where the snow had melted off a bit and sat down to rest. Aleck spotted a cow moose coming out of the timber across the Berland River and for twenty minutes we watched her slowly work down to and across the stream. She disappeared from our view under the bank and we were sure she had headed down-stream. Great was our surprise when ten minutes later she poked her head up over a clump of willows seventy-five yards from us. I grabbed the Eyemo and soon had it going but it seemed only to intrigue her for she started to circle us to get our wind. In this procedure she passed within forty yards of us and I was able to get fifty feet of film of her.

After she had departed, we dropped down to the stream where the going was easier and worked up about a mile toward the head. Suddenly Bruce spied a ram perched out on a rocky point where he could see over, under and beyond everything. His position was so well chosen that we could find no means of approach and, although we were over three-quarters of a mile away we were sure he had spotted us.

We had lunch while we discussed the stalk and finally decided to try to approach by crawling through the buck brush (stunted willow) with which the floor of the valley was covered, taking advantage of such cover as the cut banks of the stream and clumps of jack pines afforded.

We progressed by one guide watching the ram through his glasses and when the sheep's head was down or turned, the other guide and I crawled vigorously forward on hand and knees in a foot of snow. We stopped and froze when the watcher signaled the ram was looking again and sometimes we literally froze, as the ram knew well something was wrong in our direction and often watched steadily for fifteen to twenty minutes while we lay in the snow. As fast as we succeeded in getting out of his sight he would craftily feed to a new high point that forced us to entirely alter our plan of approach. After nearly three hours of this back-breaking crouching, we had covered half a mile and, while he was still 500 to 600 yards away we could see that we did not want his head. It was fair-sized in circumference but the curve was not long. It then became a problem how to pass without alarming him to see whether there were any other rams in the basin. We finally left him watching Aleck while Bruce and I slipped under the hill on which he was perched and so into the basin.

At once we found the tracks of two big rams, but hunt as we would, we could not locate them. We had passed around behind our first ram and were paying no attention to him. Suddenly, he discovered us out in the middle of a snowfield. His astonishment was visible and he stood on the skyline and watched us for a quarter of an hour. I do not know whether he finally decided we were dangerous or whether he caught our scent, for the wind was now entirely wrong from our position. He started on the run for the mountain behind him and an hour later we could still make him out climbing toward the very top of this peak. It was 4 p.m. and we were eight miles from camp so we headed home, arriving at 7:15 p.m., footsore, wet, tired and hungry.

It was a hard first day's hunt as we must have covered more than sixteen miles, some of it in terrible going on account of the snow, but the sight of the cow moose and the ram in the basin of the Little Berland paid for it all.

We broke camp at 9 a.m. the next day. No matter how early we got up or how fast we worked, it always seemed to be 9 a.m. before we were on the trail. Joe, the cook, arose at 4:30 a.m. on this morning. Abe, the horse wrangler, started out for his horses at the same time and we two dudes were up at 6 a.m. Still 9 a.m. it was before we were off. Abe had driven the horses up the valley and built himself a bed of spruce boughs alongside the trail. Twice during the night the horses had tried to work down the back trail past him, but he turned out of his blankets and drove them back up the valley.

We retraced our former trail four and a half miles and turned off it through Eagles Nest Pass. This was a defile through the mountains with nearly sheer cliffs rising both sides of the narrow pass. In it I set up the Akeley camera to take the pack train as it came through and just as I had finished, another outfit appeared behind us. It was one of Brewster's parties led by a man named Jimmie Lamb, who sure had not been shorn for "lo these many years." He was a "beaver" and a "royal" at that, and, mounted on a little goat of a horse, he was a most grotesque sight.

The two outfits stayed together for four hours till Lamb camped on Rock Creek, which we had followed for seven miles through a long flat. We stopped for a few

Pack horses in camp at Willow Creek

minutes at the head of this seven-mile flat while I climbed a small hill to photograph the magnificent panorama. At the far end towered white mountains above the brown of the valley and the green black-timbered sides of the surrounding hills. The sun was getting down and the lower half of the distant range was purple in the shadow. Sombre thoughts came to my mind born of the cold desolation of the scene. It seemed to me that if anything happened to me I should select this spot of all I had seen to rest peacefully in forever before the ever changing, everlasting mountains. We climbed up through a nameless pass and dropped down to 6,300 feet on the headwaters of the Sulphur River. We had covered more than twenty-two miles this day and, strange to say, saw no game except a porcupine.

We had intended to stay at least one day at Seven Mile Flat to hunt the adjacent mountains, but when we awoke on this morning it was raining and the clouds hung low down on the mountains. Sheep hunting in a fog was out of the question, so Bruce allowed, "We'd wheel 'er." But it was a lot easier said than done because the horses had departed. It was not until 11 a.m. that the boys located them and brought them into camp. They had wandered six miles up our back trail, passing tons of good feed enroute. Finally they were brought in and Bruce, Shep and I started ahead as soon as we had saddled, as we hoped to find something along the trail that would give us fresh meat to break the awful monotony of bacon and beans.

We were afraid of the weather and anxious to get down to a lower level if we were to have more snow. Besides, we expected to make our next camp on the Sulphur River our permanent camp. We started out and the prospect of staying more than one night in a camp was alluring to us dudes.

In intermittent rain we "wheeled 'er" till 5 p.m., when we rode out on Big Grave Flat. Facing a biting cold wind we headed for the lower end where a clump of jack pines promised shelter. We had had a most uneventful ride of sixteen miles and had not seen a thing that looked like game except one spruce hen that refused to let us hit her with rocks, despite our best efforts. The pack train came in just at dark and in very short order we had tents up and fires going.

We awoke to find three inches of snow down and more falling in big flakes that Joe, the Blackfoot, called Hudson Bay blankets. Big Grave Flat when we last saw it was covered with stunted willow. This morning it was carpeted with soft down and the wooden shelter over the grave of Delarme, a Cree chief, loomed black in the

Guides in Canadian Rockies "boil the kettle."

center of a white field.

There was no chance of hunting in such weather, as we could not see fifty feet ahead, so we settled down in the tent before a roaring fire to dry the dampness out of our soggy clothes and bedding, oil up the guns and rearrange our gear. There seemed no end of things to be done so that we had begun to long for a day in camp. Finally I wound up the housecleaning by taking a grand bath in a basin before the tent with the snow flakes dropping all around me. After lunch Shep and I started on a light hunting and fishing expedition. Armed with a rod and the "over and under" gun, we attacked the Sulphur River. Never a rise did we get to the fly in its muddy waters, but a bit of bacon on a Parmechenee Belle, weighted down with a pebble, soon produced four bull trout of about a half-pound each. We saw nothing in the way of game and both the guides who had gone in different directions returned late swearing at the snow and general difficulties of travel, but without having seen any game.

Just as we were straightening up our beds after supper, Joe, the cook, stopped at our tent for a chat on his way to the spring.

He glanced up on the hill fifty yards behind us and whispered, "Get the guns, there's a bull moose."

Before we could get the rifles out and loaded, however, the moose had started and Shep and I never saw anything of him but his tracks in the snow on the hillside.

The next day broke clear and sunny so we were away before 8 a.m. headed down the Sulphur to hunt a creek with an unprintable name that we will for these purposes call Terrace Creek. It flows into the Sulphur River about five miles from our camp just below one of the large sulphur springs that gives this river its name and which can be smelled for a long distance to leeward. We turned up this torrential creek through almost a blind entrance so close did the precipitous cliffs press in on both sides, forcing us to stay in the creek bed practically all the first mile.

Then it became impassable for the horses, nimble-footed though these mountain animals are, and we left them. We alternately waded in the creek or sank knee-deep in the snow on the banks so that at the end of two miles we were tired and thoroughly soaked. We boiled the kettle at 11 a.m. and ate our lunch.

Another mile and we located a bunch of ewes and lambs, ten strong. After looking them over carefully for a ram, we continued up the stream seeing constantly small groups of ewes and lambs from two to seventeen till we had a total of thirty-six, but never a ram.

From this elevation of 6,300 feet, the peaks paralleling the valley of the Sulphur River stood out with vivid distinctiveness. To the westward the mountain masses of the top of the Continental Divide were piled one on top of another till their summits disappeared in the fleecy white clouds. It was a superb panorama such as we had not dreamed of from the floor of the valley. With all its beauty, at the moment it spoke to us only that somewhere in that jumble of cliffs and peaks was an *Ovis canadensis* ram that we wanted and to get him meant miles of heart-breaking climbing and a succession of disappointments.

It was now nearly 3 p.m. and we had reached the basin at the head of the creek. We decided to climb to the top of the ridge and gradually work our way back to a bunch of sheep we had seen earlier in the day, but which were too far off for us to be able to tell their gender with certainty.

Our sheep had fled and the reason was still present in the form of a black bear, gorging himself on berries where they had been. What was worse, the wind had shifted and to approach him we had to drop down to the floor of the valley, a matter of 2,200 feet, and climb up at least 1,500 feet to timberline to leeward of him. This took an hour and a half, as most of the going was through most damnable windfalls. My poor legs would just not lift at all when finally we found ourselves on a level with the place where the bear had last been seen. We made a careful stalk, but he had gone and his tracks indicated a leisurely retreat into the timber. Probably he just naturally had finished feeding.

Wearied to the breaking point, we climbed down through the windfalls and reached the horses at 6:50 p.m. It was nip and tuck whether we would get out of this box canyon of Terrace Creek before it was too dark to see, but just as the last light was failing we emerged and forded the Sulphur River, belly deep on the horses.

As we straggled home along the trail in the midst of a dense growth of spruce and jack pines, we heard a coyote howl on the hill above us. He was answered from across the valley and soon a chorus of unearthly noises reverberated between the narrow walls of the canyon. We knew they were coyotes, but it sent a cold shiver down our spines thinking of the lonely trapper on his line hearing the big grey wolves that had been driven down to the timber of the valleys in search of food. We had seen the tracks of one that morning on the headwaters of Terrace Creek and in size it was double that of the coyote.

We reached camp at 8:30 p.m., cold, wet and very hungry, and found that Shep, sitting in camp nursing his injured leg, had seen four rams on the opposite hillside and had watched them for an hour and a half.

Because of these four rams opposite the camp we spent all of the next day encircling the mountain. We rode five miles up Kvass Creek on the south side of the mountain till we had reached the summit, which leads over into the Smoky River. On the trail we met Mr. Homer Seargent of Pasadena who was on his way out after fifty-five days on the Smoky and the Jackpine. He reported very poor luck, as he had killed only a small caribou and a small black bear. He had, however, been beaten by the weather, as this was the first decent day he had had. Several days, said he, the thermometer did not get above twelve degrees all day and sometimes not above twenty degrees.

This day was, however, like June, warm and balmy without a cloud in the sky. As we ate lunch on the banks of Kvass Creek I found my flannel shirt warm even without a coat and I was glad everytime Bruce dismounted to look over the mountain for rams, because, as we had only one pair of glasses, it gave me a chance to bask in the sun and stretch my muscles, which had suffered a full strain the day before. I had no desire to try them out again so soon climbing hills or crawling over windfalls and, as I lay back content in the warm sun, I almost dreaded that Bruce would say, "There's the old fellow we've been looking for."

We returned past camp in the early afternoon, but kept on down the Sulphur River for three miles to look over the east side of the mountain. It was in vain, however, and we reached camp again at 5 p.m.

Aleck came in about 6 p.m., tired and wet after a long day on foot spying out the country to the south of us. He reported lots of ewes and lambs and a few goats.

For two days Shep had stayed in camp putting hot applications on his leg and painting it with many kinds of evil-smelling concoctions. As the time that he could stay was limited, he chafed under the enforced idleness and finally decided to risk hunting. We were up and for an hour rubbed in more dope and strapped his leg with several layers of adhesive tape.

Aleck, Bruce, Shep and I started for two creeks that flow into the Sulphur south of our camp. We separated on the divide between the two creeks; Aleck and Shep taking the westerly one, and Bruce and I working to the east.

About an hour after we had tied our horses, we heard a bull moose grunt. I

Glassing for big game on mountain ridges from Terrace Creek

replied in my best Quebec style with astonishing success. The bull, who was way below us in the creek bottom, started up hill on the trot, grunting at every jump. We encouraged him and our grunts were followed by renewed crashing of brush, vigorous snorts and more speed. Unfortunately, Bruce and I were in a thick clump of spruce and could not see far in any direction. This was a great mistake, but after the bull started we did not dare move as every step on the crusty snow could be heard a quarter of a mile. So there we were anchored and the bull approached to within sixty feet when he got our wind and with a great wheeze turned and fled. As soon as we heard him go I ran up the hill, but found no way out of the spruce clump although I took three snapshots between the branches as he passed along the sidehill about 125 yards away. I missed badly and was very sore.

We left our horses at an elevation of 6,300 feet and dropped down to the level of the creek at 5,250 feet. We then toiled up the creek bed to the basin at its head and climbed up one of the side walls to an elevation of 7,300 feet. From here we could look into another basin and high up on the walls saw four nannie goats and three kids. Later we located two small rams below them on the same slope and gradually the nannies and kids drifted toward the rams so that they were all feeding within a circle of 300 feet. This rather upset the old saying that goats and sheep never range on the same mountain.

They were all more than two miles away with a deep valley between us. Further, it was after 4 p.m. and only by sharp work and direct travel could we reach the horses and get off the mountain by nightfall. So we started at once and after a hard ride reached camp in a pouring rain at 7:30 p.m.

Glory of glories, Shep was in a few minutes earlier and had killed a splendid goat with a nice set of 9 1/2-inch horns. He told me about it in this way:

After we left you, Aleck and I made our way slowly down the opposite side of the low peak we had all just come up, and after an hour's travel without a trail, down sharp and slippery slopes, through thickish pine and spruce growth, over numerous windfalls hidden by the snow, and through several bad bits of bog where we and our horses narrowly escaped being mired, we arrived at the bed of a creek. It runs into the Sulphur River, it is white and sulphurous, and Aleck says that it has no name. Then, for three quarters of an hour we made our way along this bed, picking footing for the horses wherever we

Searching for game on a basin at the head of Terrace Creek

could find it - on either bank or in the stream itself, and I will be able to remember our tortuous travel by noting the fact that in forty-five minutes we crossed and recrossed the stream (eighteen inches to two feet deep) thirty-two times!

At 10:45 a.m. we reached the small basin that collects the headwaters of the creek as they come down the mountain sides. We tethered our horses, lit a fire, made tea, ate our sandwiches and rested for ten minutes. We then saved the remaining tea and sugar, tied it, and all our leather, woolen and rubber gear to the horses' saddles (out of the way of porcupines) - and at 11:30 a.m. we started for game.

So far, except for certain places hard on the horses, we had ridden, but from now on progress was to be on foot. From the creek we cut west for half a mile up grade through snow and timber; from there a short but stiff piece of climbing up a bare hillside - perhaps 300 feet of slippery slope. From this point we swung to the left, looking for rams and following the mountain side just a short distance, crawling up to the edge of one depression after another, lying on our faces, and peering over for signs of sheep. But we saw nothing except a few ewes and lambs.

Now the day before, on his twelve-hour circuit of these basins on foot, Aleck had seen one goat at a long distance on the top of a mountain. And as we ended our fruitless series of blind stalks for rams that did not exist, we brought up again in a valley, and from that point Aleck's mountain was in view. Was his goat in view also?

To my surprise, having decided that our yellow patch two miles away might be a goat, Aleck at once became cautious. We sat down behind a tree and planned the approach. Mr. Goat lay on a high hogback ridge, running north and south. We were to the south of him, and the ridge rose directly out of the head of the valley in which we sat, as if it were a convex continuation of the valley. On either side of the hogback ridge was a basin - one to the west, the other to the east. It would have been relatively easy to proceed up the gradual slope of either basin. But the wind was from the west, and if we had gone up on that side our scent would have reached him soon; as for the eastern basin, the goat was overlooking it, and, as far as we could guess with the glasses, was surveying it from one end to the other. There was just one course; to forget the climbing advantages of the two basins, and to go straight up the ridge of the hogback, for he would thus get neither our wind nor a sight of us.

This being decided, the long stalk began. For three-quarters of a mile we made cautious progress, from tree to tree, for even at this distance the goat's sight is said to be very sharp indeed. At the end of this march, we were so far under the base of the hogback the goat could no longer see us. On the other hand, as he was equally hid from us, we could not follow his movements, and we were undertaking a hard blind stalk of a mile and a quarter with a fair chance that our goat by then would have peacefully wandered to another grazing ground.

At the head of the valley the climb began. The first part was over shale, which gave way under our feet as we tacked across it; but though dangerous as footing, the distance down was not very great, and one had the feeling that even if he should go along with a shale slide, it would probably be a slow performance, and that he would come out of it with only some torn clothes and a general shake-up.

The next section was among rocks, tacking backwards and forwards across the hogback for about 200 yards. This was not so pleasant, especially with a rifle to handle. At one spot, where the only way was across a cliff, and over a gap as far as one could step, I had to take both hands to the face of the rock, and hand my rifle over to Aleck, for I was not sure just how much distance and extra strain my propped up leg would stand.

We were now up about 500 feet - or so I guessed it on the way down, for I wasn't measuring distances or examining what was (or wasn't) beneath me as we climbed. The last 500 yards or so were over bare surface, with fine footing, hard ground, stout tufts of grass, but so steep that we had to crawl up on all fours. Except for a piece of most unfortunate luck, there was no real danger here, because the footing was honest and not treacherous. Except for half a dozen short snow patches, we were able to avoid snow entirely.

Aleck, a few feet in the lead, came on the goat's winter cave, just under the ridge, and slightly on the eastern side of the hogback. It was six feet deep, and perhaps four feet high - bedded down with several inches of dung. Clear across the basin was another cave that we guessed he used when the prevailing winds were from the east.

So we climbed on, waiting for breath every twenty feet, until we were just under the crest, and not fifty feet from one of the many depressions that combed the back of the mountain. From now on we would have to be cautious, for in one of these depressions the goat, if he had not departed, would be found. I threw a cartridge up out of the magazine into the chamber, put the gun on "safety," and we crawled forward a dozen feet. Aleck motioned me down, and as he did so, rose to his knees to look over the ridge. He was down like a flash.

"He's there," he said, "not forty feet away. Stand up and get him."

I stood up, saw the goat three-quarters on and shot him through the neck. He took two steps and fell. It was, of course, a magnificent stalk on Aleck's part. To travel a mile and a quarter, blindly, without sight of your quarry, and for the first time to raise up, look for him and find him not more than forty feet away, is an extraordinary performance.

But even though it was my first shot at a wild animal, and went straight, a man could hardly have missed it. There is no joy in the shot, and there was no joy in the killing. As it was my first head, so it may be my last. I don't know.

He was a big "billy" - heavy and powerful. His coat was long and a good white color. His horns have not been carefully measured, but Aleck estimates them at 9 1/2 or ten inches. And as Aleck took the head and horns at 1:30 p.m. on the top of the mountain, the sky grew darker, the wind came up and a storm of driving snow swept down. It was bitterly cold. We were on the bare ridge, with not even a bush for shelter, and our coats were with the horses two miles away.

We came back down one of the basins, across knee-deep snow patches and timber, slipping and sliding down the bed of a stream and walking in water much of the way. Soon after 3 p.m. we were at the horses, had a fire going, tea on the boil, and a change of shoes and stockings for the homeward trip. We were off by 4 p.m., following the trail along which we had come that morning, and arrived in camp at 7 p.m., just as a cold and windy rain began to fall.

At breakfast Shep decided that having killed a goat and therefore having experienced both the hunt and the kill, he would go out. He had been anxious since we started to gain a few days in order to go on to Vancouver, returning to Edmonton on October 12th as scheduled.

As I wanted to make an overnight side trip up the west branch of the Sulphur where we had seen goat yesterday, I said goodbye to him, although he did not leave our permanent camp until the next day.

While at breakfast our tent caught fire and we nearly lost it all. One of my socks, laid on the woodpile to dry, caught and soon the whole pile of wood was ablaze. Bruce saw it just in time, and we saved our tent and its precious contents. Another moment and there would have been a grand explosion of films and ammunition.

Bruce and I started at 9 a.m. with one packhorse loaded with our bed rolls and food for a couple of days. Abe came along to bring back the horses, as there was no

Snow-capped mountain tops and tree-covered valleys - where Shep took his goat

feed for them at all in the basin where we proposed to camp.

The previous night's rain that we had at camp we found to be snow a short distance up the mountains, and every tree was laden with it and seemed to be waiting with foul intent to dump it down our necks as we rode underneath.

It was a hard climb over the ridge as the trail was even more slippery than the day before, and it was a most difficult job to get the horses up the little creek that we were to follow to its head. There was a good deal of muskeg on the lower end, and a thick tangle of willow and dwarfed spruce as we approached timberline.

We reached a camping spot that was dry in the last timber and here we unloaded and cooked lunch. After the dishes were washed, Abe left us and Bruce and I moved up into the head of the valley. We soon spied two goats, which we concluded were billies, on the same mountain where we had seen the seven goats the day before. We watched them for a couple of hours as it was too late to try such a long stalk.

Slowly they fed over the crest of the ridge. Then another goat appeared, the forerunner of eleven more, all nannies and kids, but as they kept at a long distance from the first two, we did not lose faith that the first were billies. They were still feeding on the grassy slope when we returned to camp at 4 p.m.

Here Bruce built a wickiup consisting of five poles leaned against a tree like a tepee and covered with spruce boughs. With a fire before it and a good bed of "mountain feathers" underneath, it was as comfortable a camp as one could want. We had supper cooked and the dishes washed by 7:30 p.m. and after a pipe (and a chew of tobacco by Bruce), we turned in to gather enough knee power to get up that mountain after the goats.

We rolled out of our blankets just at daylight and, while I was scraping up some snow to fill the tea kettle, I heard a moose grunt down the creek. I called Bruce and we started down to investigate. We had gone only 100 yards when we heard him plainly near at hand. We squatted behind a spruce thicket and I got off a couple of grunts. Not forty yards away, out stepped a bull moose full of pep and high purpose. We took a good look at his head, but it was small, not more than a thirty-five-inch spread. We decided not to shoot. We did irritate him considerably by grunting at intervals and, as he could not locate us, he went through some of the most amusing antics, perhaps supposed to fascinate a cow moose, but to us produced much suppressed mirth. He pranced about in front of us, crossing the little valley half a

"The grassy slope where we saw both sheep and goats."

dozen times and working up to within twenty-five yards. He thrashed the thickets with his antlers and pawed the earth, grunting all the time. As no lady friend appeared he finally tired and started off. He passed to leeward, but did not seem to get our wind and Bruce and I paralleled him back to camp. The last we saw of him he was still traveling up the valley grunting his way along merrily.

Bruce was a little sore that I did not kill him in spite of the small head. He seemed to be generally sore at moose and as I questioned him he told me he had had a deep hatred against them ever since one winter in the Kootenay District where he was packing in supplies for a mine. He had left the dynamite till the last so that it would freeze and be less dangerous and also to get the horses more accustomed to the work and the trail. Finally they had nothing else left to pack but sixty cases of dynamite and caps, so these were loaded on the thirty-six horses and started, not without some trepidation. After an hour on the trail a bull moose appeared, charged one of the horses and stampeded the others, spreading packs, dynamite and caps over half a county. It was no use to run, for if one stick had gone off everything would have gone up, including everybody within half a mile. Fortunately, the stuff was too cold to explode and after much effort they chased off the moose and gathered themselves and the pack train together again. Since that day Bruce acknowledges a great delight in seeing a moose killed.

We cooked breakfast as fast as possible. Just after starting for the grassy slope where we had seen the goats, it began to rain, but between showers we located our two goats on the very highest peak. It took us more than two hours to get near the top and on the way we saw a cross fox trotting along the hillside within easy range.

We did not dare shoot as we were after bigger game, but Bruce said ruefully, "There goes $25."

At the top of the open slope two ewes were grazing and it was the hardest kind of crawling through two feet of soft snow to get past them without their detecting our presence. We were afraid their flight would start the goats. Just as we had succeeded, we nearly stepped on a yearling ewe that was feeding apart. For some peculiar reason it did not seem to resent our presence and after trotting fifty yards it started feeding again. During most of the rest of our stalk it was within plain sight of us and seemed to feel no fear.

We approached the very highest peak of the mountain with a vicious snowstorm swirling about us. All around the packed white blanket stretched to the top unbroken except where here and there a rock protruded a few inches above the surface. We crept on until I saw Bruce suddenly drop. I went down, too, and from a flat position on the snowbank I could see a pair of black pointed horns just over the snow crest in front of us. When they disappeared, as the goat lowered its head, we rose and crept forward until we were within thirty yards.

Bruce studied the situation for fully ten minutes while we lay in the snow. We were in a bad place if the goat looked our way over the ridge. We were without cover of any kind and, as we had reached an elevation of 7,400 feet, there was no shrubbery behind which we could hide.

We finally decided to stand up quickly and shoot. We arose, but to our utter disgust, instead of two billies, there before us were fourteen goats. Most of them were lying down in a slight depression. Two or three were standing, and the horns of one of these, an old nannie, we had seen over the snow crest. They were all on their feet in short order and we expected headlong flight. Just to be contrary, instead of running when they made us out, all fourteen came to attention and fixedly looked us over. There they stood for fully ten minutes while Bruce tried in vain to pick out a good-sized billie. There were big nannies, little kids and small two- and three-year-old billies, but no head worth shooting in the whole fourteen.

We were sick with disappointment, but, against hope, Bruce kept looking and to my plea to let me take a picture he replied, "There may be an old billie in the bunch and if you fool with that d_____ thing you'll miss your shot."

Right there I missed one of the best pictures I'll ever get. One old nannie, the largest in the bunch, took her position in the forefront and glared at us steadily, stamping her foot continuously. She questioned our right to be on her territory and yet she was inordinately curious as to what we were. The spell of their interest was broken occasionally by a ubiquitous kid who frolicked about until his mother gave him a butt to suppress his levity and chasten his soul.

After they had finished looking us over, they milled about and for fully twenty minutes the bunch stayed within thirty to forty yards of us showing no fear, but watching every move we made. Finally, they began to work off down the farther side of the peak into some steep, rocky slides from which pinnacles of rock jutted up. In and around these and sometimes over them they climbed slowly, working downward and away from us. We climbed down the east side of the mountain and, very cold and very wet, built a fire of the first stunted spruce. We felt better after a pail of tea and a couple of sandwiches, and decided to hunt a basin that now opened up, which we had not seen before.

It was very likely looking country, but produced nothing but two ewes and a lamb. It did, however, furnish more thrills than I care to collect in one afternoon. None of it was easy climbing, but one particular shale slide was frozen underneath with about an inch of loose stuff on top. We started across and when we had nearly reached the middle it was so bad that Bruce decided we should go back. But that could not be done since we could not get a toe hold on the ground over which we had come. Bruce dropped his mitten and it rolled 200 feet and disappeared over the edge. We looked at each other and for a minute it appeared as if J. Henry Schroder Banking Corporation was going to be short one president. How I longed for a steel plate on the butt of my gun instead of the rubber pad that was there, so that I might dig footholds in the frozen ground. Finally Bruce worked his way over to me and passed me his gun that was properly shod. With this I slowly dug out little steps so that eventually we returned to safe ground.

Both of us had had enough, so we sat for half an hour under the pretense of spying out the country. Bruce then went down below for his mitten and when he returned he looked even more scared. He allowed there was a 300-foot drop below the point where the mitten had disappeared and he only recovered it by going to the very bottom.

"Anyway," he said, "there's a two-foot snowbank under that cliff so the landing would not have been so hard if you did not go through it."

We found a way above the slide, but much of the fun had gone out of the afternoon.

Bruce unconsciously had a way of saying, "Now we'll slip over on that little point over there."

If he had only said what he meant, "Now we'll slip over to that point," I'd have felt more cheerful.

We had no luck in this basin and at 4 p.m. started for camp. On the way back we disturbed three ewes and a lamb, who when we last saw them were still going strong up a snowy peak toward heaven. We saw two goats across the valley, and after a careful study decided they were billies. Just then a kid appeared from behind some brush and changed our idea as to their gender, thereby saving us a long hike. Finally at dusk we reached camp, and I was so tired I could hear the angels sing.

Prentiss Gray's mountain goat held by guide

THE CANADIAN ROCKIES

After a good night's sleep we were away at daylight, leaving a note for Aleck scribbled on a blaze on a tree with a cross stick notched in above it telling him to pack our stuff back to the main camp and that we were hunting on our way back home.

We then crossed over the divide into the basin and the one next to it and in each saw both female sheep and goats. At about 4 p.m. we crossed another divide and dropped down into a third basin. From this basin ran a creek which poured into the Sulphur River close to camp. We were moving along the creek bottom at a good pace when Bruce and I simultaneously saw a lone goat far up above us grazing on an open patch of grass. We contemplated him long and earnestly for it was a devil of a climb and it was late. He appeared to be entirely alone, so the supposition was that he was a billy.

At 4:50 p.m. we started the climb and, as usual, when we started a stalk, it began to rain. At 5:40 p.m. we came out where Bruce said the goat had been, although I felt sure we were too high, and it was my eyesight as well as my lungs that told me so.

We looked everywhere in vain and no billy. My remarks to Bruce that we were too high went unheeded. Suddenly I heard a shout and thirty yards below us the old fellow broke out of a patch of stunted spruce. He had no chance to get away for it was rock slides in either direction for 400 yards. I felt sure I could kill him before he could get out of range no matter which way he ran, so I took plenty of time to sit down and aim carefully. When I pulled he was not more than sixty yards away. The gun misfired. Five times I drew a careful bead and nothing but a dull click resulted when I pulled the trigger. I reloaded with fresh shells and on the sixth try the gun went off. I was so surprised that I pulled the shot to the right. I continued to pump out unexploded shells till the ninth, which went off and the goat dropped. He was by this time more than 200 yards away and it was a blow to see him stagger to his feet again and start on, but going very slowly. After the tenth dud I reloaded from shells I had pumped out, hoping they would fire on the second try but, though I tried seventeen shots all together, none went off after my ninth.

Bruce yelled to me that the goat was badly hit and that he would follow him up and for me to go back for the camera pack that we had discarded during the last part of the stalk. I got the pack and tried to follow across the rock slide over which the goat and Bruce had traveled. In the middle of it I decided it was no place for me

[151]

Gray, left, skins mountain goat with guide.

as the whole thing appeared to be on the verge of going off down hill with me in the middle of it. I gingerly picked my way back to my starting place and descended to the valley. I stood there for some time wondering what I should do next. Bruce had gone down the valley toward camp chasing the goat. Camp was 4 1/2 miles away through very rough going down a creek swollen waist- deep by the warm rain and melting snow. It was 6:10 p.m. and before 7 p.m. it would be too dark to travel. I knew I could not make camp, but decided to get as far down the creek as possible and then "siwash it" ("jungle it" they call it in Alberta) for the night under a spruce tree. I traveled over windfalls, waded the creek, stumbled over boulders in the semi-darkness till I dared not risk a broken leg any longer. I sought a clump of spruce and in the pouring rain tried to start a fire.

My first two efforts were in vain, but finally a blaze was going and I set about to gather enough wood to last through the night. In the dark and without an axe it was hard to find sufficient wood of decent size to last, but eventually I had a sizable pile and set about drying my clothes. We had eaten two sandwiches at 11 a.m. and I was feeling a little hungry, but I had the tea pail and a handful of tea in the pack and they helped a lot to cheer up the picture.

All this kept me pretty busy until 10 p.m., when Bruce suddenly appeared. He had followed the goat till dark and then had come down the valley to camp. He had started a fire but, when he saw sparks rise up from my fire as I threw on wood, he had come along a mile down the creek for company and for tea. I was very glad of his help as we carried in two big logs that I could not lift alone. We kept busy till midnight cutting boughs to lie on and to shelter us from the rain that was coming down in sheets.

Bruce reported that he had followed a clear blood trail of the goat till too dark to see, but hoped if it did not rain too hard to pick it up in the morning and find him. We lay by the fire and at first sleep would not come. Gradually, after putting on more wood at 1:30 a.m., I dozed off and only awakened about every hour and a half when the fire got so low that it was cold. I did not have a bad night, but at the first crack of dawn we were up and away.

Our only idea was to get into camp for breakfast, so we hurried the three remaining miles to camp and, after wading the Sulphur up to our waists, arrived for a large breakfast. After a couple of hours sleep we started back to look for the goat. We found him not 300 yards from where Bruce had lost the trail in the darkness.

[153]

He was lying dead on a snowbank and we were surprised at his size. His horns ran full 9 5/8 inches and he was in fine pelage. We skinned out the head and made a short trip to look into the basin for sheep, returning to camp just at dark.

We intended to move camp back to the Eagles Nest Pass to hunt the basins that were too full of snow when we came in. But the weather stayed bad, raining at camp level and snowing like blazes on the mountains. It did not let up till noon and I spent the morning trying to persuade my rifle to go off. After my experience with the goat, I cleaned the firing pin, but it still refused to fire. Everyone helped with advice; extra washers to stiffen up the spring, etc., and finally it did seem to improve.

On this afternoon Bruce and I rode up to Terrace Creek and looked the country over for rams. We saw five ewes and lambs, but no rams. For the life of me I can't figure out where the fathers of all these lambs have gone.

At dark a trapper, Jean Weber of Entrance, appeared with his winter supplies for a five months' stay in this neighborhood. This was his trap line and he was moving in before deep snows closed the passes. It looked as if we had better get ready to move out, so we decided to hit the back trail and hunt the country as we moved along.

Camp was astir long before daylight, but it was 9:45 a.m. before the tents were down and all the horses packed. After I had packed the loads for my two horses and taken down my tent and stove, I took a number of pictures of the mountain on which I killed my goat, both with the Akeley and with the long lens on the still camera. With the glasses from camp we could see the exact spot where I shot the goat at least four miles away.

After we had been out a couple of hours we came out onto a flat and spied a young bull moose at the edge of the timber watching us. Aleck and I stopped our horses and I gave a "plaintive" call. The young bull started for us at once, and I believe would have come close enough to photograph if the rest of the pack train had not arrived with bells ringing and Joe in the rear shouting at the top of his lungs. As it was, the bull came to within 150 yards and then sort of sidled off into the timber.

We reached Little Grave Flat (Mile 65 1/2) at 1:45 p.m. - eleven miles in four hours exactly. Here we camped, as we proposed to hunt the basins in this neighborhood for a couple of days. I asked Joe why the Indians preferred to be buried out in the middle of a flat instead of on a hill facing these majestic mountains. He replied that the deceased were not consulted, but they buried them on the flat because the digging was easier. The grave was a rectangle of logs five-by-eight feet, three or four tiers high, notched together at the four corners with a split shake roof over the whole. The wooden affair is in the nature of a monument, as the body is placed in the ground.

One of the great pleasures to me of hunting various kinds of game in various parts of the country is to experience the complete difference in the method of hunting. Since 1904, when I hunted Osborn caribou in the Cassiar Mountains, I have not seen the tactics employed by Bruce and Aleck on this trip. To a certain extent hunting elk in Wyoming and Montana is similar, but there more chance is laid on stumbling onto a band of elk or seeing them at a range not exceeding a half mile. During the rut the hunter is greatly aided in locating his quarry by the bull elk's "bugle" or whistle.

Here, no trust is placed in anything but the binoculars and hours are spent in scanning the country at distances that seem a day's travel. Tracks are looked for first and each is followed with the glasses both ways in the hopes that it will lead to the game. Tracks across snow can be seen easily with eight-power binoculars up to three miles, although it is not generally possible to tell what made them, it is a fair assumption that if they are above timberline in steep country they are made by sheep or goats. Sometimes in soft snow a wolverine will leave a track that at a distance is deceptive, and in our recent hunts we have been fooled often by these.

If a study of the tracks is not productive, one's attention is turned to the southern grassy slopes where the snow goes off first. Here will most likely be noticed bands of ewes and lambs or nannies and kids, but here also by themselves may be seen single rams or billies, or sometimes bands. If it is the middle of the day, the game may have retired to a position on the bluffs or cliffs just above these grassy slopes. Billies may have sought their rest in some rough, steep slope that is standing almost on end, while the rams will try to find a rocky point on which to lie down, which commands a view in all directions for miles. Their eyesight is far keener than man's, supplemented even by binoculars, and their position above allows them to look down into any sort of brush cover that would afford protection if the game were lower.

Our method of hunting has been to work up the small creeks that lead off from

Mountain range where Prentiss Gray found his goat.

the main river. These usually run back two to four miles through well-timbered sidehills. Gradually the timber thins out until the bed of the creek itself is above timberline. Its head is generally in a basin surrounded by majestic peaks and it is after we pass timberline and get among these mountains that we really begin to hunt. As soon as we can get a view of the upper slopes, progress is slow as every bit of country, except the north slopes where the snow already lies deep, must be looked over most carefully. Constant stops are made and twenty minutes to half an hour consumed in each study of the hillsides. If nothing results, as is usual, we move on until a new vista opens up, when the process is repeated. If a height can be gained it adds to the expanse of country that can be covered with the glasses.

When we have hunted out a basin in this way, we climb over the lowest pass that offers into the next basin and repeat the process. It is entirely a game of looking, and sometimes days will go by with no reward except bands of females. It appears that the country has been denuded of game, but when you consider the great distances, the enormous surface in these broken-up valleys, and realize that probably even with the most careful study you do not see one-third of the area because of the dips and depressions and the ground behind rocks and shrubs, it perhaps is stranger still that you see so much game as you do.

On this day Bruce and I wanted to hunt out a creek that flowed into the Sulphur at the upper end of Little Grave Flat. The pack train was to move on to the summit at Mile 61 and unpack for four days, or until we got a ram.

Aleck started at 6:30 p.m. for the horses, but at 8 p.m. was back again with only two. He had twice waded the Sulphur River, waist-deep, and as soon as he came out his pants froze stiff as boards. It had been a bitter cold night with snow flurries and everyone was about half-congealed and in none-too-good temper. The names those horses were called was a caution. Bruce and I decided to walk, and Joe and Aleck started horse hunting again. They did not find them until 2 a.m. We had arranged to have two horses left for us so that when we came off the mountain we could ride the four miles to the new camp.

We struck up across the flats through a mile and a half of very bad downed timber. Finally we started to climb and had not got up 500 feet before we saw a two-year-old ram on the canyon wall opposite. He watched us, but as we drew away he went about his feeding and paid no further attention to us.

Up above the timberline we laboriously toiled without seeing further game and

Up above timberline the men toiled.

so came out onto a sort of mesa where the snow was two-feet deep and everything was white. Here we found lots of tracks, but all leading down into the valleys below, and we concluded that the last few days snow had driven the game to lower levels.

We were loath to turn back and continued over the summit and down a ways into the headwaters of the Big Berland. No sign of game rewarded us, and we returned to the vicinity of the young ram we had seen earlier in the day. As we approached within 400 yards, he watched us without great interest. Just then I saw a good mule deer come out of a little pass and yelled to Bruce who was twenty-five yards ahead to know whether I should shoot and risk scaring any good rams that might be about. He could not see the deer for a moment and finally told me to go ahead, but by this time the buck had put on speed and was just topping the ridge when I fired. Of course I missed badly although the distance was only 150 yards, and the bullet hit the ground between his hind legs, throwing dirt and enough snow on him to scare him to death, if the length of his jumps going down the hill on the other side were any indication. The strange part was that during all this excitement the young ram never moved, and before we were out of sight lay down contentedly.

We saw two bunches of ewes and lambs and another two-year-old ram, but no heads. However, golden eagles were quite numerous and on several occasions flew fairly close to us as they hunted the mountain slopes.

When we dropped down off the mountain we found our horses and stopped to make a cup of tea at a trapper's line cabin belonging to Jean Weber. We arrived at camp very cold, as the temperature had taken a decided fall, but the boys had my tent up and a fire going so I could get into dry, warm socks and boots at once.

As we needed no horses for our hunt the next day, we were away early, despite the fact that it was snowing heavily. We hoped that before we reached the upper ridges the snowstorm would have passed. We slowly worked our way up a creek bed a couple of miles, but the clouds hung low on the hillsides and soft flakes drifted down.

Sometimes a bright disk in the sky showed us the position of the sun and quickened our hopes. Once it broke through enough to cast a shadow for five minutes. Three bunches of ewes and lambs appeared to us through the mist and we did our best to make horns grow on them through the glasses.

Finally we reached the basin at the head of the creek and decided to cross the summit into another creek. This looked very simple as an unbroken snowfield stretched right to the top. However, as we got within 100 feet of the crest, we found the previous snows were frozen with a hard crust and this day's fall had placed on top of the icy surface about two inches of soft, feathery stuff that would hold nothing. Unless we could make this last 100 feet, we should have to climb down two miles and then a like distance up the next creek. We tried in vain in three places, and at last, by digging out footholds with the butt of Bruce's gun, slowly, and with much trepidation on my part, we reached the crest.

We had spent an hour at the job and when I was halfway up, holding my breath and fearing to look down, Bruce, who was one step above me digging out another step above him, remarked, "What a hell of a slide a feller would get if he started from here." Bruce always has a cheery word to say just at the right time.

When we were fairly on top, a shift of the wind gave us a view of a splendid basin below us with majestic walls and three peaks towering around its rim. The quiet of it all was broken only by the "peep" of a rock rabbit. The fog came down and smothered us with a white pall so that we had to look carefully or we would have stepped off the skyline.

We concluded that this made hunting hopeless, and carefully picked our way down to timberline, 1,500 feet below us. Here we boiled a pot of tea and had our lunch which, since the clouds did not lift, we stretched out for three hours.

We could see little, but once through a rift we made out two mule deer feeding in the brush across the valley. The buck did not have a decent head and their position was almost impossible to approach without considerable traveling. Once again, a small two-year-old ram appeared on the skyline, but he, too, held no interest for us and we watched him feed away. At 4 p.m we gave it up and returned to camp where we answered Joe's query with the usual and too-often repeated reply, "No luck." Another precious day of the all-too-few passed without even sight of a decent ram.

Before daylight I heard someone rattling my stove and slowly awakened to the fact that it was 6 a.m. and that Joe had kindly come in to start my fire. As the tent warmed, I raised one eye above the eiderdown sleeping bag and peered out through the opened tent flap to see what kind of a day had been provided after the storm. The high snow peaks across the valley of the Sulphur were gradually turning pink at the first touch of the sun. The skyline was clear and slowly the mountains stood out well-defined against a cloudless blue sky.

I lay a while and dreamed, but, strangely, there crept into this glorious picture of the rosy hand of dawn, painting snow-capped peaks, thoughts of how cold my underwear would be when I started to pull them on. Even my special pride and joy and the object of Shepardson's envy, my Eskimo suit, which was carefully folded beneath my pillow, would probably be frozen quite stiff. While each day I snuggled in its warmth, it had no great reputation for retaining body heat when taken off at night, and especially when the temperature approached zero.

I thought of how I had purchased these magnificent garments in a store in Jasper. They were ample in size and the clerk assured me they would not shrink. I hope he's a liar because they have stretched so that they go around me twice at the waist and I can nearly make a union suit out of the shirt alone. However, their half-inch thickness intrigued me so I bought them. Possibly I was also attracted by a label on them that said, "Direct from lamb to man." I sort of figured that if I wore them I might be lead direct from man to lamb - or rather to a lamb's daddy, which was the object of this trip. But Shep said if this was my purpose I ought not to wear outer clothing or the paternal ancestor would never recognize his offspring's wool. However, I had lain long enough in bed and with one superhuman effort I crawled out of my bag, snatched the woolen garments from beneath my pillow and spread them quickly before the fire while I crouched over it and smoked a cigarette, waiting for the heat to penetrate one-half-inch of wool.

Dressing after that was quickly done as nothing inspired languid movements, and soon, in the warmth of the cook tent, I drank several cups of strong tea, ate oatmeal and two moose steaks, two large slabs of bread covered with jam and topped off with a bowl of stewed fruit. I was then ready for the day.

Bruce and I planned to hunt a basin about two miles below camp. We started up the little creek that flows out of it and had not gone a half mile when I saw a cow moose and calf on the hillside above us making their way along above timberline. I remarked to Bruce that with all this snow one would expect moose to be lower down. A grunt of a bull moose close at hand brought us up with a start and by his continued grunting we located him in a patch of stunted spruce about fifty yards below the cow. He was working his way toward her as fast as he could travel. The glimpses we caught of him in the timber and as he plodded up the steep sidehill

Top of the ridge - picture perfect

showed him to be a very large bull. His antlers looked big; he was going almost directly away from us and we could not see the web.

He was rapidly getting out of range and was now more than 150 yards away when Bruce said, "It's a good head. Plug him."

I sat down and drove the first shot home. I could hear it hit and the bull stopped and swung sidewise, but did not fall. I fired four times more, hitting each time, but he would not come down although he had only moved a few steps from the place where he was originally hit.

I reloaded my gun as he slowly took a few steps forward, and taking careful aim, fired again. This was too much for him and he dropped, rolled a few feet, and then started a mad fall over a bluff and down a rock slide. I never heard such a racket as he crashed through the brush at the bottom and we figured he was coming all the way down into the creek where we were. As it was, he stopped because his antlers caught under a log not twenty-five paces from where we stood. We approached, expecting to find his antlers badly smashed, but strange to say, only one little tip was gone. The head was a disappointment since its spread measured only 41 1/2 inches, and for so large an animal it was almost a freak.

I walked back to camp, brought up a packhorse and enlisted Aleck's aid. The three of us skinned out the head by noon and Aleck took it back to camp, while Bruce and I went on for rams. I saved the head thinking Shep might like it as a reminder of the days we lived together on tough moose steak.

We had only just left the moose when we saw two rams high up on the skyline watching us. We studied them carefully and one seemed to have a fair-sized head, but Bruce turned it down flat. One small moose head was enough and he did not propose to take in a small ram as well. It is true it would probably only measure fourteen inches and did not have much of a curl, but I have seen a lot worse sent to Jimmy Clark's to be mounted. (James L. Clark was a Boone and Crockett Club member and director emeritus of preparation and installation at the American Museum of Natural History, New York City. He was a member of the original committee that devised the Boone and Crockett Club's copyrighted scoring system.) It was a four- or five-year-old ram and Bruce would have nothing else than that we should let him grow for another four years.

We hunted the ridges all afternoon, but did not see a sign of game until just as we drew near camp, when we spied a little bull moose standing in the middle of the

Prentiss Gray tracks a trophy moose and finds success.

meadow not 100 yards from the cook tent looking the outfit over. He stood there entirely unconcerned as we approached and my hope was that I could reach my tent and get the camera into operation on him. But as I was setting up the tripod he turned and trotted off into the woods.

The next day Bruce and I were off just at daylight. We wanted to get in as full a day hunting as possible and still make the next camp at Mile 52 where the pack train would stop. It was snowing when we left camp and by the time we reached the summit it had become a real blizzard. You could not see ten paces ahead and before we reached Seven Mile Flat there were eight inches of snow down. Fortunately, the storm was from the west, behind us, so that the horses hurried on with their tails toward it. The wind had a full sweep at us down Seven Mile Flat, but there was nothing to do but pull ahead. So we kept on and reached the proposed camping place at Mile 52 before 10 a.m.

Here we boiled a pot of tea and ate a couple of sandwiches before starting our hunt. We left the horses behind and, to my great regret, my slicker and sheepskin coat also. But the storm gave signs of letting up and we were anxious to climb as fast as possible to get up to the sheep ranges. We toiled up through the woods to timberline and followed this for a couple of miles above a small creek into whose basin we were headed.

In a little gully I saw a good-sized mule deer watching us from a point not forty yards away.

I called to Bruce and all he said was, "Crack him."

The deer started up the hill, but I had lots of time for he could not get out of sight for another 100 yards. So I took careful aim and at eighty-seven paces, I let go. The bullet took him through the spine and before he stopped rolling downhill he was dead.

The antlers were not much, having only four points on each side, but the deer was fat and in excellent pelage. I particularly wanted a scalp to fit a pair of antlers I had at home and I have never seen a finer marked scalp than this deer had. We skinned out the head and dressed out the hind quarters, which was all we could carry and after an hour's delay started once more after sheep.

The first time we could see into a basin we sat down under a lone spruce tree to have a look over the country. We had been sitting there only a few minutes when we heard a scratching and as I turned around a flash of white disappeared into a hole at the foot of the tree. In a moment a little white head with beady black eyes appeared and, standing on its hind legs with fore paws on a scraggly root, regarded us. For the twenty minutes we were there this little ermine popped in and out of the hole trying to make out his strange visitors. Once he came out entirely and climbed the tree. After going clear to the top, he scrambled down again and took refuge in his retreat among the roots. He was hardly three feet from us and gave us ample opportunity to satisfy our curiosity about him, even if his seemed insatiable. He was not yet prime fur. Some of his summer coat of brown still appeared along the spine, but his head and under parts were white and the black tip on the end of his tail was clearly defined. We left the little fellow still popping in and out of his retreat.

The day was "dirty," snowing hard at intervals and misting all the time so that it was very hard to use the glasses effectually. We were in beautiful sheep country, but the only trouble was there were no sheep.

We moved about slowly just at timberline so as to keep as well under cover as possible, but, although we looked over a lot of country, we did not see a thing until after 3 p.m. Then we spied a small ram and a few moments later two more, but none with "shootable" heads. Later we saw a single big sheep way up on the mountain, but he was at least four miles away and it was too late to even try getting nearer to see what kind of a head he had.

At 4:30 p.m. we started back to camp, stopping to pick up the deer's hindquarters and head. It was a very heavy pack for Bruce, but we made camp before dark and found it completely established.

What a glorious day greeted us the next morning! Brilliant sun shone on the snow-covered ridges. Every tree glistened under its white load and there was frost enough in the air to make us feel glad we were alive. Our last day's hunt was starting gloriously, but that's all it did do - start. Soon after leaving camp we spied two rams and crawled within 225 yards of them. From this point we examined them carefully, but finally decided they were too small to shoot. The head of the largest would not have measured fourteen inches. When we stood up they went out of their beds like a shot out of a gun and the last we saw were two faint dots going over the top of the highest peak.

Then began a series of ascents and descents of every ridge and mountain in sight. I never crawled up so many hills in my whole life put together, and "crawl" is literally the word, for most of them were not far from perpendicular.

Bruce thought no more of a 1,000-foot climb than I would of going to the spring for a bucket of water. As soon as we had reached a crest and he had looked over the country, he was sure there was a ram in the next basin. Whereupon we must descend into the one we were looking at and crawl up out of it over the ridge to see into the next. We boiled the kettle over a tiny fire of dry willow; we had seen one more small ram and two mule deer, none of which interested us for shooting purposes.

After a pail of tea Bruce said he could see better and surely he could, for from the next ridge he spied a sheep (gender unknown, but size described as big as a grizzly). Only this sheep was on the summit of the fifth ridge from us and there was no way around. We spent the next five hours getting over the intervening country. I was ashamed to look at my feet, they were being treated so badly, and my knees had long since passed the numb stage.

When we finally crept up to the last ridge and lay down in the snow to locate our ram we feared only that the lengthening shadows would leave no time for a careful stalk. But no ram was in sight and telltale tracks in the snow on the ridge opposite showed where he had moved over the next ridge. This was too much and besides it was 5 p.m. and we were a long way from camp. We reached camp long after dark dog-tired, but satisfied that we had hunted hard and that no lack of effort on our part had caused our failure to find the big ram I had come so far to get.

As Bruce put it, "I never hunted so _____ _____ hard for a sheep before in my life. We have looked over every G____ D____ creek from Eagles Nest Pass plumb to the Smoky and not a _____ of a ram have we seen worth taking a crack at." It was over for this year and the next day we "wheeled" for Jasper.

It was now October 14th and our bad weather still continued. Snow was coming down when Joe called me at 5:30 a.m., but it seemed fitting that inasmuch as we entered this country in a snowstorm, we should quit it the same way. Fortunately the horses were not far away and we soon started packing. This was dirty work in the snow. The ropes were cold. The tents were wet and heavy and our fingers did not seem to exist at all. They were so cold.

It was the usual 9 a.m. before we quit Mile 52 camp and took the trail over Eagles Nest Pass. The snow continued and a strong wind drove it straight in our faces. There were eighteen inches of snow down already in the pass and the horses

The men hunted all afternoon at Seven Mile Flat.

had hard work getting through. Across the meadow on the Hay River side the full force of the blizzard hit us, and we were almost tempted to take refuge in the deserted cabin on the edge of the flat. As if discouraged by its failure to turn us back, the wind gradually diminished and by the time we reached the green timber around Errington's, it had died out completely. Only the steady, persistent fall of fine snow continued unabated.

The whole country was tracked up by coyotes and we had seen literally hundreds. One of the results was that we saw on the entire trip very few grouse and very little other small game. It was, of course, the first year of the new seven-year cycle of rabbits and they were very scarce, although traces were numerous of the last few years when the bunnies had been plentiful. In one patch of burnt timber there were thousands of young spruce trees that had been chewed off two feet above the ground. For every fifty stubs so killed there was one little tree that had escaped. It showed the foraging of rabbits when the snow was deep and when the only thing they could find to eat were the tops of these young spruce seedlings that were just tall enough to protrude above the snow. Only those escaped whose tops were covered by the snow or were too tall already for the rabbits to reach. It may be that with the dearth of rabbits and small game, the coyotes will cease to multiply as rapidly, but at present they are undoubtedly turning their attention to the young of the larger game because rabbits are scarce.

Ahead of us we had four miles of trail through downed timber after we left the government's forestry service trail. This could not be called a trail, it was simply a way. We feared that a foot or eighteen inches of snow in this stuff would make it impassable as the horses could not see to step over the logs and might catch their feet and break a leg. Bruce was most anxious to get through before more snow came down, so we pressed on as fast as possible. By some strange miracle we found only six to eight inches of snow here and so got through nicely.

After this was passed we contemplated camping, but the warmth and comfort of Ranger Alex Nelles' cabin at Willow Creek tempted us and we pushed the horses on. He received us effusively and turned the cabin over to us. A hot rum punch, a hearty supper and a pipe dissipated all the memory of cold hands and feet of the past 8 1/2 hours. We turned in with the feeling of a good day's work behind us, for we had covered twenty-four miles of bad trail.

While we were at breakfast the next morning, I looked out of the cabin window

Bruce told Prent to "crack him" when tracking a mule deer buck.

and saw a cow moose and calf crossing the flat not more than 100 yards from the cabin. Although the wind was blowing in their direction they seemed to pay not the slightest attention to us.

The weather had moderated and, while it was still cold, the snow had ceased to fall. There were fourteen inches on the level at the Willow Creek cabin and as we took the trail, we passed through miles of small spruce and jack pine forest with every tree laden with white, feathery masses of snow. About noon the sun came out and the trees began to spill this surplus weight till it looked like another snowstorm. And may I add that it was cold and wet when a bucket load of it came down on top of your head!

We had only a short pull of fourteen miles to Shale Banks, but the trail was very slippery and it took us five hours. Ranger Nelles traveled with us, so at Shale Banks we pitched only a tent to sleep in and cooked supper in his cabin. While we were unpacking, a small ram appeared on the bank across the river and I set up the Akeley camera and ran off 200 feet of film on him. The bank is about half a mile long and rises precipitously 500 feet above the river. No human being could possibly scale it without a rope, but sheep and goats navigate it in every direction without any apparent difficulty.

The next day took us easily to the Athabasca as it was only a ride of twelve miles. Here we camped. I wanted to put in a couple of days photographing sheep and goats in Jasper Park. We swam the horses across the river where they evidently found the feed so much better that the next day they could not be located until noon. Jake Otto also took his time about bringing down our supplies and mail for which we had phoned, and as the boat was on the other bank of the river we were stuck in camp while precious hours of good sunlight passed, separated from the place where we wanted to try to photograph sheep by only two miles. At last we built a raft and after much hard work and some precious navigation, for the current was swift, Bruce got across and brought back the boat.

At 10 a.m. Clausson Otto appeared with the car and my mail and provisions. I ran through the most important letters and then persuaded him to take me and my photographic equipment down to a sheep lick. As soon as we landed there I saw a bunch of ewes high up on the hill. I started after them with the Akeley camera, and they led me on a merry chase all over the Roche Miette for two hours. However, I got 200 feet of film and also got thoroughly exhausted carrying seventy-five pounds

Ranger Alex Nelles' warm cabin tempted the men at Willow Creek, but they moved on.

in camera, plus extra film in every pocket of my hunting coat.

About noon Aleck arrived with the saddle horses and a packhorse to carry the camera back to camp. Otto went into town for hay for the three horses as we proposed to keep them up so as to have them on hand for the morning, the last day of our hunt.

After lunch Aleck tried to work a bunch of sheep down toward the place where I had the cameras set up and I could see him far up on the mountain crawling around them to head them in my direction. But they ran every way except where he wanted them to go, so finally he gave it up and we started home at 4:30 p.m. On the ride in we saw a mule deer doe standing by the skeleton of a horse and chewing a piece of bone. She obligingly let us approach within fifty feet and we took some film with the Eyemo, which as usual refused to work except spasmodically.

When we returned I found the boys had been busy and had put up a splendid camp. Never had my tent been so well-rigged - pegged down all round and a big log laid across the back behind which was a bed of spruce boughs a foot deep. All my panniers were neatly arranged and there was a pile of firewood big enough to last a week. It was to be our last night in camp and they had spread themselves.

Joe built a splendid dinner and the last bottle of Scotch helped start it. The only thing that marred the festivities was that Bruce had nearly frozen all day in the cold wind because he could not find his coat. About 5 p.m. he discovered that Joe had used it, plus most of the saddle blankets, to wrap around a can of yeast which he was trying to raise to make biscuits for dinner. Joe was afraid the yeast would freeze in the cold wind, but Bruce was sore as hell.

Before daylight I was in the cook tent, as we had a long last day before us and the stars shining clearly told us we could expect a decent one. Aleck and I were away just as it was getting light, headed up Rocky River for pictures of goats.

After six miles travel over gravel bars of the lower Rocky River, we entered the gorge. It was an extraordinary thing even in this land of wonderful scenery. The river cut straight down through the rock for more than 1,000 feet and the sheer cliffs rose almost perpendicularly. We climbed up and followed the rim and expected to take our pictures of goats across the gorge on the opposite side. In no place were these rims more than 400 yards apart and some of our shots were not more than 150 yards distant, so that the sheer drop of the walls with the river 1,000 feet below can be visualized. We had proceeded only a short distance along the trail at the top

Snake Indian Falls

when a black bear appeared not far off in the brush and caused my horse grave concern. As the trail followed the edge of the cliff I concluded that the ground was the safest place for me. I slid out of the saddle as quickly as I could get my legs untangled from the mess of saddle bags, tripods and sheepskin coat - with which my poor horse was always burdened - and did my best to quiet the steed.

The bear worked off and we started ahead, but I remembered those sidewise jumps my horse had made at Little Grave Flat when she came on the grave from around a willow bush, and I calculated where we would land if the same performance were repeated on this trail. I walked.

We saw three nannies and a kid feeding on a grassy slope and prepared to operate on them. We decided that by packing the camera down on a point of rock we could get within good range, and so we shouldered all the impedimenta and started. I hadn't known we had so much and after I had packed fully 100 pounds for a quarter of a mile I almost threw part of it over a cliff.

We set up in a spruce thicket, finally, and put on the seventeen-inch lens. For ninety seconds we had a wonderful time getting good footage of the goats as they made off. They discovered us as soon as I started turning the crank and did not care for us even 150 yards away. They made a most wonderful group as they hesitated on the topmost rock for a last look at us.

After this short but busy session, we traveled three miles and saw three more old billies tucked away at different places on the cliff opposite. None of them offered opportunities of successful pictures, so we boiled the kettle and had lunch.

On the way back we located five more goats, three alone and one nannie and kid. We tried every lens we had, but they were long shots, up to 400 yards, and my hopes for these pictures were not strong. It took a lot of time, however, and before we knew it we had long passed the hour when we should have started back to camp where Clausson Otto was to meet us at 5 p.m.

Clausson had waited for us, however, so I piled my cameras in his car and started with him for Jasper. A truck was to have brought the rest of the stuff, but we found it on the road half-way to Jasper with the engine dropping out, so we had to go back and get the balance of my duffle, as well as the men. We all piled in the car and loaded my duffle on top and reached Jasper at 8 p.m.

Food was first in order and we nearly bought out the restaurant. After that I parked on Otto's front porch till 11 p.m., and then started the process of cleaning myself at the Pyramid Hotel. This was quite an operation and two weeks beard came off not too easily. However, it was done in a couple of hours, and clean sheets welcomed me.

On October 19th I left for Vancouver, but the "head of heads" stayed behind to grow in circumference and spread for another year.

———————

Whitney Shepardson was a dear friend of Prentiss N. Gray. When Prentiss was killed, Whitney became the legal guardian for Sherman and Barbara Gray whose adventures with their father are detailed in the last chapter of this book.

Wyoming pronghorn graze in lush grass.

[177]

Jenny's Lake

Wyoming

1926

Gray spent October of 1926 exploring Montana, Yellowstone National Park and the mountain range that became Grand Teton National Park. Gray documents his travels in the journal that becomes the sixth chapter of this book. Gray and his wife visit with Horace M. Albright, who is superintendent of Yellowstone National Park at the time. Albright was discussing in 1926 the establishment of the Grand Teton National Park with John D. Rockefeller, Jr., who purchased land that became the park by an act of Congress in 1929.

The journal containing his Montana and Wyoming trip in 1926 is combined with the journal on his trip to Antelope Island which took place in November of 1926. This journal, one of the smallest in the collection, is bound in navy blue leather and cloth with printed marbled endsheets of cranberry, navy and light blue and cream colors.

After a month's hunting in the Canadian Rockies, I met Laura in Butte on October 22nd and together we reached Bozeman, Montana, the same afternoon.

Here Mrs. Miller, Mrs. Pouch and Mrs. Livingston Delafield met us with a truck. After an hour and a half spent in buying the necessary stuff to fill out our equipment, we finally started for Elkhorn Ranch, arriving there at 7:30 p.m.

Coulter Huyler, Ed and Livingston Delafield and Ed Pouch were camped up on Taylor Creek not far from the ranch trying to hunt elk and praying for tracking snow. The weather was too good for hunting but I determined to make use of the brilliant sunlight for photography, putting off my hunt till snow flew.

We were fairly busy all the first morning getting settled, loading film and straightening out our equipment so that we did not get started on our first camera hunt until 11 a.m.

We took the trail up Tepee Creek into the Game Reserve and after an hour's ride located a fine bunch of elk of about twenty head. We tried to move the cameras up to them on our backs but the elk slowly worked off and probably in the shifting wind caught our scent. We could not get within a quarter of a mile of them and finally gave it up.

After lunch we tried the higher ridges but, aside from jumping two bulls that were lying down in the timber, we saw nothing. These two splendid elk made off across the sagebrush hills and would have afforded an easy rifle shot at fair range but were useless to us armed only with a camera.

In a crossing much frequented by elk, as evidenced by the deep game trails, we built a blind of jack pine boughs. An hour's watching produced nothing and so when the light became too dim to photograph, we returned to the ranch.

We were away from the ranch before daylight the next morning and by 7 a.m. were settled in our blind. It was not a moment too soon for before we had finished mounting the camera and making our hiding place a little tighter with extra boughs we heard a "bugle." It was rather late in the year for the bulls to be "bugling" as the rut was almost over and most of the bulls had left the cows. However, this old bull was very noisy and it seemed that he was just over the hill from us and, with his herd, working our way.

First, a cow, a calf and two heifers appeared trotting to a little pool within forty yards of us. We let them come but as they finished drinking and the rest of the herd had not appeared, we took a few feet of film of them. The whir of the camera disturbed them and after a moment's hesitation they made off. This was most unfortunate, for just at that moment the balance of the herd of about twenty-five with a fine old bull in the middle appeared and became alarmed at the flight of these four. We got some footage, however, as they strung out along the side hill and, with a shot on the skyline as they topped the ridge, completed 200 feet of film.

We waited till 10 a.m. but nothing more appeared so we put in the next two hours building another blind to which we could shift if the wind changed or if the elk approached from a different direction. We returned to the ranch for lunch and found Ed Pouch and Coulter Huyler there. They had come in from the hunting camp and, so far, had not had any luck. Liv Delafield had missed a fine bull but the rest had just been out of luck and had not seen a "shootable" head.

We started out again at 3 p.m. and just as we topped the ridge above our blinds we saw smoke in the valley of Daly Creek. We galloped as fast as we could push the horses toward the fire and when we arrived found that the game warden, Frank

Marshall, and one of the forest rangers were already there and had it fully under control. It had not done any great damage except to burn about ten acres of grass and sagebrush, but it was just entering the timber and might have been a real hot fire if not attended to at the start.

This put an end to our photography for the afternoon but before dark we had time to make a fly camp in which we proposed to spend the night. We put a pack cover over a log and Laura and I placed our blankets under this. We did not dare build much of a fire for we knew there were elk all about us but we cooked some soup and with some bread and jam did very well.

The next morning we were in the blind just as it came light but although we nearly froze we did not see a thing to photograph. When Frank arrived with the horses from the ranch at 9:30 a.m., Laura decided she had had enough for one day and started for home. Ernest, Frank and I ate a second breakfast of a cup of tea and a sandwich and started trying to find a few elk that might have stayed out late feeding. About 2 p.m. we saw some cows a long way off lying down in a little park in the timber but we could not get to them before sundown so we set up a blind facing a large park on Daly Creek. I sat there till it grew almost dark while Ernest scouted the nearby country for the elusive elk. Just as shadows crept up the valley where the cameras were set up, Ernest appeared and announced that a large herd had come out of the timber high up on Specimen Ridge. I demurred at his suggestion to pack up the ridge because the light was getting bad, but he assured me that if we hurried the sun would still be shining on the high ridges when we arrived.

We ran fully three-quarters of a mile with the camera, seventeen-inch lens and tripod and it was all uphill. We relayed carrying the outfit but I confess that the limit of my endurance did not let me pack the load over one-third of the distance. How Ernest can do it is a marvel to me but even with his game leg he climbs easily with a load that would kill me.

Finally, we came out on a high point a full half-mile from the elk but I could see the shadows crawling up the hillside as the sun sank behind the opposite ridge and I knew we had no time to approach nearer but must set up at once where we were to get a few feet of film. I ground off seventy feet before the sunlight passed but it was a long shot and I had grave doubts of the value of such a picture as the light was only passable.

It was dark before we were back to the horses and it seemed a never-ending ride

Specimen Ridge in Wyoming

down Daly Creek to the Gallatin Road. After that it was four miles to the ranch so it was 8 p.m. before we were home.

We took a day's rest in camp doing nothing more serious than setting out the Nesbit Flashlight camera for a coyote. The Pouches and Coulter Huyler rode in after dark from a three day trip to Jack Creek and the Madison. They had wonderful fishing and caught a large number of rainbow trout up to three and a half pounds. In the evening I developed test films and found the results satisfactory.

Laura, Miller, Frank and I started for Mammoth in the car quite early the next morning and covered the eighty-five miles via West Yellowstone before noon. We called on Superintendent Horace Albright at Administration Headquarters and he offered us everything in the Park and invited us to put up at his house. It was delightful to find a government official so anxious to be helpful and Albright seemed to take a real keen interest in the pictures of his animal charges that I was trying to make.

As the light was perfect, we did not spend much time visiting but drove the five miles down to Gardiner for lunch, as we had learned there were antelope already down on the flats close to town. We found this game much less shy than in September of last year when they were annoyed if we appeared nearer than 250 or 300 yards. We could approach within 100 yards without disturbing them but if we moved closer, they gradually fed away from us. There were at least 200 head in sight most of the time and some splendid bucks among them.

We took 600 feet of film and a few dozen stills but looking back I fear that most of our pictures were taken as the antelope were feeding away from us and that we did not get much except rear-end views.

They are a wonderful little animal, so graceful and light in all their movements. Their "contrasty" coloring with back of tan and sides of almost white, and particularly the white rump, destroys all the theories of protective coloration. When startled, the white hairs of the rump rise and make a target that would be hard to miss at any decent distance. However, their keen eyesight prevents most hunters from getting within a decent distance and their fleetness soon puts them out of range.

As the afternoon wore on, Laura offered a few cautionary remarks about saving some film for other game and so we took an inventory. To our horror we discovered we were running short and had only 1,000 feet of film left, including the Eyemo film that was wrapped on special spools in 100-foot lengths. We cut off on the

A fawn eats tender shoots.

Fresh beaver cuttings at Goade Creek - network of natural patterns

antelope and decided to ration the balance, 400 feet for deer and 600 feet for elk. Also, we wired New York for 2,000 feet more film to be sent posthaste by airmail.

On the way back to Mammoth we spied an old black bear sunning himself in the upper branches of a pine tree. It was such an unusual occurrence that we decided to use up a few feet on him. Sometimes in the fall just before they hole up, a bear will climb up into a tree to get the full play of the sunlight. Here he will stay for hours dozing in the warmth.

We were anxious to get started early the next morning for our pictures of mule deer so as to work as long as the deer stayed out and catch them as soon as they started feeding after the midday rest. Most animals have a very disagreeable habit (from the photographer's point of view) of appearing in the open only very early in the morning and very late in the afternoon. During all the hours of good light they are lying down in the thick brush. Deer are the worst offenders in this regard and retire to their beds very early and emerge generally only after the sun has set. This is emphasized during periods of full moon when it is light enough all night for them to feed, and as the moon now was at its fullest we realized we should get no pictures if we waited long after sunup.

We did not wish to disturb the Albrights' breakfast and so while it was still dark set off for Gardiner to breakfast at the Shaw Hotel. While we were running down the road, there loomed up in our headlights a doe and fawn crossing the road. We swerved a little to miss them when suddenly from out of the darkness a small buck jumped directly into our path. Frank slammed on the brakes but the fender struck the buck's antlers, upsetting him. We ran back just in time to see the deer pick himself up, shake his head in a dazed way and trot off up the hillside. I'll wager he had a bad headache for a day or two but as there was no sign of blood I do not believe he was hurt.

On our way back from Gardiner in Boiling River Canyon we found a small bunch of five mule deer and for two hours took their pictures. We worked very carefully and slowly so as to get all we could of one bunch without having to locate game again. Finally, they fed off into the willow thicket and although the hour was late we started hunting again.

Luck was with us for we came on at least twenty-five deer in a willow thicket. After I had set up my camera to windward behind some cover, Frank went downwind below them and gave them his scent, working toward them very slowly. One by

Mule deer on a ridge

one they got up from their beds and came out of the thicket onto the open hillside just as we hoped they would.

There were two good-sized bucks in the bunch and while I was taking a picture of one with the 12-inch lens the other approached and without any preliminaries they locked antlers and started pushing each other about. I signalled Miller to take pictures as rapidly as possible with the still camera and I ground film. I don't know the details of the fight because I was so busy keeping them on the ground glass field and in worrying about exposure and focus that I paid no attention to the result. It was the chance of a lifetime to get two good bucks fighting with perfect light and good distance. The battle ended abruptly, as it began, with one buck backing off and the victor returning to the herd of does.

It was now noon and we started for Gardiner for lunch. We had just reached the pie course when Sam Woodring, Chief Forester, telephoned that 250 buffalo were down in the flat near the Buffalo Ranch and we had better move out there (thirty-four miles away) quickly. We were off at once, picking Woodring up at Mammoth but we did not reach the buffalo herd until nearly 4 p.m. as the road was bad.

Here Bob Lacombe, head of the Buffalo Ranch, took Laura and his wife in a Buick sedan while Woodring, Miller, Frank and I started in a buckboard to work the herd. Before we had approached within 300 yards the herd began to move and Lacombe drove ahead to try to head them off. Woodring put his horses into a gallop and the three of us tried to hang onto the buckboard and steady the mounted camera while we tore over the prairie at a mad pace. It was a wild ride but we drew up within a hundred yards of part of the herd and I jumped off, set up the camera and ground film.

Meanwhile, Lacombe was tearing across the same sort of ground at thirty miles an hour, blowing his horn and yelling from the window of the car at the top of his voice. Laura and Mrs. Lacombe were down on their knees in the back to keep from bouncing through the roof. One old bull charged to within thirty feet of the car before Lacombe could swerve and get around him. All his efforts to turn the herd were in vain and the animals strung off across the Lamar Valley and up the hills on the farther side.

We returned to the ranch for a cup of tea and just at sundown started for Mammoth. In the dusk we passed a good many elk feeding on the slopes above

Chapel in the woods - Church of the Transfiguration, Moose, Wyoming

Wyoming bison

Goade Creek and decided to return to this section the next day for our try at this game, which last year, and so far this year, had practically foiled us. We drove into Mammoth at 7 p.m., very cold and tired but more than satisfied with the day's work.

Elk feed a little later in the morning than deer but still we wanted an early start as it was to be our last day in the Park, so we were away just as it came light. After a run of ten miles along the Tower Falls Road, we spied a large bull feeding up the sidehill.

With cameras on our backs we started the sharp pull uphill and approached within a couple of hundred yards. From here Miller crept ahead and came back with the report that there were two small ridges between us and the bull, and that he was feeding quietly.

We moved on without great caution and as we topped the first ridge ran right into Mr. Elk headed in our direction. He had finished feeding and had started for the timber, which happened to be in our direction. He was gone so quickly after he spied us that we did not get a picture. It taught us a lesson, however, and hereafter we will not move the cameras up without keeping one man out ahead at all times.

I scouted around the hill while the boys were resting from the climb and spied another bull lying down in the timber not far off. We quickly moved our gear to his neighborhood but, as the shadows were deep in the woods where he lay, we decided to try to force him out into the open by giving him our wind. Therefore, we sent Frank to windward of him and fifteen minutes later saw the effect. The bull threw up his head, sniffed and started at a trot but, alas, he took a direction that we had not counted on and he was almost completely screened by clumps of trees all along his course. What was worse, four more good-sized bulls followed him out but we did not get a single picture.

We returned to the car feeling thoroughly discouraged that our luck of last year still held over us. We drove along to Goade Creek, scanning the hills for elk. Suddenly to the south we saw a herd of more than a hundred head cross the skyline. They were traveling but we decided to try to cut across their trail ahead of them.

We raced up the hill as fast as our seventy-five pound pack of cameras, tripods and lenses would allow and came out onto a high plateau. Along the south edge of this was a deep coulee partly timbered and we crawled to the edge and looked over. Here and there, among the trees in the ravine, we could see elk and, glory be, they

Laura and Prentiss Gray, center and right, enjoy a cup of tea with a guide.

were not more than 125 yards away. We set up the Akeley low down to get the only cover offered, which was sagebrush, and as the herd worked out of the timber onto the opposite rim of the coulee, I stood ready to grind. I glanced at the register and, to my horror, noticed I had only forty feet of film left in the magazine. I whispered to Frank to go back to the car a mile and a half away for another and he started to crawl back out of sight. Miller and I froze and prayed fervently that the elk would neither see us nor feed off before Frank returned. With straining eyes we watched our back trail for Frank, keeping an eye on the herd so we could get forty feet of them anyway if he did not return in time. In a remarkably short space of time, but which seemed hours to us, we saw him crawling toward us on his stomach through the sagebrush. With the extra film at hand I started to crank and he reached me just as the film ran out. Either the whir of the machine or the movement of my hand, cranking, startled the herd but they tarried long enough to give me the forty feet and allow me to change film and get fifty feet more before the last of them straggled over the ridge.

We were tired and nearly starved, as it was 2 p.m. and we guessed that Laura at the car might also be hungry. So we moved down to the mouth of Goade Creek and cooked lunch below one of the tallest beaver dams I have ever seen. In the narrow creek they had built a dam fifty feet wide and nine feet high. Fresh cuttings of good-sized poplar trees were all about and before setting out for more elk we took some pictures of the work of these industrious animals.

Before coming down we had seen a very large herd of elk, probably more than 200 head, back about a mile from our position. After lunch we decided to work this bunch for close-ups, even though it meant a long pack with the cameras. We came up with them about 3 p.m. and, keeping well to leeward and working very slowly and carefully on groups of the larger herd that could be stalked, we succeeded in getting considerable footage of cows and calves as well as herd pictures during the next two hours.

Just at 5 p.m. we found a bunch of more than sixty head feeding along the skyline. It was a wonderful picture but no camera can ever reproduce those splendid elk silhouetted against a sky of flaming red. Our last foot of film went in the effort to record some idea of the grandeur of the scene.

When we reached the car at dark we could not find Laura. We figured she had started for Mammoth and so it proved, for we picked her up in about a mile entirely

Grand Teton from Jenny's Lake in Wyoming

congealed after a three-hour wait in the cold for us.

I sat up late that night rewinding film from the Eyemo reels to fit the Akeley camera. It was all we had left and we could not risk starting home with an empty camera. Game always appears when you are not loaded for it.

The next morning we headed back to Elkhorn Ranch but had not gone five miles before we saw a bunch of elk lying down on the edge of timber. We worked up very close, not more than thirty-five yards, and got some splendid shots of cows and calves. Finally, the herd bull walked out onto a pile of rocks in the open and we got a few feet of him. We were not satisfied and followed, but the best we could get of the bull was in the woods as he stepped across little openings at about 150 yards. I took it because it is about the sort of view of a bull elk that the hunter generally gets.

Our run home after this was without incident except for an effort to photograph a badger. We could not persuade him, even after a half-hour wait, to poke any more than his head out of his hole, so we did not waste precious film on him.

We were all pretty tired when we reached the ranch, after four strenuous days, but Laura heard about a dance at the Sappington's Ranch fifteen miles away and nothing would do but I must take her and Julie Pouch. We demonstrated to the natives the complete ignorance of the effete East in the science of square dancing but made up for it by eating full rations of sandwiches, pie, cake and coffee at midnight and afterwards washing all the dishes.

There were about thirty people present and only fifteen chairs in the two-room cabin where the dance was held. Most of us sat on the floor, as a poker game in one corner of the room monopolized six or seven of the chairs. Music was furnished by a phonograph with records twenty years old, a harmonica that nearly everybody tried to play and an organ that could not be brought into tune with the harmonica. The dancing wound up with a Virginia reel that I danced with Mrs. Sappington, the hostess. As she measured four-feet, two-inches in height and four-feet, six-inches in diameter, it was quite a sight. We reached the ranch at 3 a.m.

Coulter Huyler expected to leave the next morning but at breakfast we all decided on the spur of the moment to go to Jackson Hole. We chartered the Miller car and Huyler, the Pouches and ourselves, with Frank driving, started on a 135-mile trip through Yellowstone Park to Moran. We pulled in just at dark but the towering Tetons were still vivid against the fading light in the west.

Mt. Moran majesty

WYOMING

We saw very little game in the Park, only one coyote, but late in the afternoon after we reached the Hole, elk began to come out of the timber and we saw several hundred head. At one place thirty were feeding on a single hill across a coulee from us and directly below us in the bottom stood a bull moose not twenty yards from us.

We were greeted at Moran by the sight of two nice six-point elk heads and a 59 1/2-inch moose head, which a hunting party had just brought in. It was sad for Huyler and Pouch who had both hunted hard and had seen nothing worth shooting.

We awoke to find that somebody had sent us a perfect day so we were soon bowling down a good graveled road to Jenny's Lake. The water in Jackson Lake had been pulled very low this year for irrigation and as a result it looked like a mud hole in front of Moran. Jenny's Lake, a little gem set among the pines, was a delightful contrast. Above it rises the Grand Teton in all its glory, towering 13,500 feet.

We drove on to String Lake to see a piece of property but the owner was not even disposed to name a price on it so we returned to Jenny's Lake and loitered there for an hour taking pictures and reveling in the warm sun.

From here we drove to the Seebahm Ranch at Kelley and saw Harold Elkins who had just purchased it. He was unable to give us lunch so we crossed the valley to Mrs. Seebahm's new place and had soup and sandwiches. About 3 p.m. we started for Jackson but stopped off at the Harrison Ranch, Circle H, as Laura thought he was an old friend with whom she had gone to school in Salt Lake City. So he proved to be and also he had the most attractive ranch we had seen. The ladies fell in love with it because of its outlook and the decorations of the living room. We men agreed because his very pretty wife greeted us in a gorgeous suit of Chinese pajamas. We all concluded we wanted his place.

We arrived at Jackson after dark but found a splendid dinner and housing at the Crabtree Hotel. A council of war after dinner decided that Huyler should stay over a day and try to buy the Circle H Ranch.

It was cold and there was a skiff of snow in the air when Huyler left the next morning in his rented car for the Circle H Ranch and we in our car for the 175-mile drive back to Elkhorn Ranch. We made good time and by 1:30 p.m. had reached Old Faithful where we cooked lunch and watched the geyser spout twice. We half hoped the Queen of Rumania would pass as she was booked to tour the Park this day but she did not come and at 3 p.m. we left for the last drive home.

[195]

We saw a number of elk on the Madison River and came close to two big bulls with herds of cows. Alas, it was too late to photograph. A golden eagle and badger completed the list of game for the day but a wonderful sunset cheered us on our way as we crossed the divide between the Madison and the Gallatin. We reached the ranch at 6:45 p.m. and after dinner packed until 11 p.m.

We were up at five the next morning packing and at daylight I left with Raleigh to bring in the flashlight camera. At 10 a.m. we started for Bozeman but the road was in very bad condition and we slid all over it and did not reach Bozeman until nearly 2 p.m.

Here we found a wire from Huyler saying he could not buy Circle H but had bought 187 acres next to it called the Grant property.

We left in the afternoon via Butte for Salt Lake City where I hoped to kill a buffalo.

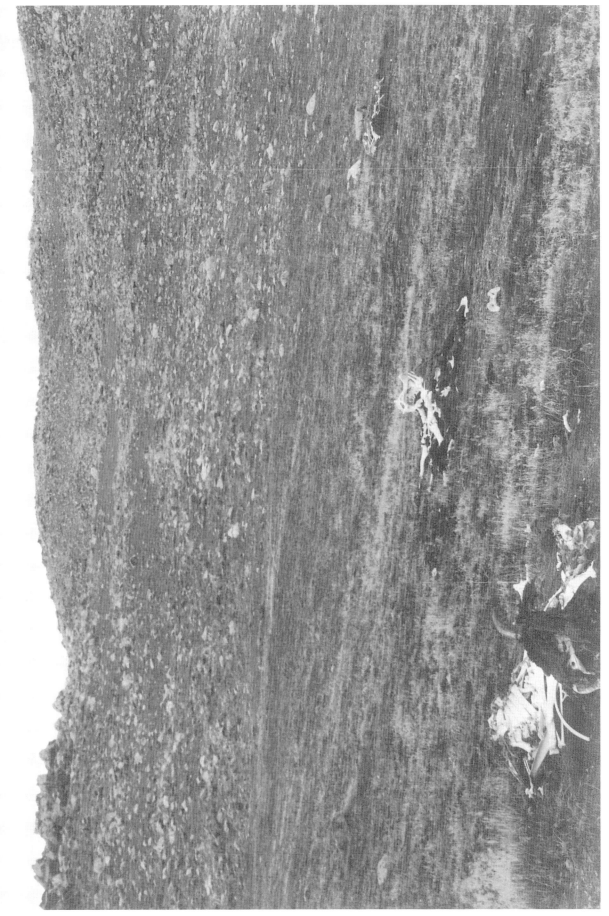

Bleached buffalo bones on an area called "The Plains" on Antelope Island, Great Salt Lake, Utah

The men land on Antelope Island on November 7, 1926.

The Buffalo of Antelope Island

1926

*This journal is contained in the same journal as the September trip to Wyoming and
Montana in 1926. This is the smallest journal kept by Gray during his thirty-five years
of writing and becomes the seventh chapter of this book.*

To complete my collection of horned mammals of North America I wanted
a buffalo head. I knew that of the 20 million buffalo that once roamed the
prairies, the slaughter of 1865 to 1875 had nearly exterminated this animal.
The buffalo was originally found in almost all parts of this country except the
Northeast and Southeast. A few buffalo were reported in North Carolina in
revolutionary times and a herd of about a thousand once roamed the present state
of Kentucky, according to Daniel Boone. But over a hundred years ago these animals
had disappeared from east of the Mississippi River, and by 1850 they had been
driven back to the dry plains and the region of the Rocky Mountains.

By 1875 the immense herds had dwindled until there were but two remnants -
one in the Panhandle of Texas and the other in Montana. By 1888 both of these
herds had been broken and slaughtered, and the only buffalo that survived were
scattered bunches existing in isolated spots.

Records compiled by the American Bison Society show that in 1889 the American
buffalo was at its low ebb, there being only 835 wild and 256 captive buffalo in
existence. In 1913 there were 3,500 head; the last thirteen years have seen the herds
multiply until there are now something like 8,000 buffalo.

I knew my only chance of getting a head was from privately owned herds, as all
other buffalo were protected in the national parks of the United States or Canada.
Therefore, I obtained a record of all the private herds and found that the one on
Antelope Island in Great Salt Lake City, Utah, was living under conditions most
closely approximating their wild state and had been less accustomed to man than
even the large herd in Yellowstone. Here I hoped to get some semblance of sport.

The camp on Antelope Island

THE BUFFALO OF ANTELOPE ISLAND

Before I could complete my arrangements with the owners of the island for the privilege of shooting a buffalo, the herd was sold to the Scotty Phillips Buffalo Ranch of Fort St. Pierre, South Dakota, and preparations were started to capture the 250 head on the island and ship them to South Dakota.

It was with great joy that I read in August that all efforts to round up the herd for shipment had failed because the animals were too wild and the terrain too rough to work over. The attempt had been abandoned.

I renewed my negotiations with A.H. Leonard, head of the Scotty Phillips Buffalo Ranch, for the right to shoot on Antelope Island and it was finally arranged. So on November 4th I arrived in Salt Lake City and on the morning of November 7th started for Antelope Island. We motored to Saltair, where Leonard greeted us decked out in a red sweater with blue collar and cuffs, and loud checked pants tucked into blue cowboy boots. His Stetson was enormous and banded on the edge of the rim with red. A wonderful apparition and indicative of much that was to follow.

There was a considerable sea running on the lake after the gale of the previous day. We were put aboard a 40-foot launch which, while a good sea boat, rolled and pitched tremendously during the crossing, throwing plenty of spray over us. The shallow water and the high percentage of salt in the water (22 percent) made the waves heavy and short. When they hit the boat it was like a hard blow from a hammer and the spray that drenched us left a white deposit on our clothes. When the engine broke down halfway across, as was to be expected of such a rattletrap craft, we fell off into the trough of the sea and rolled our scuppers under. Finally, after an hour and half's run, we landed on the lee side of Antelope Island at a dilapidated dock that had been used for shipping cattle and sheep.

A quarter of a mile from the dock we could make out two tents and an unpainted building and toward these we made our way. These proved to be the main camp of the Buffalo outfit and, besides the cook and two roustabouts, there were three guides and a couple of horse wranglers gathered here. There was also a taxidermist named Jack Miles from Denver and a man named Slight of the Pathe News Service who was trying to make a movie of the buffalo.

To my great disappointment I found I was not to go out this first afternoon so after lunch I climbed to the top of the ridge to look over the country that we were to hunt. The island was about seven miles wide at its widest point and stretched away to the north for twenty-one miles in a succession of peaks, the highest of

Brigham Young's Ranch - a site to explore

which rose 2,000 feet above the level of the lake or 6,000 feet above the sea. These mountains were bare except for a few stunted cedars, many of which had been killed by fire six or seven years ago when much of the island was burned over. On the top of the ridge among the rocks I found seven old buffalo skeletons bleached white by the sun. Far below, the lake shimmered in the last light of a dying sun. Gold and amber and brilliant purple streaked the sky, throwing in silhouette the rugged mountains on the western shore of the lake. I sat there until dark and then made my way back to camp.

I was up early the next morning but there seemed no excitement in the camp and it was 8 a.m. before breakfast was ready and 9 a.m. before we started in a wagon for the ranch seven miles north. This old ranch was formerly owned by Brigham Young and consisted of a couple of adobe buildings and several frame barns and granaries. The old adobe barn was struck by lightening two years ago and was in a sad state of repair.

Before we reached the ranch we saw a small buffalo bull and I took a few feet of film and some still pictures of him. He had come down to water at one of the numerous springs that occur along the flat shoreline. He was small and his head did not tempt us, so we left him to grow a few more years.

On arrival at the ranch it was the work of only half an hour to rope enough horses and saddle up. My guide was Bill Powell, a full blooded Sioux Indian who has been with the Scotty Phillips Ranch for many years. We were accompanied by two wranglers and the Pathe man. Two other men drove behind us in the wagon to which four horses were hitched. This wagon was to bring in the meat, hide and head, in case we killed in an accessible place.

We left the ranch about 10:30 a.m. and climbed to the top of the ridge, which at this point was about a thousand feet above the lake. There was no road and the wagon had hard going bumping over rocks and pulling up out of the coulees.

Finally we reached the summit and searched the western slope of the island with our glasses. Nothing was in sight so we left the team on top and rode down toward the western shore. About halfway down we spied a solitary bull standing on a point between two deep ravines. He was in a commanding position but from the top of the hill had been out of sight. It was now nearly 11:30 a.m. and the sun, reflected from the bare rocks, was very warm.

We were able to get our horses down into a coulee and rode to within 600 yards

Prentiss Gray with Springfield rifle beside his buffalo. Sherman Gray in 1994 still owns this favorite hunting rifle.

of the bull. From here we looked him over carefully and I was assured by the guide that he was worth shooting. We started the stalk and the whole crowd came along. The Pathe man was furious because I insisted they all stay behind with the horses but it was my hunt and I did not want an audience. Our stalk was fairly short and the last half of it I insisted on making alone without even the guide, as I wanted to get some fun out of it and, so far, it had been a regular gang party.

I worked my way carefully between the rocks, keeping a clump of cedars between the buffalo and myself. Finally I passed these trees and nothing more offered as cover except sagebrush. However, I saw a particularly high bush that stood fully four feet and was very thick. Behind this I crawled along on my hands and knees until I was only twenty-eight paces away from the bull.

Slowly I raised up and fired. The bull went down, shot through the top of the shoulder. It so happened that this was the first buffalo killed on the island with one shot and Bill Powell yelled to me to fire again quick. I could see no reason to do so as the bull was prone and refused to shoot again, to Bill's great disgust and annoyance. He came up yelling to shoot again and was tremendously surprised to find the bull down.

My shot startled a coyote. I only caught glimpses of him as he ran through the sagebrush until he was about 600 yards away. I knew I could not hit him at that distance but fired two shots to stir him up. Both times I overshot and I was greatly surprised at the carrying ability of the 180-grain bullets.

As soon as the bull fell, the entourage moved up and one of the men signaled the wagon to come on. The buffalo lay in a devilish place for the wagon and we had to block the wheels and ease it down the last slope with a rope. It was 12:30 p.m. when the bull dropped and by 1:30 p.m. we had him skinned out and loaded on the wagon.

Then all the riders hitched their lariats to the wagon and with the four horses straining their utmost we started up the hill. Halfway up the steepest pitch a "hame and belly" band on one of the lead horses broke and his whole harness came off. The wagon started down-hill and it certainly looked like a wreck. However, the outriders held it until the wheels were blocked with rocks and when the harness had been repaired we pulled it out and finally reached the summit.

As I hoped to catch the afternoon boat back to Saltair, I took a short cut and did not go back to the ranch with the boys, but rode direct for the camp at the

Sunset on Antelope Island - Peace, satisfaction and love of the wild

landing. Here I arrived at 3:30 p.m. but the boat had not been heard from. It arrived at 5 p.m. and everybody aboard was so drunk that I did not care about returning to Saltair with them that night. We had to hoist the captain up onto the dock with a derrick. Meanwhile, the wagon had arrived and when Miles skinned out the buffalo head we carefully compared its measurements with the best head taken to date on the island. Except in width between the eyes it exceeded all the heads taken so far, measuring:

Length of horns 16 1/4 inches
Spread between tips 20 1/2 inches
Greatest spread 25 1/2 inches
Circumference at base 14 inches

The boys estimated the buffalo weighed more than 1,800 pounds alive. The surprising thing to me was the thickness of the skin over the forehead, which was 1 5/8 inches thick. I had been told that no high-powered rifle would shoot through this skin over the forehead and that the day previous to my arrival a man had tried it with a .303 Savage without success. While I appreciated that it was like hitting a chunk of rubber with an axe, I doubted this statement and challenged Miles, the taxidermist, on it. We repaired to the shed where the head and hide was hung to dry and set up the head of the buffalo that I had killed. At ten paces I fired at a cigarette paper laid on the forehead where the skin and hair was thickest. The bullet tore through the skin, through the frontal bone of the skull, through the lower jaw, through two thicknesses of hide of the back skin and buried itself in the ground. So do many hunting myths disappear.

The next morning I started back to Saltair to put the buffalo meat into cold storage and ship the head east to be mounted.

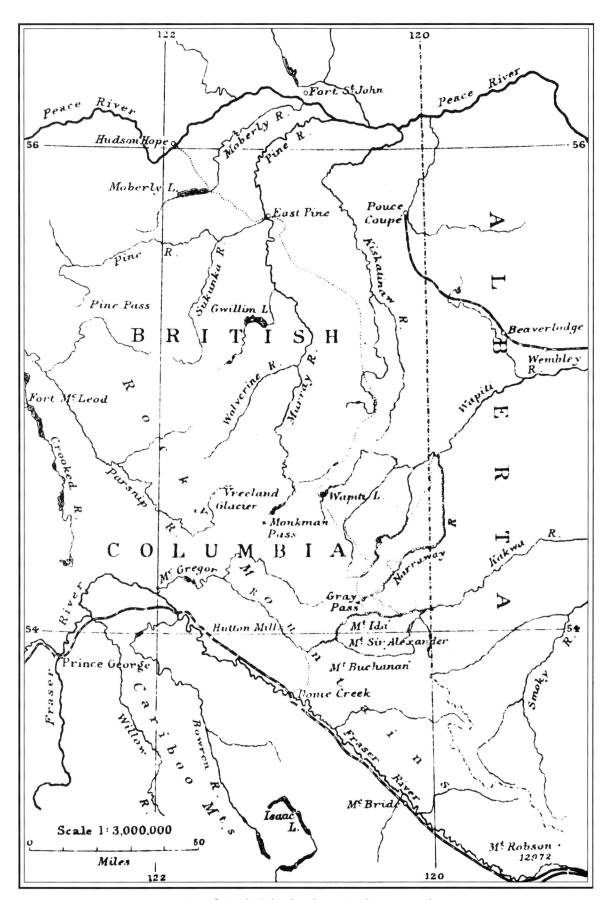

Map of British Columbia shows Gray's 1927 travels

From the Peace to the Fraser

1927

The eighth chapter of this book is the entire journal of Gray when he traveled along the Peace and the Fraser Rivers and charted lakes, rivers and mountain peaks never before charted for Canadian government maps. This journal, the thickest of his North American journals, contains fabulous photographs of scenery and wildlife and documents many big game hunts. The original journal, twelfth in the series of 21 journals, is bound in navy blue leather and cloth and contains printed marbled endsheets of pale blue, cream and gold colors. Spectacular scenic photographs highlight this chapter.

After three days and nights on the trans-continental train, the cool sheets and hot baths of the Hotel Macdonald at Edmonton were a great relief. When I awoke a sea of fog covered the valley of the Saskatchewan River, but an hour later a brilliant sun had chased it away, and directly below the hotel the river was disclosed winding its tortuous muddy way. It was Harvest weather, snappy mornings and warm middays. The town thought and talked only yields of wheat and prayed that the frost would hold off a fortnight more to let the last fields of grain reach maturity. Threshing hands were pouring into town by every train from as far east as the Maritime Provinces to gain the wages offered in the wheat fields. Even local political issues had sunk beneath the all-important question of the operations of the Canadian Wheat Pool.

Our day was spent in getting our baggage, rifles and cameras through the Canadian customs. The last few things on our list were finally purchased and we started out with Elmo Essery to meet the notables of the city. We were introduced to the Governor of Alberta Province, Dr. Egbert; the Manager of the Bank of Montreal, Mr. Pike; and what was a stranger to us from the United States, a "Beer Parlor." By 4 p.m. we were fully ready to take our train for the north and were escorted to the station by several autos, loaded with distinguished citizens who bade us a vociferous and tuneful adieu. It's a good town - Edmonton.

FROM THE PEACE TO THE FRASER

We were on the last lap of our railroad journey. From Edmonton to Grand Prairie is 406 miles and the timetable said it could be done in 23 1/2 hours. Our experience, however, made this seem very doubtful. For the first few hours we ran through a country that had been fairly well cleared - wheat fields just beginning to ripen stretched away for miles on either hand. Toward evening more uncleared land began to show itself; brush piles showed the process of clearing and the rough first plowing told a story of the making of new fields to add to the tremendous acreage on which Canada is already producing a large part of the world's wheat. The talk in the smoking room was of queer sounding places that had never appeared in the geographies of our days at school - Slave Lake, High Prairie, Winagami, and Sexsmith - all were catalogued by their yields of grain per acre. Here before us was the making of a new empire - another Nebraska or Iowa was being carved out of the wilderness.

As late as 1890 this country was condemned in no uncertain terms by one of its most noted explorers, Warburton Pike. He states:

I made careful inquiries and observations along the whole length of Peace River, and I do not deny that in some parts of its course crops of wheat and barley may be raised in favorable seasons, as the well-managed farms of Mr. Lawrence at Vermillion, and Mr. Brick higher up at Smoky River fully attest: but their farms and all spots in which grain ripens are in close proximity to the bed of the river and there the amount of arable land is limited. Climb the steep banks and take a glance over the millions of fertile acres that the philanthropic politician wishes to see cultivated: notice the frost on a summer's morning, and make the attempt, as has often been made already, to raise a crop on this elevated plateau. In ten years' time this may be a cattle country, although the hay swamps are insufficient to ensure enough feed for the long winter; but let us have an end of this talk of sending poor settlers to starve in a land unable to supply food to the Indian, who is accustomed to a life of continual struggle with a relentless nature.

This same country, "this elevated plateau," raised nearly eight million bushels of grain in 1927. Herman Trelle, a homesteader of Wembley, won the world's championship at the Chicago Fair for both hard wheat and oats. The suitability of this region for the production of most kinds of grain as well as the raising of hogs and cattle has been abundantly demonstrated.

The train creaked and swayed and threatened to leave the rails. It even acquired a hot box doing sixteen miles an hour, but it was far better than we had expected to find - an ancient but clean Pullman and a very excellent dining car. At last, toward 3 p.m., we pulled into Spirit River where we met J. McDermott, the factor at the Hudson Bay Post at Hudson's Hope. He was on his way out to see his wife but she had died the morning we left Edmonton and we had been asked to bear the sad news to him. While we were talking to him the train suddenly started to back out. I got aboard but Frank Dewing could not make it and we pulled away leaving him disconsolately standing on the platform. He commandeered an auto and started after us in the hope that he could catch us at the next station, five miles below. I pleaded with the conductor to hold the train there, but he was adamant. After loafing all night and getting behind schedule several hours, he was possessed with the idea of making up all this lost time in the remaining thirty-five miles. Frank dashed into Roycroft just as we were pulling out and by a quick run, swung onto the train.

At Grand Prairie Mr. R.O.G. Bennett, manager of the Bank of Montreal, met us and turned us over to John McEachern, who was to motor us to Rolla. The car was loaded and away a half-hour after the train pulled in and covered the 104 miles to Rolla by 9 p.m. The road was fair and for the most part led through the same endless wheat fields. Just before we reached Pouce Coupe we crossed the boundary line into British Columbia.

On our arrival at Rolla we located McGarvey, who operated the boat on the Peace River from Rolla Landing to Hudson's Hope. He was full of "Spiritus Frumenti" and assured us that he would "start sometime tomorrow and get there anytime in the next four or five days, but, "You will have a hell of a good time loafing along in the boat." As we did not care to do any loafing after hurrying three thousand miles to get this far, we sat up half the night trying to find a way to speed him up. At midnight he woke us up to be sure we had enough liquor to take us upriver. I told him we had only half a quart and he wanted us to drive back to Pouce Coupe at once for more. We declined and compromised on an ice cream soda with a large shot of Scotch in it which cleaned out our remaining supply. A more awful combination I never tasted. After this we went off again to bed and McGarvey to Pouce Coupe for more booze.

He appeared, however, the next morning at 11 a.m. to our great relief. While

Prentiss Gray begins his trip along the Peace River from the town of Rolla in 1927.

waiting for him we had been interviewing the natives about their winter trapping country. One W. (Curley) Cochrane told us much about the country north of the Peace toward the Nelson and Liard Rivers. All agreed that Stone's sheep did not exist south of Peace River nor *Ovis canadensis* north of the river, nor, in fact, north of Wapiti Lake.

We decided to have dinner before starting and so did not leave Rolla until 1 p.m. A Ford car took us the nineteen miles to Rolla Landing over the roughest road I have ever seen an automobile tackle. The last mile and a half you could have used a parachute; I chose to walk.

At the landing (elevation 1,425 feet) there was much fixing of the boat to be done, the mail to be loaded and fifty gallons of gas (cost one dollar per gallon up here) to be pumped aboard. Finally we were away at 4:30 p.m. and for the first time we realized the volume of water and the strength of the current of the mighty Peace River. McGarvey's boat, called "Starvation" because he said it did not earn enough to feed even a porcupine, was capable of doing fourteen or fifteen miles in still water, but headed upriver we hardly moved in places against the current. The average drift of a log from Hudson's Hope to Rolla Landing is about ten hours, indicating a current average, at high water, of nine- to ten- miles-an-hour. Just ahead of us was a powerboat pushing two barges, freight-laden, upriver. It was making less than two miles an hour, and in the swiftest water was forced to tie one barge up to the bank and take one ahead at a time.

We bucked the current, twisted and turned over shallow bars for five hours. When it became too dark to run farther, and we tied up at Taylor Flats (thirty-two miles from Rolla Landing) for the night. A man named McKnight had a cabin there and his good wife soon had some supper for us. A couple of cowpunchers, moving a bunch of cattle south; the government tax assessor; and a bride and groom just returned from their honeymoon in Vancouver, gathered around the table, and over the after-supper pipes the conversation drifted inevitably to wheat. It was always wheat, and even back here in the bush we could not escape. Yields, markets, grasshopper pests, who was cutting - always wheat, wheat, wheat. I never wanted to see a piece of bread again.

We were up at 5:30 a.m. the next day, hopeful that our good example would bestir McGarvey, but he just turned over again and went back to sleep, impervious to our pleadings and statements that there was no fog on the river and that it was a

Frank Dewing, left, pumps water from the boat, "Starvation," as unidentified passenger steers.

long way to Hudson's Hope. It was 8:30 a.m. before we cast off from the bank and headed up stream.

We had seventy miles ahead of us and it proved a not uninteresting trip. The river for most of the distance was about 600 yards wide and ran between banks that through the centuries had been cut almost perpendicular, towering about 700 feet to the first bench. We were told that the north bench extended fairly level as far back in places as forty miles from the river. On the south side the country appeared more broken, and the higher hills showing above the bank were covered with a thick growth of spruce and jack pines.

We stopped for supper at Ardel's homestead, and after climbing the bank about 600 feet above the river, found his cabin on a flat of 200 acres. He had a most prosperous looking place, well kept and apparently well run. His Dutch wife gave us a splendid supper and reluctantly we drank our third cup of tea and started our boat again. We ran two hours more upriver before we landed and shook out our sleeping bags. Just before we pulled into the beach we caught a glimpse of our first game - a black bear that slipped into the brush before we could get a shot at him.

We had landed, however, in a mosquito bed and I have never seen the pests worse. McGarvey produced a bit of netting and with this over our heads we slept a little but the pests were troublesome all through the night and wakened us often. We did not loiter long in the morning but pushed off in the boat as fast as we could and after a short run of two hours, turned her nose into the beach at Hudson's Hope. Breakfast was our first thought and we did it full justice: then we remembered the previous night and bought thirty-five yards of cheese cloth. We arranged with Mrs. Peck, who possessed the only sewing machine in Hope, to make five mosquito tents for our party as we felt sure we were going to need them if the weather continued warm.

Mrs. Peck was a fine type of frontier woman who, when she found that I was eager to learn all I could about the country, welcomed the chance to talk. Her conversation, stored up during the many months of lonely life in the woods, poured out in overwhelming volume as her foot pumped the pedal of the sewing machine and her nimble fingers fed the muslin of the mosquito tents under the needle. She was at this time thirty-seven years old and, after serving through the war as a nurse, had come out to Canada. In Pouce Coupe, which most people would consider the edge of civilization, she had married Peck and they decided they would really pioneer,

Peace River - water highway

taking up from the Government free land, as they had no money to buy the relatively expensive land around the settlement.

Therefore, they filed on a homestead on the Pine River where their nearest neighbor was forty miles away and the nearest settlement more than 100 miles distant. They raised some cattle and enough hay to feed them. She and her husband each maintained a trapline over fifty miles long and tending a line of traps means visiting each one over this distance at least once in four days, sometimes in bitter blizzards with the thermometer at forty below; sleeping at night when away from the home camp in a brush lean-to. From their traps they earned the $500 a year necessary to buy clothes and such food as they could not raise on their farm.

For seven years they kept up this struggle while four boys were born to them. Then they decided to return to civilization and came out to Hudson's Hope where Peck obtained a job as forest ranger. Her great joy at being near other people, even if there was only one other white woman in town, was evident, but as she called in her four sturdy boys she said that she wondered sometimes if they would not be healthier and happier if she had kept them out in the woods away from the deteriorating influence of the town.

After lunch we hired a team and drove up the Canyon of the Peace. This impassable barrier to navigation extends for twenty-two miles above Hudson's Hope and is so rough that no boat can get through it. In the early days when the Hudson's Bay Company was freighting all their supplies up the Peace for the posts in the Northwest, they hauled boats and freight over a fourteen-mile portage which cuts across the bend of the river.

There was no word for us from Harry Snyder at the Hope, and he had agreed to wait for us here only until the morning of the twenty-sixth. Here it was the twenty-seventh and he had not even arrived. We visualized all sorts of accidents that might have occurred to him on his river trip and anxiously decided to cross the portage in the hope of getting some news of him.

We left the Hope at 6 a.m. in a light wagon for the head of the Canyon. At about nine we reached the end of the portage and found there a Major Anderson and guides waiting for teams to take them across the Portage. Anderson told us that he had passed Snyder at Ne Parle Pas rapids and that he was due here shortly. We decided to wait and meanwhile set off to photograph the rapids in the Canyon.

The river, in a distance of twenty-two miles through the canyon, falls 243 feet so that it is mostly fast, white water. With the exception of the Liard, the Peace is the only river in the United States or Canada that rises on the west side of the Rockies and cuts through the Continental Divide to find its way to the oceans east and north. Through this canyon the Peace makes its way through the last of the Rockies and starts on its way to the Arctic.

The walls are sheer, rising from 600 to 700 feet, and at their foot the swirling water eddies and tears its way along the narrow channel across which you could throw a stone any place. We were rather careful to keep away from the edge as once into this torrent you would do more than get your feet wet. No one has ever gone through alive and, they say, even a log thrown in at the head of the gorge is chewed to small pieces before it reaches the Hope.

All reports agree there is no considerable waterfall in the canyon, although no one has ever thoroughly explored its length. The river seems to descend in a series of rapids between perpendicular and often overhanging walls of sandstone. We heard a story at the Hope of seven Chinamen who tried to run the Canyon. They had been mining on the gravel bars above the Ne Parle Pas Rapids and having collected considerable gold dust, were in great terror of being robbed before they could reach the "outside." Just before the freeze-up, they built a raft and started down river. As they drew near the head of the canyon, they saw a number of men on the bank of the stream waving frantically to them. They misinterpreted these warning signals and concluded it was an effort to lure them ashore to steal their dust. They sailed serenely past and before they knew it they were in the swift water at the head of the canyon. Nothing more was ever seen or heard of them or their raft.

About the middle of the afternoon we heard a chug-chug upriver and soon around a bend came Snyder's two boats. We shot a moving picture of their arrival and then for several minutes told each other how glad we were to all be together. There were no teams available at the Portage to move his outfit over, as a party of politicians touring the country for votes had the previous day used all the teams in Hudson's Hope.

We had, however, arranged for three teams to move Snyder's gear over the Portage early the next day and that was the best that could be done. About 4:30 p.m. we started back to the Hope, but as the day was fine we were in no hurry. We were traveling a historic path. Mackenzie had followed it in 1792; McLeod, Finlay,

Butler and Pike had trodden it. It was a gateway to the great north land that lay behind the Rockies. As we walked through the open woods we dreamed of the long lines of Indians carrying heavy loads across its portage for the early travelers or the Hudson's Bay Company. A bear track in a boggy place recalled that in 100 years since it had been opened, the country had not become crowded with settlers.

Three spruce hens flew up with a whir that startled us. Soon the Akeley was running and we were putting away a moving picture of our feathered friends who allowed us to approach quite close, even with the heavy camera and tripod.

At the Hope we at once set about great preparations for "Snyder et al" to arrive early the next day. We were to pull out before noon, but they lost a horse and did not reach the Hope until after lunch. We therefore abandoned all thought of getting away this day and settled down to organizing the packs, balancing the loads and leaving behind surplus stuff.

We were about to see what the white spaces on the map, which had so attracted us, contained. We knew that a great country south from the Peace River to the Fraser, west to the Continental Divide, and east of the British Columbia-Alberta Boundary, stretched before us practically unknown. Few expeditions had penetrated it farther south than Pine Pass; there was locked in these mountains the answer to one biological question that we hoped to solve. How far north does the bighorn (*Ovis canadensis*) extend its range in this area, and did it overlap and interbreed with the Stone's sheep (*Ovis stonei*)? In 1912 Fredrick K. Vreeland hunted sheep on Mt. Selwyn but met with no success. They, however, killed Stone's sheep near Laurier Pass north of the Peace. In 1912 S. Prescott Fay passed through the Northwestern part of this area without seeing sheep or sheep sign. One of our guides in 1917 had killed Stone's sheep on the Wicked River not far north of the junction with the Peace, but Snyder, Paul and Bates, on their way down the river, had tried to locate these sheep without success. The most northern record of Bighorn was on the Wapiti River north of Jarvis Pass where William Rindsfoos in 1916 killed some specimens at this point. Here was a wide stretch of territory more than 200 miles in a northwest-southeast line where there might be sheep of either of the two species mentioned or an interbreeding of these species such as occurs between the *Ovis stonei* and the *Ovis dalli* in the north.

The country was not without its record of failures to solve its secrets. After the disastrous trip of Warburton Pike in 1890 around the north and west edges of this

Breakfast was the first thought at Hudson's Hope.

territory, H. Somers-Somerset in 1893 was reduced to killing his packhorses for food and reached Fort McLeod almost starving in an attempt to cross the northern section from Dunvegan through Pine Pass. We knew it was a country shunned by hunters, and trappers and all the professional guides from Edmonton north gave it a bad name and declared it contained no game. We wanted to know why.

At last on August 29th we were ready to start; by 7 a.m. the horses were in and we started packing. We found, however, that we had two more loads than packhorses and we had to swing them on two of the saddle horses. We expected to supply the deficit from the Indians at Moberly Lake.

We followed scrupulously the usual ritual of the first day on the trail. Repacking horses every few minutes, adjusting packs, and finally nursing two exhausted horses slowly along the trail for the last two miles. One old black horse started the day by kicking off his pack, and Dutch ovens and panniers flew in all directions. He broke his pack saddle into pieces but the pack cover caught in the cinch and stayed with him, flopping as he ran, and adding to his terror. It took us an hour to track him down and catch him.

As a result, we did not reach the west end of Moberly Lake until 6 p.m., and it was 7:30 p.m. before we made camp about three miles down the lake. Supper was cooked long after dark and it was only a few minutes thereafter before I was tucked in bed, very tired and both foot and saddle sore.

We had traveled twenty-two miles through a rolling country rising to a maximum of 2,500 feet, or a thousand feet above the Peace River. The woods were principally jack pines, with quaking aspen and cottonwoods around the lakes and low places. The ground was covered with low blueberry bushes in full fruit; saskatoons, raspberries, and chokecherries were in profusion, and we often halted along the trail to eat our fill.

Our crew consisted of: Jim Ross, a trapper from Hudson's Hope; John T. (Slim) Cowart, Prince George, British Columbia; Elmer Keith, Durkee, Oregon; Frank Dewing, Livingston, Montana; Joe MacFarland, Hudson's Hope; Pete Callao, Joe Callao, Sam Callao, brothers and Cree Indians, Jack Fish Lake; Harry Snyder, Chicago; George Bates, Caroll Paul, Marquette, Michigan; and Prentiss N. Gray, New York.

We were delayed the next day waiting for three more packhorses to come in from the Indian camp at Jack Fish Lake. Some of our horses were overloaded and

Men prepare for the start of their Canadian adventure on August 29, 1927.

two had barely reached camp the previous night. Therefore, after supper we sent Pete Callao to get more horses but he had trouble rounding them up and we were obliged to wait a couple of hours for him. Finally our pack train was complete with thirty-three horses.

Our trail for the first four miles led along the north shore of Moberly Lake, a beautiful bit of water eleven miles long and about two miles wide. The Indians tell that it abounds with white fish and the stakes set along the shore for gill nets seemed to indicate that the Indians were busy catching their winter's supply.

We crawled up over a timbered ridge after crossing the Moberly River where it emerges from the lake. The trail was pretty well overgrown, but not impassable and frequently we all stopped to feast on the profusion of raspberries that grew everywhere. After topping the ridge at an elevation of 4,000 feet, we dropped down into the valley of Wobby Creek. This stream's lower end, where it enters into the North Pine River, meandered through a succession of lovely meadows, where the feed was belly deep on the horses. Here there was a profusion of pea vine of which the horses were particularly fond, and it was hard work to keep them traveling to make camp on the bank of the North Pine River.

We were in camp at 5 p.m., having covered eighteen miles. It was a splendid camp at the foot of a big meadow with our tents pitched under some poplar trees. As the cook had lots of time to prepare dinner before darkness we had a large feed.

It rained hard most all the night but the morning was clear except for a few fleecy clouds in the sky. Our trail lay down the North Pine for about six miles to its forks with the Middle Pine. Here we forded and the water deepened till it looked as if we would have to swim. As it reached the skirts of our saddles it fortunately began to shoal and we came ashore without soaking a pack.

Just before we reached the ford, we came to the homestead of Frank Treadwell, who had taken up 364 acres of bottom land. If the railroad ever goes through as surveyed he will have a valuable farm, for apparently everything grows here. We bought four sack-loads of cabbages, beets, rutabagas, carrots and potatoes that we dug ourselves in his wonderful garden, of which he was justly proud. I can't say as much for his squaw. She was fat, and although young, had four kids in evidence. Treadwell was more than seventy and I asked one of our Indians if the children were his. He replied, "No, but he thinks so."

After leaving the ford we followed an old Indian trail, which had not been cut

Pack string fords Moberly River.

out for years, to get up over a shoulder of Table Mountain. We finally topped the ridge at 4,100 feet and turned almost due east through an open forest of cottonwood and scattered spruces.

After several miles we emerged into flat open land of Lone Prairie, where a man named Penwell had a homestead. The land was fertile; his cattle appeared sleek and fat, but his children all looked as if they had had the rickets and his wife resembled a worn-out dray horse. As George expressed it, "We are now among the pioneers where men are whiskered and the women are double breasted."

We made a comfortable camp early in the afternoon after covering eighteen miles; and after supper Paul fished a small stream that flowed past our tents. He soon landed seventeen grayling, which promised a change from ham or bacon for breakfast.

On two or three occasions during the day the equilibrium of our pack train had been upset by yellow jackets. Their nests were generally close to some swampy place, and the first horses floundering through disturbed the hornets and got stung. Therefore all was confusion as we crowded the rest of the string of horses through on the run. At the last one, the packhorse just ahead of me mired and stuck her nose in the mud. Just then a hornet stung her on the tail and she turned completely over and up on her feet in one action. I put my horse through and he mired just as the packhorse had done but fortunately he did not turn clear over and I stayed in the saddle. It was most amusing to see the pack train pass a hornet's nest until it was your turn to ride through.

We awoke in a downpour - breakfast was a wet affair as no cook tent had been put up. We were fairly dry under our sleeping fly but packing looked like a damp performance. We sat around camp until 10 a.m. when it gave promise of clearing and we started slinging packs. Finally we were away, but one delay after another killed time and we finished the day with only twelve miles to our credit. This was the first day we had been without a trail of any kind. Previously we had been using Indian trails such as they were, but after this camp at Lone Prairie we lost the last vestige of a trail. We were cutting "across country" from the Middle Pine to beyond the South Pine, and the country was devilish.

This day was an endless drag of repacking horses and pulling them out of muskeg, and was capped when two fell through a corduroy bridge that we had hastily constructed across a swampy little creek. My horse tore off one of my saddle bags,

Camping party enjoy a smoke and hot coffee.

and profanity was running riot all over the place most of the day. The line of conversation would seem to indicate that every horse in the train was descended from a female dog and that their fathers were all bachelors.

We were held up a bit at the South Pine to find a ford, but finally got across without swimming. It would have made but little difference anyway, as it rained hard most of the day and we were all pretty wet when we pulled up to camp at dark.

The next morning broke clear and bright and by 5:30 a.m. we had finished breakfast and by 7:30 were on the trail. Our camp had been pitched in a meadow high up on the mountain slope above the South Pine. Our view across the valley to the high hills between the Middle and North Pine was magnificent.

While we were at breakfast an old fellow, Sandy Elliot, rode into camp full of a desire to converse. He was the old type frontiersman, long curly red hair and beard, buckskin clothes and slowly recovering from a week's drunk in Pouce Coupe. He could talk faster than any three men in camp and as we thought we held the world's record with Elmer Keith, the cook, we were flabbergasted to find his superior. An hour after he left, Frank started off with a sack to find the Elliot homestead. He had been gone only a few minutes when we heard a shot and Frank came back in a hurry but with a sack full of rutabagas. He could not find the owner and had raided his garden, when the old fellow took a shot at him but fortunately missed.

For three hours after leaving camp we bucked brush; first alder brush then a small second-growth quaking aspen that had grown up through a lot of deadfalls. It was terrible going and it lasted until we crossed Cold Creek, where we entered a country of muskeg and jack pines. We plugged along all day till 5 p.m. and in spite of repacking innumerable horses and dragging pack animals out of bogs, we made twenty-two miles to Salt Creek by camping-time at 5 p.m. The cook had shot two ruffed grouse with a revolver and we four "dudes" had a supper fit for a king. After nine hours in the saddle over the worst possible country without a sign of a trail, we were entitled to it. Lunch these days consisted of a sandwich eaten in the saddle so that by night we were ravenously hungry.

Again it rained most of the night but daylight came clear. The four "dudes" with Joe and Frank took off ahead of the outfit in the hopes of picking off a moose or some other fresh meat. Our course lay almost due south from Salt Creek to the big bend of the Cutbank River. Jim Ross assured us it was the best trail we would see on the entire trip and that he expected a full twenty miles before night. We started with light hearts and our hopes were fully justified. A more perfect day never lay out-of-doors and the "going" was the best we had struck so far. For the first four hours our course lay along the bank of Salt Creek, a beautiful stream that meandered through a wide valley. Timbered slopes rose 1,000 feet gradually on either hand and the meadows through which we traveled were firm and smooth.

After we passed the big bend in Salt Creek and had climbed over the hill, we dropped down to Muskeg Lake which was well named. We, however, kept up a little on the sidehill in the timber and had better footing. About an hour later we came on an abandoned trapper's cabin that was the only sign of human habitation we had seen since we left Elliott's.

We pulled into camp on the West Branch of the Cutbank River after nearly nine hours of steady travel and estimated that we had covered twenty-four miles. Paul tried to land some fish in the river but could not get a rise. We all shaved and cleaned up, principally because it was Saturday night.

Moose sign was abundant and we again took the trail, passing one moose wallow after another, on the constant lookout for a "piece of meat." All we saw during the morning was a large owl who refused to tarry long enough for us to get his picture.

We were following the west branch of the Cutbank River and after three or four miles of easy going we plunged into a mess of downed timber that would be hard to beat. For the next four hours we floundered and stumbled through this. Horses were down with their legs caught in the tangle, which had to be chopped away to get them on their feet again; lash ropes pulled loose and packs were pulled sideways by the snags and the few standing trees. It meant endless work for the two packers at the end of the train.

Our order of procedure was about as follows: the four "dudes," Pete, the head Indian, and Frank, with the camera horse left camp at 7:30 a.m. after a 6 a.m. breakfast. At 8 a.m. the pack train with Joe in the lead and a man behind each six horses moved out. Sam, the third Indian, rode alongside and pulled out any horse whose pack showed signs of loosening. This horse was picked up by Elmer Keith and Jim Ross at the tail of the train and repacked. They averaged repacking about twenty horses a day in this sort of country.

About noon the advance party of "dudes" made a pot of tea and ate their sandwiches. By the time the pack train had caught up, a bowl of tea was ready for each man, who drank it, so to speak, on the fly.

About 4 p.m. the guide at the head of the train began to look for a camp site and sometime before 5 p.m. his hand went up to indicate a halt. Whereupon all of us breathed a sigh of relief and perked up considerably. Eight or nine hours in the saddle was long enough and with the horses loaded as heavily as they were, it was plenty for them.

We ended the day after sixteen miles travel at a splendid campsite on the Cutbank River in a grove of spruce. Paul and George went off at once and soon had caught a mess of grayling and rainbow trout that did well for dinner. George pulled one splendid two-pound rainbow out of a pool and was correspondingly proud.

Again it rained at night. Breakfast was a moist party and packing a slippery mess, but finally we were away shortly before 8 a.m. Our trail at first lay along gentle grassy slopes but soon we were in the endless windfalls only to emerge into bottomless muskeg. It was a busy day for the packers and a wearisome day for all hands and all horses.

About noon we reached Bear Hole Lake, that does not appear on any map but which is a sizeable bit of water about two miles long and averaging over a half-mile wide, with a little island in the middle of the lake toward the northwest end. The lake is located on a high plateau entirely surrounded by dense jack pine and spruce woods so that it is not visible for more than 200 yards from its edge. There is no commanding hill near it from which it can be seen and it is not surprising that the government surveyors, in making a topographical survey of this country, missed it.

We followed its shores for about two miles and found its outlet draining east to the East Branch of the Cutbank River. The elevation of the lake is 3,725 feet and to the southward a gently sloping timbered ridge rises to 4,250 feet. From the top of this ridge we had our first view of the promised land to the south. Bold and clear rose the Fortress with its black sides beyond the sharp-pointed Mt. Ida. On the other side should have been Mt. Alexander but it was hidden in a mass of clouds. Running across the southern horizon and then stretching north was the crown of the Rockies. The peaks were all snow covered for evidently the rain and hail of the previous night had been a heavy snowfall in the high mountains. The sight cheered our hearts and when a half-hour later we camped on a delightful flat, we all felt very happy to be at least in sight of the hunting country. We had made seventeen miles and were out of the territory covered by the government maps. More important, the high mountains gave promise that we were out of the land of muskeg.

Indian grave in the wilderness along the Peace River

Volumes could be written on the evils of muskeg but with most of it behind us our happier frame of mind called for neither a diatribe nor a philippic. After floundering in it for eight days, we thought we knew most of its evil ways but it played its most disastrous prank on us just at the end of this day. We had covered a bad bit of country and all of it was muskeg and downed timber and in many places both. An hour before we pulled into camp we came to an innocent-looking bog. One of the first horses stepped off solid ground and disappeared up to his head. His flounderings soon created a pool and to our horror we discovered that it was Bates' panniers that were slowly filling with water. The men worked fast to unpack the horse and by vigorous tugging on head and tail finally got him out on solid ground.

In getting across this place we mired two more horses and all hands were thoroughly glad when this hole was at our rear. This was our hardest day and by camping time we had gained less than any day so far - eleven miles. As we were off the mapped area, the streams were indicated only by dotted lines, which in most cases proved to be incorrect. Believing, however, that the high peaks were more likely to be correctly placed, we triangulated the position of our camp from Lone Mountain and the most easterly of the Quintette Peaks.

The day ended with a gorgeous display of northern lights and with a moon three-quarters full hanging in a dark blue sky over the snowy peaks and to the south. Great shafts of green light in the north flamed and flared and kept us from our beds.

Camp was called at 6 a.m. as usual but two horses were missing and could not be found until 9:30 a.m. Then the four "dudes" with Joe and Frank started out ahead of the pack train. We headed west in the valley bottom for three-quarters of a mile and then entered the burnt timber 100 yards west of old Callao's trapping cabin, which had been built in 1901. We started a stiff climb through windfalls, finally emerging into a lovely green forest which, however, as we gained elevation, turned into scrub at timberline. It was a hard pull for the horses and I eased up on mine by walking the distance. From on top we could look back over the muskeg country we had traversed in the past two days. From our elevation it was innocuous enough to look upon as none of the bog holes and unfathomed depths of mud showed. Lone Mountain now stood out clearly, whereas from the trail in the valley we had trouble locating it on account of its gradual sloping sides. We had passed

Fording the South Pine River in British Columbia

over one shoulder of it without knowing it.

We could not actually see Wapiti Lake to the south of us but we could make out a small lake that the Indians said was only four miles from Wapiti Lake. To the south was a jumble of peaks, many snow covered and steep. We thought we could see Mt. Alexander and certainly Mt. Ida was clear before us. Just over a saddle rose in the mist a higher peak that may have been Mt. Robson but, if so, it was 135 miles south of us.

Our camp was located on a little creek that the Indians call Parsnip Creek, which flows into the East Branch of the Cutbank River. It apparently heads in a small lake and near it, from another lake in the muskeg, Kinoosao Creek flows west into the Pine River.

As we were making the climb I had plenty of time to think and decided, in spite of the short time remaining, to make the trip to Kinoosao Falls if we had to backpack it all the way.

We boiled the kettle on the south slope and while there part of the pack train caught up with us. They had lost eleven horses in the timber and were having a terrible time rounding them up so we left them a pail of tea to cheer their lagging spirits. About 3 p.m. we jumped two good bull moose and Paul and Bates each killed one. Paul's moose measured forty-five inches spread and had good palms. The one that fell to Bates' shot was a year or two younger and measured forty-one inches but with smaller palms. The first had just finished rubbing but the second moose was still fully in the velvet.

Here was fresh meat at last and more than enough. I took pictures of the game and left the boys with the guides to bring in the meat and the heads while I went on a short distance with the pack train to make camp by the side of a small lake, which nestled among the high hills.

As we cooked dinner, five caribou strolled up onto the ridge to look us over and a big bull moose came out on the skyline 1,500 feet above us to see what it was all about. We seemed at last to have reached real game country.

It was surprising what a difference the killing of our first game made in the attitude of everybody in camp. We had had a hard day, tediously covering only eight miles but the campfire shone on a laughing, happy crew because there was fresh meat in camp. I was not able to unroll my blankets till quite late as I had test films to develop and the repacking of my duffle for the side trip to Kinoosao Falls that was to start the next morning.

I was up at 5 a.m. "raring to go" but eight horses were missing and among them my saddle horse. It was 7:30 before they could be found but within fifteen minutes thereafter we were off, leaving the rest of the camp busy preparing the two moose heads.

Our trail for the first five miles lay in a direct line to Wapiti Lake. It was a stiff climb but Jim Ross had blazed it on his way back when he laid out the caches. There was of course no sign of a trail underfoot but by following the blazes we found that enough brush and small trees had been cut out to allow the pack animals to pass.

As we left camp we climbed 1,000 feet straight up. After catching our breath we dropped down into a narrow valley and worked our way slowly to the head of it. Here we found a delightful glacial lake (elevation 5,100 feet) set in behind a typical terminal moraine and hemmed in by steep mountains that rose 2,000 feet on all sides except at the head of the lake, where there appeared to be a pass. We took the horses part of the way around the lake on the gravelly beach but then had to cut a track through the woods to pass some steep cliffs.

We traveled slowly up to the Pass that had an elevation of 5,700 feet; or about 500 feet above timberline. Here we lunched and while we were waiting for the kettle to boil located two billy goats on the opposite mountain. They were high up and I was not greatly interested in goats unless they were big and nearby.

We were on the trail again as soon as the tea was cool enough to drink but instead of dropping down into the valley of the Wapiti, Pete decided to bear off to the west and circle the mountain on this side of the Pass. Before we were around it we had reached an elevation of 6,300 feet and could get a comprehensive view of the country. To our southeast lay Wapiti Lake, which we had come so far to see and near that we hoped to locate our permanent camp. It was only three miles away but we were not to walk on its shores till we had photographed Kinoosao Falls. It is the headwaters of the Wapiti River, flowing east to the Smoky and thence to the Peace River. We had to get over the divide to find water flowing west into the South Pine.

From this height Pete laid our course through a valley running to the Pine River that seemed to offer the least difficulty in the way of downed timber and muskeg. It was a tough trail over mountains, through green and downed timber but in five hours we had made our objective with only one accident. In a small creek one of the packhorses mired down and as he had our bedding rolls aboard it was lively work to get him unpacked before they were soaked. We camped at 5 p.m. and I must confess it was a relief to make a small camp without all the noise and conversation of our caravan. The gang of men and horses with us made for confusion and the endless conversation of our cook (Elmer Keith) destroyed all the quiet I had come to get. Therefore, I was particularly glad to get off on this trip with only Pete Callao and Frank and with only two packhorses besides our three riding horses.

It was such a beautiful night that we had not bothered to put up a fly. The moon, almost full, sailed through a sky of scattered small clouds. The alternate light and shadow on the surrounding mountains was fantastic. Daylight saw us stirring and before 7 a.m. breakfast had been stowed away and the horses packed. Just before we left our camp I spied a bull caribou on the top of the mountain opposite, standing out clearly on the skyline as he fed along.

The first mile took us through a park-like country where we could ride comfortably without "chopping a road." Then we plunged into thick timber where Pete labored industriously with his axe to make it possible for the packhorses to pass.

We struck a grizzly track so fresh that the leaves were still wet with the water splashed on them as he waded a little creek. Dung in the trail was still steaming and we expected every moment to get a shot. We covered the country thoroughly, working up onto an elevation from which we could see the slopes of the surrounding hills. We searched in vain but never did we locate the bear.

After this the going became about as bad as it possibly could be but at 10 a.m. we came through a cut in the mountain and there was the Valley of the Pine at our feet. We had struck it just where the river forks and on the west fork not more than two miles above the junction was a fair-sized lake that we named Dewing Lake. It was about one mile long and a half-mile wide. Pete assured us that on the same branch six miles farther up was a larger lake two miles long, but we did not see this.

The only evidence that we found so far of anyone else having been through this country was some axe cuttings eight feet above the ground, which Pete told us he had made when he had a trapline into this country eight winters before. He allowed he had made these cuttings on the level of the snow to make a martin deadfall.

From 10 a.m. to noon we traveled down the Pine River high up on the east bank; at least we tried to travel. The timber was very thick and in the two hours we

Much time was spent dragging horses from the muddy bog.

certainly did not cover more than one mile. Pete and Frank both were out ahead chopping for most of the way. After they had cut a "road" I would bring up the horses.

We had lunch just as we emerged from the green timber and felt we must eat before we tackled the expanse of windfalls that stretched ahead of us. From this point to the falls, about 15 miles, it was all downed timber. We struggled till 4:30 p.m. in the worst tangle I have ever seen and finally gave it up. The poor horses were completely exhausted from jumping windfalls. They got all tangled up in the mess and one after another would quit and lie still till we prodded them on their feet again for another effort. In the whole afternoon we did not make two miles.

We decided to camp but even that was a problem for it took some time to make a space big enough for the fire and our beds. It was apparent there was nothing else to do but leave the horses in the morning, and, carrying the cameras, try to reach the falls on foot.

The map was a snare and a delusion. It showed the falls less than four miles from the camp, but Pete insisted that it was a long thirteen. We hoped he was wrong but knew in our hearts that he was right.

We were away bright and early on our backpacking adventure. The sun had just touched the small glacier on the mountain opposite camp and turned it a delicate rose, when we shouldered our packs with light hearts. Pete had the DeVry camera weighing twenty pounds and his axe; Frank, the Eyemo, weighing sixteen pounds and the tripod weighing ten pounds; and I carried the Una and extra films, changing bag and small tripod weighing about eighteen pounds, plus my gun, giving me about twenty-five pounds.

We fully expected to be back the same night, but for lunch and against the contingency of having to stay out all night, we carried six sandwiches each and some tea and sugar. From the moment we left camp we were in windfalls and from there to the edge of the falls it was just plain hell. Nothing else can describe it. Windfalls with snags, windfalls piled higher than our heads, windfalls lurking in every bit of grass to entangle our feet. If a square foot of ground was not covered with downed timber, it was muskeg into which we sank above our ankles. Sometimes for 200 yards we never touched the ground, climbing over all sizes of downed timber that crisscrossed each other like jackstraws. The constant effort of stepping up and down, straddling logs, which always seemed to have a projecting sharp snag just

Downed timber on the way to waterfalls made travel slow.

where you sat on them to get over, wore down our strength and frazzled our tempers.

Pete and I were wearing moccasins and rubbers and they were less slippery on the logs than Frank's hob-nailed boots. He was slipping and sliding dangerously. My feet were tender and the moccasins offered little protection from the sharp-pointed spikes that projected from every log. Altogether we were having a rough time of it and by 12:30 p.m. we were about done in. We boiled the kettle and rested for an hour. I dug out an extra pair of socks to reinforce my foot gear and discovered that my left shin was skinned from ankle to knee. This gave me a lot of trouble afterwards as the bone was bruised and whenever I fell, which was often, the pain was terrific.

After lunch when we ate our six sandwiches Pete showed us the location of the falls from the top of a hill but he was not sure, as he had not seen them for eight years and then only in winter when the windfalls were buried far below his webs. It did not look far off, say eight or ten miles, but it was farther than we expected in the distance and in traveling effort it was 100 miles. I don't believe I was ever so tired in my life as when we stopped for lunch, and that after only six hours of it.

About 3 p.m. we heard a terrific crashing of dead limbs and two moose came out of a small clump of green timber. One was a splendid bull whose antlers, still only partly peeled, would have measured more than fifty-five inches. He stood broadside at seventy-five yards for a moment or two, but nothing on earth would have tempted me to pack his head out of that place and we let him go.

We struggled on and at 6 p.m. began to look for a place to camp. Water was scarce on the bench where we were traveling but finally we came across a small stream and stopped at once.

It was not much of a camp. By dint of considerable axe work we cut enough wood off a space fifteen feet square to keep our fire going all night and also to allow us to get down to the ground where we spread spruce boughs for our beds. It was a sad performance going to bed supperless except for more tea, but just as the sun sank we were cheered by a sight of the Continental Divide due west of us across the area marked on the map as unexplored. There on the topmost peak hung the Vreeland Glacier capping the mountain, with a long tongue extending down the Eastern Slope. It was one of the things I had come to see, and while on our diminishing grub supply we could not hope to reach it, forty miles away, we had seen it and in the morning light would photograph it.

Bear Hole Lake

FROM THE PEACE TO THE FRASER

I did not sleep a great deal; I was too tired and my leg pained me greatly. Further, I was dripping with perspiration and it took me three hours to dry out my clothes enough to lie down in them. I cannot say I have ever been comfortable sleeping out without blankets and this night was long. Tired, hungry and cold, we huddled over the fire.

Daylight came through a leaden sky that had crept far down the mountains and was pouring its contents of rain on us. We were soon drenched through but our wet clothes warmed to our body except when the bushes or a spruce bough unloaded a fresh shower of cold water on us.

We each ate our remaining three sandwiches and drank much tea huddled over the fire. We were cheered by the fact that the falls could not be far off but puzzled that we could not hear them, if they had as great a drop and volume of water as reported by Pete.

We started again at 6:30 a.m. and had two hours of terrible going in windfalls before we reached the edge of the Pine River. It was forty hours since we had first seen the river from the hills and had expected to be drinking its water in a couple of hours. We found several gravel bars on which we could travel, relieved of the monotony of windfalls, but here and there we had to go back into the brush to get around cut banks. At 9:30 a.m. we reached the top of the falls (elevation 3,250 feet) and what a sight met us! A great river, swollen since we first saw it by three tributaries from the unexplored territory to the west, poured over a series of shale ledges that extended across the river bed. Then it made a sudden drop 235 feet to a deep pool. Perpendicular from this pool on both sides rose black cliffs that seemed to frown down on the river for having escaped their iron grasp. From the pool the Pine River took up its peaceful way, dividing into two channels and leaving an island directly in front of the falls. I was most anxious to get out to this island as it would have afforded the best view of the falls but both streams were deep, wide and cold, and wet though we were, we had no mind for swimming. It would have been a long hard job to even get down to the river below the falls as the cliffs continued sheer for more than a mile.

We contented ourselves with taking pictures at the top of the falls and from a point a quarter of a mile below the falls but still on the high bank. It was raining all the time we were working with the cameras but we took two dozen stills and 200 feet of moving picture film and then started our homeward march shortly after

[241]

"Muskeg," the pack horse, takes an unscheduled break.

noon.

We had decided to try a new way back on the theory that nothing could be worse than the route we had followed. We thought that from the hills we could see more green timber along the river bank than we were experiencing up on the bench. This meant less downed timber and possibly an easier trip, though longer. This proved to be correct for by 5:30 p.m. we figured we had covered six miles and had had much less downed timber. We were, however, wet to the skin from the constant rain and the downpour we received off every branch we touched. We made camp in a grove of spruce and built ourselves a "wickiup" of boughs. With a roaring fire in front we began to steam out and by 9 p.m. were in dry enough shape to lie down and try to sleep.

Frank's trousers were nearly torn off and only by patching with slivers of spruce could he maintain any semblance of covering his underwear. Mine were snagged in a dozen places and my socks were both torn at the tops and burned where I had tried to dry them too close to the fire. We did not sleep a great deal as we were hungry to the backbone. I had a can of Oxo in my emergency pocket with my compass and matches, and two cubes were doled out to each man, which, with tea made by reboiling the tea leaves used at noon, made the meal. It rained all night and besides our wakefulness due to our discomfort, we were damp and very cold.

We could not sleep after daylight and as breakfast was a light affair of two bouillon cubes each and more reboiled tea, we were on the road early. There was not nearly so much windfall as on the way down but it was bad enough. Also, we found some country that had been burned over after the first fire had gone through and this was fairly easy traveling except that the rain had made the ashes that covered the ground very slippery and we did a lot of sliding on the steep sidehills. A final handout of two bouillon cubes each and tea seemed inevitable at noon till Pete saw a spruce hen and I shot its head off. It was very shortly thereafter roasting on the end of a pointed stick. Divided into three portions it did not go far but it helped to keep our backbones separated from our wishbones.

All afternoon we struggled on in really tough windfalls. Frank had one bad fall, and he thought he had hurt his back. All of us were down often enough but we were as careful as possible as we realized that a broken leg meant building a cabin and staying till one could travel out by sled on the deep snow. A horse could never have carried a man out of this tangle even if the invalid could have stood the pain of

Callao Lake - named for Prent's guide

the ride.

It was a gladsome sight to find the five horses as we neared camp about 5 p.m. We had worried a good deal that they might have pulled out for parts unknown as we left them in a tangle of windfalls where there was very little feed. One of the horses had its front feet over a log and it was evident that it had been standing in this one position for at least twenty-four hours. I learned for the first time that if a horse gets its front feet over a log or wire fence and cannot step over with its hind feet it will make no effort to jump but will stand there till it drops of starvation.

Three hundred yards farther we could see camp and even our stoical Indian let out a whoop. We had considered it a poor camp, just a cleared space in the windfalls by a muskeg pool, but under the tarps was food and warm blankets. We wasted no time in fancy cooking. Frank had left some rice soaking and in twenty minutes we had boiled it and had it under our belts. This was just a starter. Biscuits, moose steak, a gallon of coffee with sugar, fried potatoes - we ate till we could only just roll over on our blankets. We had been seventy-two hours on six sandwiches each, a spruce hen and a box of Oxo cubes.

Our trip home was made in thirteen and one-half hours traveling time against fifteen hours going out, largely due to fewer windfalls, although we figured we had covered more miles. We estimated the distance going out at thirteen miles so that we had made less than a mile an hour in the downed timber.

The government map names these falls "Kindasao" but this is evidently a misspelling of the Indian name for them, which is "Kinoosao," meaning fish in Cree. They are also called "Kapaca Tignapy" by the Indians, which means falling water.

As far as I can learn, these falls have only been visited once before by a white man. They were discovered and named by S. Prescott Fay in 1912 and his trip is described in the June issue of *Appalachia 1915*. We believed we were the second white men to see them and the first to bring back a moving picture record of them.

We did not get away from camp very early. We were in no hurry to leave our warm blankets and then there was a large breakfast to be eaten so that it was 8:30 a.m. before we hit the trail.

We had good going after the first two hours of windfalls; that is, there was only the usual amount of downed timber and bog. At 11:30 a.m. we were working our way through some scattered spruce on a steep sidehill when my gun caught against a tree and held up my horse that I was leading. I went back to disentangle it when I heard a series of grunts and Frank yelled, "Grizzly." Pete was ahead of me perhaps 100 feet when he had come on a bear feeding in a berry patch not fifty feet from him. The bear rose on its hind legs and looked him over. He did not dare move for fear of scaring the bear, expecting I would come up any second. Suddenly the bear let out a "woof," dropped on all fours and started up the ridge away from us. I arrived at Pete's side just in time to make out the bear as it ran through the brush near the top of the ridge. I waited a second, hoping to get a better view and just as it topped the ridge it crossed an open space possibly the length of the beast. It was going straight away from me so I had no choice of shot, but as I touched off the gun we saw the bear rise, spin on its hind legs and plunge into the brush.

I was all for letting the bear alone to bleed to death or at least stiffen, for I confess I did not relish the idea of ploughing around in thick brush looking for a wounded grizzly. However, the boys insisted we would lose the bear unless we took up the trail at once. We found lots of blood at the top of the hill and a clear trail where it led down on the other side toward a little stream.

The brush was very thick and I thought nothing of this procedure. Frank said afterwards I looked at my gun at least twenty times to be sure there was a shell in the barrel. Truthfully, I was scared. The trail led straight down the hill but as we proceeded the blood sign became less and less. We were getting pretty discouraged when we struck the creek, for we had trailed it more than 300 yards in the past half-hour. But here the bear went on down the creek bed instead of climbing up the other side and we felt sure it must be pretty badly hurt. Fifty yards further on we saw it lying under a clump of spruce, about thirty feet away and as it lifted its head I shot it through the neck. That ended Mrs. Bear, for it proved to be a bitch grizzly about four years old. We estimated her weight at 400 pounds and her length taped seven feet, two inches.

It was just noon when she was finally killed and the next two and a half hours we were busy photographing and skinning out this silver tip. Meantime, it had come on to rain and later to snow so we were glad to get started again.

It was a cold but happy ride into camp. Happy because we had Kinoosao Falls in our camera box and a grizzly hide in a sack.

We left our comfortable camp on the flat and headed for the permanent camp somewhere on the other side of Red Deer Creek where the rest of the party had already been camped for three days. We crowded the horses pretty hard and as the trail was easy, although wet and boggy in places, we made excellent time. We covered the nine miles to Wapiti Lake in three hours.

This was our first close-up view of this lovely lake, which had been one of the goals of the trip. It is mapped as one body of water but in reality it is three lakes separated by narrow strips of marshy ground. The main lake is 2 1/2 to 3 miles long and 1 3/4 miles wide. It nestles among high mountains that rise high above timberline.

We struck the lake at its extreme western end and found a sizable stream entering there across a series of flats that were boggy in the extreme. On the south shore where we left the lake (elevation 3,975 feet), the mountains came down precipitously to a gravelly beach. We had a considerable climb up this slope but after we had gotten up above the first bench, we found that our route lay through a wide pass that rose in a series of park-like openings to timberline. It was a gorgeous ride and the thought that just beyond was permanent camp, food and a bath helped a lot. It was quite a distance to the top (elevation 5,650 feet) and in one of the last openings, as we rode into it, I saw something black run for the timber at the other end. I jumped from my horse and yelled, "Bear!" As I ran forward I caught a fleeting glimpse of the animal as it made off through the trees but I saw it was not a bear but a black wolf. This whetted our appetites for his hide the more, but hunt as we did, we never caught another sight of him.

Pete called in what was supposed to be a wolf-like manner. It was at least as children we had been taught that wolves howled. Greatly to our surprise the wolf answered repeatedly but we could not coax him out into the open.

We fooled around for half an hour but to no avail, so cooked lunch of three spruce hens, which I had shot, biscuits and tea. It took all the last of our supplies but we felt sure that we were close to permanent camp. We topped the ridge at 4 p.m. and the other side of Red Deer Creek looked a long way off to us.

The descent was a terror; straight up and down in places, and we thought for a while we would have to unpack and lower the packs down with the lash ropes. To add to our joy (?), the crowd ahead had carefully blazed the trail in all the soft places where the twenty-eight horses had plowed out a "road," but on the hard rocky ground they had left not a blaze. So we lost some time hunting trail and it was nearly 5:30 p.m. when we reached Red Deer River (elevation 4,250 feet). For three

Pete Callao laid the course through a valley running to Pine River.

miles along the river the trail wound through dense green timber so that it was not until almost dark that we found the cache that had been put down for us by the boys in July. We knew then that permanent camp had been moved nearer hunting country and decided to camp for the night here. Vanished were the ideas of a hot bath and clean dry clothes. However, at hand was lots of food in the cache and we took all we needed for dinner, breakfast and for three more days, as we did not know how far they had gone ahead. It had been a delightful but long day, putting twenty-five miles behind us.

We got an early start at 6:30 a.m. and climbed the ridge to 5,425 feet. This took us more than two hours but from the top we could see the permanent camp a mile away in a little basin. It was a welcome sight and the boys were hearty in their greeting.

One of the guides, hunting horses on the ridge, had seen our fire at the cache the night before so they knew we were getting near. A bath, shave and clean clothes and then a general overhauling of gear took all the rest of the morning and most of the afternoon. At 3 p.m. Snyder and I looked over a lot of country from the top of a ridge back of camp but saw nothing in the way of game except two ptarmigan. We nearly blew off the ridge, however, and returned to camp to anchor all tents doubly strong to withstand a terrific gale that threatened to blow us off the mountain.

We found that Paul had killed two goats, the best of which had fallen 700 feet and smashed his horns to bits. Bates had killed a caribou so the camp was well supplied with meat.

About midnight the storm that had been brewing all day hit us in full force. A terrific gale of wind swept over the peaks and across our valley - our tent rocked and strained at the guy ropes. Finally one blast ripped loose the lean-to that formed part of our sleeping quarters and left Paul out in the rain and the breeze. All hands were up at once to cover up the duffle as best we could and we spent the rest of the night trying to hold down what remained of our bedroom.

As soon as daylight came we started to move camp into the shelter of a clump of spruce. It took us most of the morning as it was still raining hard and only one tent could be moved at a time. Then its contents were hurried up as back packs before they were soaked. Toward noon the rain ceased but the clouds hung low on the surrounding mountains, so that it was not until after lunch that we decided to look for goats even though it was late for a real start.

[249]

Paul, Snyder and Prent went for a "look-see" to find the falls.

FROM THE PEACE TO THE FRASER

The ability of the Rocky Mountain goat, which is not a goat at all but an antelope, is well-illustrated by the following letter to Mr. W.W. Seymour of Tacoma, Washington:

Dear Mr. Seymour:

Last August, on our climb of Summit Chief, we saw a mountain goat working his way up the almost sheer rock ledges of Little Big Chief. It seemed so desperate a venture that we stopped and watched him climb. We became so intent that I forgot the quarter-mile distance and the fact that a goat does not deign to learn English. At a seemingly impossible place of the climb I yelled involuntarily, "Don't go there, you idiot - you can't climb that!"

But he did just the same. In several places the goat leaped his whole length (not height) upwards to the next ledge. Finally he tried one jump he could not make. It was more than a large goat-length above him. His front feet just reached the rim of the ledge, but were not over enough to pull up. His hind feet struck, as usual on these leaps, against the side of the ledge.

We expected the goat to be dashed to pieces in a fall. Instead, he pushed against the side of the ledge with both front and hind feet, turned a complete somersault in the air, and landed securely on all fours on the ledge below from which he had sprung.

He then, evidently content for the time, worked his way back to the snow-finger below and gave us another thrill. The snow-finger was as steep as snow will hold on a chimney. The goat huddled his four feet close together and coasted. His sharp feet cut the snow and left behind him a veritable shower of flying, trailing snow.

These are the facts as we saw them. It stands to reason that our attention did not wander - the successive feats were too thrilling to miss.

We, the undersigned, offer this account of what we saw as a just tribute to the most skillful mountaineer we know - the mountain goat.

Signed:

Joseph T. Hazard
Harriet M. Taylor
Florence McComb
Glen F. Bremerman

Kinoosao Falls - What a sight!

We reached camp at 7:30 p.m. after dark to find George there with a splendid nine-inch goat.

The next day was gorgeous after the storm; the sort of warm, lazy day when you just want to lie about on the soft grass and spin yarns. It took the guides until 10 a.m. to stir our enthusiasm for hunting but finally we started for goat country with all the cameras on a packhorse. We sat on a high slope in the warm sun and looked the country over, taking a few pictures of Paul's mountain goat while Slim Cowart scouted for goats that we could photograph.

Slim came back after an hour reporting no goats in sight and only one basin into which he had not looked. We decided that I should move on ahead with Pete hunting, while Snyder and Paul followed along slowly with the camera horse. We looked into the last basin and there was a "thumping-big billy." There was no cover and no means of approach nearer than 250 yards so we abandoned the idea of getting his picture and decided to take his head.

Pete and I crawled up a little ravine on hands and knees till nearer approach was impossible; then I shot and the goat dropped. He had still a lot of kick in him and his final efforts threatened to push him off the ledge on which he fell. Pete yelled to me to "kill him dead," and I fired three more shots. It was useless for he kicked over the ledge and started to roll, finally coming to rest within fifty yards of us.

The volley of shots started another goat out of his bed and as he was making off Pete yelled that his was a bigger goat and I fired at him. He dropped on the first shot although the distance paced 276 yards. At the shots, Snyder and Paul hurried along with the cameras so we gathered a lot of pictures of the dead goats.

We were two hours skinning out the two animals and just as we finished, Pete discovered fifteen goats, mostly nannies and kids, on a grassy slope not over a half-mile away. We hurried up our work and started in their direction with the cameras as fast as possible. At 600 yards we began taking pictures and moved up finally to 400 yards before they became nervous and started off.

Meanwhile, Paul and Slim had gone after a big goat that they had spied on the very top of the next mountain. They had a hard climb and no luck as they could not locate the goat when they reached the top.

While we were packing up our cameras we saw a small goat high up on the ledge about 600 feet above us and 500 yards away. Snyder started throwing lead near to him to make him run so as to give life to our moving picture.

Pine Valley from the top of the 3,250-foot falls

FROM THE PEACE TO THE FRASER

We returned to camp to find Jim and Joe back from their backpacking trip to Jarvis Pass. They had been out six days trying to find a pass to the south of us through which we could take the horses to reach the lower country along the Fraser and the railroad. We had no mind to return over muskeg and downed timber to Hudson's Hope and felt sure there was a way out to the south.

They reported they had found a passable route and that within ten days we could reach the railroad via Jarvis Pass. They had gone far enough to see that we could make the base of Mt. Ida from which we knew we could find the trail from Jarvis Pass to McBride on the railroad. This report was all I had been waiting for as I was already overdue at the end of the telegraph wire.

We said our farewells the next morning and stole as much salt as we could get away with for heads we might kill. It was sad to break up the party so early because we had had such good times together. My party consisted of Slim Cowart, Joe Callao, Frank Dewing and myself, six packhorses and our four riding horses. We were headed across country marked on the latest government map, "High Snow and Glacier Peaks - Unexplored Country." Anyone who has traveled the mountains knows there are few, if any, places remaining on the American continent unexplored by white men. Prospectors and trappers have combed practically every foot of it and unmistakable signs in the forests bespeak human visitation - axe marks ten feet above the ground where a trapper has cut a drag log for his trap when the snow was deep, or breast high where the prospector has cut away a snag to get his packhorses through. The map called this country "unexplored" and on the particular trail we followed through the jumble of peaks and passes we saw no signs of previous travel. Even our Indians claimed they had never heard of any of their people visiting this territory and possibly we were the first white men to cross from the Peace to the Fraser by this particular route.

However, Wapiti Lake had been visited by Beau Gaetz in 1898 when he spent two winters trying to find a route to the Klondike through this country. R.W. Jones, searching for possible passes to the Pacific Ocean for the Grand Trunk Railroad from 1900 to 1905, must have covered a great deal of this country, although his final choice of Pine Pass was far north. Jarvis had covered the country around the headwaters of the Porcupine River, finding the pass that bears his name as well as naming Mt. Ida.

S. Prescott Fay had crossed from Jasper to Hudson's Hope in 1914 but his route

Harry Snyder of Chicago cleans a rifle in camp.

lay some miles to the east of ours and south of Wapiti Lake. Despite these, and possibly some other excursions into this wilderness, the country was unknown and unmapped and our feelings as we journeyed into this little-known section were a mixture of awe and expectancy. We could not hope to find any mountains of great height that had not been located before. The country on all sides of this unexplored area had been covered by sportsmen and mountain climbers if not by government surveyors. Only this little area about forty miles wide by sixty miles long had turned most of them back and we hoped to search out its mysteries. As we passed through the wooded areas I searched in vain for axe marks that would tell us at least that some Indian trapper had had his line through this section.

Their lack made the forest more wonderful. The high passes between us and the railroad had turned back others - perhaps we should not get through.

Our course out of the valley of the Red Deer, which is really the southwest fork of the Wapiti River and so called by the Indians, took us first northeast to get into a little tributary valley, then southeast and southwest along this valley to a 6,000-foot pass where we crossed back into the valley of the Red Deer. We had to make this detour to avoid a terrible tangle of downed timber that lay for three miles above our permanent camp.

We looked down on the headwaters of Fish Creek but skirted the head of the basin and went down through a lower pass into the upper reaches of the Red Deer. Just in the pass we saw a young bull caribou but did not bother him as his antlers did not appeal.

As we were about to camp, Joe discovered a bull caribou. He declared it a big one but I could see only its hindquarters sticking out of the brush. I missed disgracefully on my shot and we spent an hour trying to hunt out this bull. Finally Joe returned to bring up the pack train while I waited on the sidehill.

As I lay there in the warm sun I made out a big white-necked bull caribou with a single cow feeding slowly up the valley and for half an hour I studied his antlers through the glasses and watched them feed along. They were nearly a half-mile away but I could see that while the "tops" of his antlers were good, the "shovels" were just spikes. A single cow came out above them and watched them carefully. Luckily the old bull did not see her or he would have added her to the harem he was evidently beginning to collect.

The last part of our day had been through a splendid forest where tall trees filtered the sunlight onto a grass carpeted ground. There was little downed timber and practically no underbrush. We wound our way among the trees following a game trail, not because a trail was needed but because it was headed in our direction and gave a comfortable feeling that we were going some place. We came out into open meadows where we could see the trees straggle up the hillside to timberline and end in a tangle of stunted balsam. Here we camped by a brook that came down from the snowcapped pass that lay between us and what we hoped would be sheep country.

The next day started auspiciously with the sight of seven caribou on a hill a mile away. Two bulls and five cows made up the herd but one bull was hanging on the outskirts and we could make out with the telescope the threatening advances of the old herd bull toward this smaller male whenever he came too near. We decided not to go after them as we were anxious to clean up our sheep hunting as soon as possible and to hurry on to the railroad.

It was a hard climb up to the pass (elevation 6,050 feet) leading from the Red Deer into Fish Creek. As we crossed a small glacier that lay in the pass, there burst on our view the most gorgeous valley I have seen in the Canadian Rockies. It was a mile wide between steep walls of limestone, and stretched away for about five or six miles before, swinging to the north, it passed behind projecting mountains.

At our very feet, down a slope so steep as to prove dangerous for the packhorses, nestled a tiny lake, deep sapphire in hue. Beyond it stretched long meadows between clumps of timber that gave the valley the appearance of a cultivated estate. Farther away, a dense growth of dark spruces extended across the valley from rim to rim and even in places straggled up the talus slopes. Several of the peaks towered 2,000 feet above the floor of the valley and the general average of the encircling wall of mountains was about 6,000 feet.

We had considerable difficulty getting our pack train down the eastern slope of the pass but finally it was accomplished while I photographed the performance from the farther side of the lake.

As we reached the floor of the valley we saw a cow caribou and calf moving off slowly as if they had no fear of man. A few minutes later we jumped a big grizzly but he made off hurriedly at the sight and scent of our cavalcade and we found we had disturbed him at his meal on a freshly killed caribou yearling. It was a big bear but I had my full quota and sat my horse and watched him go.

We were interested in the fact that the bear had been able to catch and kill this caribou. Many writers contend that grizzly never kill game, but here before us was the indisputable evidence of a freshly killed caribou with a broken neck, part of the entrails torn out and the loin partly eaten. Down the valley was the grizzly that we had disturbed at his feast and his track, 10 1/2 inches wide, indicated a big bear.

Our scouts, Jim Ross and Joe, had told us that here they had found their first and most northern sign of sheep, so here we decided to begin our hunt. We dumped our packs beside a clear stream and turned all but the saddle horse loose. As soon as possible we started down the valley, studying the grassy slopes on each side above timberline. After about two miles Joe jumped off his horse and announced, "Sheep." High up on the northern rim on a sunny slope we could see first one and then gradually six more sheep feeding around a bunch of scrub.

We watched them for half an hour through our glasses as they were more than a mile away and with the fifty-power telescope made out a good ram. We planned our stalk, which was to be through the timber to a point a half-mile beyond, then up the farther side of the ridge and over its summit above them. It was then 11 a.m.

By 12:30 p.m. we reached a point at the edge of timber at an elevation of 5,250 feet beyond which we could not take the horses. Above us extended a grassy slope that seemed to rise almost straight up. For an hour we toiled up this slope, our feet slipping and our lungs screaming for breath until finally we had risen 1,100 feet, when we sat down for a blow.

A shot rang out below us but not far away and our hearts dropped into our boots. Some other hunting party had found this Eden and was just a few minutes ahead of us. We ran to the edge of the canyon to our east and looked over. Far below we could see a lone figure walking along. He stooped and started to dress out a sheep he had killed. We called and he jumped a yard, as surprised as we were. We studied each other through our glasses and finally he toiled up the slope to us. It was Jim Smith, a prospector of Dome Creek, who for years had roamed these mountains alone, always in the hopes of finding a pay streak.

We had a five-minute chat and he promised to visit our camp before we left. Then we parted and took up our hunt. Five hundred yards farther and Joe, who was in the lead, motioned me down. I crept forward and looked over the brow of the hill at a good ram that I decided to shoot. Then and there I gave the most marvelous exhibition of rotten shooting I have ever seen. At seventy-five yards,

Prent Gray downs a mountain goat near the Peace River.

sitting down with carefully collected aim, I missed the ram three times. Finally, another ram walked into view and I decided to change my luck by a change of rifle and target. I fired at this second ram and he dropped. My first ram had meanwhile walked away and passed out of sight behind a clump of scrub. One was down and I started forward with Joe beside me when a third ram ran out from under the hill and Joe yelled, "Shoot, shoot; he biggest." I fired twice before I dropped him. However, he struggled to his feet and disappeared in a gully.

We looked over the first ram and found it to have a 14-inch base and 36 1/4-inch curl, but the ends of both horns were badly broken and broomed. The second ram had not gone far and proved to have a compact set of horns with a 14 1/2-inch base and 35 1/2-inch curl.

We all went to work skinning and photographing till it occurred to me to look over the next ridge to see what had become of the other sheep. I crawled to the top and in the little swale below was a good ram. I hurried back, collected Frank and the DeVry camera with the 6-inch lens, and started up for a try at a moving picture.

As we topped the ridge we saw not one but twenty-six sheep lying down or feeding nearby. The one I had seen was off at one side, but as soon as they detected us, which they soon did, they all bunched up. They were not nervous or excited so I took time to set up the camera on a tripod. Then Frank drew back, slipping downhill to reappear below them so they would be sure to start uphill. The maneuver was entirely successful and after he had waved his hat at them several times they moved off slowly. They were led out by the biggest ram I have ever seen. His horns were certainly more than seventeen inches, but my quota was full and I had to let him go. Meanwhile, the camera was running and we were making a real picture of real sheep. This just topped off our day.

This bunch of sheep was particularly interesting in that it contained one splendid old ram, several seven- or eight-year-old rams, some younger rams and both ewes and lambs. We had always been told that before the rut the older rams are never found with ewes and lambs and in my limited hunting of sheep I had never seen them together. Yet here they were and before we left this sheep range we saw these mixed herds repeatedly. Possibly it was because these sheep had never been hunted before and the old rams knew no more need for caution than the ewes and kids.

This was indeed a happy day. Down below me were two fine specimens of *Ovis canadensis* that I had hunted unsuccessfully the previous year. Twice I had crossed the continent for this day. Miles I had ridden and more miles I had walked for this moment. I had shot badly when the final test came but by shooting often enough I had killed all I was allowed and besides had a wonderful picture to remember it all by. I knew this was the last year I could hunt sheep - my knees and wind just would not stand it - but I was content. This one day was to be long remembered.

Photographing the sheep and skinning out the heads took more than two hours, but finally the four packs were made up of meat, cameras and guns. They were heavy, as each sheep head alone weighed more than forty pounds and each man had a head plus meat or camera. We were some time getting down the hill but finally we reached the horses. As we rested we decided there would never present itself an opportunity so favorable to get sheep pictures and therefore we would lay over a day to try for them. Therefore, we left the cameras cached in the brush and loaded the camera horse with heads and meat.

The next day proved perfect for photography. As we passed down the valley from camp, we stopped only long enough to locate the sheep feeding on the slope to the north of us. They were all headed in the direction of the little coulee where we had hunted the day before.

We picked up our cameras but decided we could not take a horse farther up the mountain and that the Akeley must be carried up on our backs. Therefore, we made up three loads of the outfit, none of which weighed less than forty-five pounds, and started slowly up the ascent. It took us more than an hour and a half to climb 1,000 feet in elevation, but fortunately we located a band of sheep lower down than we had expected and we set up the cameras and went to work on them.

We first cut a few spruce boughs and camouflaged the tripod using some bushes that were already in place. From behind this blind we reeled off foot after foot of film and shot several magazines of still pictures at a bunch of six sheep about 300 yards away that paid but little attention to us. Occasionally a ram would lift his head and watch intently in our direction. Once or twice a quick movement on my part would attract the notice of all of them but they soon went back to feeding or laid down. For an hour we photographed, then the sheep slowly moved off and Frank went in pursuit to see if we could get any close-ups.

While he was gone, three rams came along over the same route and got themselves onto the screen. Frank returned and reported that the sheep were traveling probably to their bedding ground higher up but that he had located some ewes and lambs over the ridge.

We found this small bunch of ewes and lambs grazing on a rocky slope. We watched them carefully for half an hour to see which way they were feeding and then hurried on to get ahead of them to set up the cameras.

We had picked out a spot where we figured they would pass within seventy-five yards of us and hastily constructed a blind of brush. We set up the Akeley with the 12-inch telephoto lens and the Soho Reflex with a 37 1/2-inch lens and waited. We had ample time to see that everything was in proper adjustment as no sheep came within camera range for an hour. Suddenly, Frank nudged me and I looked up to see and old ewe looking in our direction from the top of a little rise. She evidently noticed something different in the landscape, but as we "froze" no movement betrayed us and after careful scrutiny lasting twenty minutes she decided to come on. She was followed by a younger ewe, a yearling ram and a lamb.

They came within fifty yards of us before we started the cameras but although they looked up at the whir of the machine, my moving hand grinding the machine was screened by my hat and they could detect no movement. They soon settled down to feeding again and we took film till we were tired.

These sheep paid no attention to noise, the whir of the moving picture machine or the click of the focal plane shutter in our still cameras, which sounded like a crash to us. It is impossible that they did not hear these sharp metallic noises as they were not more than thirty-five yards from us at times. Although the wind was from them to us it was not strong and if they had been deer instead of sheep I should have been surprised if they had not scented us at this short distance. However, not once did they appear disturbed by anything except motion. I was very careful to keep my hand, which was cranking the Akeley, screened by my hat, but once or twice during the hour and a half that we were photographing these sheep I inadvertently exposed my hand above the shelter of our blind in reloading the cameras and instantly the sheep were alert and staring in our direction. It was often a tedious business because I did not dare withdraw my hand or move a muscle till they went back to feeding and on one occasion the suspense lasted fifteen minutes.

We were in camp at 4 p.m. and I was just taking a bath when Smith, our prospector friend, whom we had met the day before, came along for supper. He had only just arrived when we saw the pack train of Snyder, Paul and Bates coming through the pass. Within an hour Snyder rode into camp full of excitement thinking

[263]

Sheep country – "Scouts tell the men that sheep are found."

somebody was hurt and that an accident had caused our delay. We reassured him, telling him we had stayed over to photograph, and our reunion, plus my sheep, was the cause for a real jollification. During the party Smith produced a bottle of moonshine, which, plus a bottle of Scotch from our stock, was soon finished. Result: Smith was tight and we put him to bed and picketed his horse. However, before this occurred he agreed to show us a route to the railroad that would put us through in four days as against ten days via Jarvis Pass. This pleased us no end and the next morning we were in the saddle early.

However, Smith had had such an evening of it that he did not meet us as agreed until after 10 a.m. As we were dependent upon him to show us the short way to the railroad, we had to wait. We sat in a clearing and watched four rams feeding on the mountain opposite; a small bull caribou came out and when he saw us pranced down the meadow. He had nothing to fear and seemed to know it, for he executed some fancy steps and proudly moved away disdaining all appearance of haste.

Snyder described their sheep hunt after my departure as follows:

As soon as Prent and his boys were ready to start I had my horse saddled and rode down as far as the forks of the creek with them. We waited there until 10:30 a.m. for Smith to appear and while there Frank and I located four rams on the northern-most lateral ridge of Sheep Mountain.

I returned to camp at about noon and told George and Paul that we would now go on our first sheep hunt. We saddled horses and with Jim Ross and Sam Calleo started for the mountain. Riding as far as timberline we commenced our stalk and came out on top of a knife-like lateral ridge immediately above where I had sighted the sheep in the morning. It was 4 p.m., the sun was bright and the sky perfectly clear and there below us were two beautiful specimens of bighorn, both lying down sound asleep. Bates had brought his camera and he started to take pictures while Paul and I studied the two rams. I finally selected the largest ram and told him that it was a perfect head and estimated the range at 125 yards. Paul undershot his first three shots but the fourth shot registered a hit. When the shooting began, three other smaller rams ran out into sight. Paul fired eleven shots in all, seven of them taking effect. About the time George had quite a good footage on his camera, two more large rams came into view from underneath the cliff at the base of our ridge. One look and I shouted for Bates to take the larger ram in the lead. He did so. His second shot registered a hit and the third shot brought his

The DeVry camera captures a successful sheep hunt.

sheep down. With some little difficulty we descended the precipitous ridge and started measuring the sheep. Paul's sheep was a perfect head, both horns with 36-inch curl and both points perfect. Bates' sheep measured 17 1/2-inch base on both horns, one horn 38 1/2-inch curl and the other thirty-five. I measured Bates' head first then proceeded to Paul's sheep and while measuring and admiring the wonderful head, heard a shout from Bates. All of the time we had been measuring these sheep there were two smaller rams watching us on the same hillside at about 100 yards distance. At Bates' shout, I looked up and there silhouetted against the sky was the granddaddy of the herd that Prent had seen and photographed on the two preceding days. One good look and I picked up my 7mm Mag. with the scope attached, sat down and, figuring the distance at 250 yards, with the first shot registered a hit, but low down on the left shoulder. The second and third shots were also hits and the old fellow laid down. I then called to Sam and we got ready to climb up to him.

Just as we were ready to start Paul shouted, "He's up and going over the hill," and there stood the ram again on the skyline with a very bad list to port and apparently his right foreleg entirely shot off. Standing, I fired a fourth and fifth shot at the old fellow and at both reports we heard a thud and I could see him flinch through my scope. He then laid down and Sam and I started our climb up a terrifically steep slide rock slope.

Just before we reached the ram, the old fellow struggled to his feet, although apparently two legs were entirely out of commission and started staggering toward the edge of the declivity. I knew if he fell he would roll at least 1,000 feet and I shouted to Sam to run and catch him by the leg. Sam was able to do so just as the old fellow toppled toward the cliff. Sam held him by the left hind leg until I got up within about fifteen yards, when I shot the old fellow in the breast and gave him a "coup de grace." He was a very much larger ram than the other two, but the base of his horns only measured seventeen inches. The curl, however, was 42 1/2 inches and a very magnificent specimen indeed.

The sun was just setting and we hurried the skinning-out process as much as possible, then climbed the ridge we had descended and on down to our horses. By the time we reached the bottom of the gulch it was pitch dark, and without a trail through the thick woods it took us until 8:30 p.m. to reach camp, but we were a happy crew. One big drink all around and supper and we were ready for bed.

The next morning we decided to go camera hunting, saddled our horses early and rode down to Sheep Mountain and ascended in the same place that Prent had made his ascent both days he was after sheep. We rode up as far as timberline and then climbed the rest of the way on foot, but a diligent search of the entire mountain revealed the fact that every sheep had fled and left no definite trail.

Pete Callao and I then ascended to the very peak of Sheep Mountain, an elevation of 7,350 feet, and searched the adjoining country in every direction. On a knife-like ridge running due north from the northernmost slope of Sheep Mountain, we discovered six rams at a distance of about three and one-half miles and on the same slope within fifty yards, twelve goats, three billies, seven nannies and two kids. But it was 5 p.m. and we were a good five miles from camp so we decided to hunt these sheep another day.

On the road down I spied a goat, a big billy about 1,000 feet below us, and Paul wanting another goat, he and I made the stalk. The goat saw us several times but since we were above him he paid no attention until just as we reached his level. He then started to run. Paul sat down; the first shot registered a perfect miss but the second shot was a perfect hit and killed the goat dead. When the goat fell we paced off the distance and found it to be 204 long paces; we measured the goat to be a 9 1/2-inch goat with a very wonderful coat. It was so cold and so late that we decided to send the boys up to skin him out the next day and proceeded to camp.

The next morning there being about two inches of snow on the ground, we decided to go grizzly hunting and went up the adjoining valley a distance of two hours travel. It was here that Bates secured his large caribou. We returned the next day and decided we would make one try for the six rams that I had spied two days before and, regardless of whether we secured them or not, start the following day for home.

When we awoke the next morning there was a terrific wind blowing and it looked as if it might snow or rain again any minute, but we had the horses in by daylight and Paul, Bates and I, Jim Ross, Pete Callao and Elmer Keith started up for the high pass immediately back of our camp to get into the main valley, from which we could ascend the knife-blade ridge on the opposite side of which I had spied these rams. I conducted this stalk again, as I had the previous sheep hunt, and after a very steep climb of 900 feet we reached the top of this ridge. A careful stalk to the edge of the ridge disclosed two rams at the far end, one of them very peacefully asleep and the other one grazing. We retreated to the west side of the ridge and approached about 200 yards nearer; again we crossed the top and I spied a third ram. It was agreed that Bates was to have his first choice, Paul the second choice and I was to take the third ram. We then retreated back on the west side and went clear around the north end of the ridge and approached within about 150 yards of the two rams, the third being invisible. Some pictures were taken and Paul, at the command of fire, killed the first ram with one well-directed shot at a distance of about 125 yards. George's ram started to run and he missed his shot; the third ram then sprang into view at a distance of about 220 yards from where we were standing.

The wind was blowing so hard and the ram was so far down the hill that I had to jump to my feet in order to get him on my sights, but at the first shot from my .300 Mag. he started rolling down the hill. One ram continued running straight away from us but for some reason Bates held his fire.

I shouted to him with a great deal of emphasis to "Shoot, damn you, shoot!"

The ram stopped a minute to look back at us; Bates fired and much to the surprise of us all, not only hit the ram but killed him. It was the best shot I ever saw either accidentally or otherwise, as the distance was a full 500 yards. We discovered it was almost impossible to stand on this ridge it was so steep, but providentially both Paul's ram and mine landed on little level spots just big enough for them to lay on, close to the place where they were shot. Paul's ram measured sixteen inches and each curl was thirty-four inches long; and again both points were perfect. My ram measured sixteen and one-half inches with a curl of thirty-five inches and another magnificent trophy; Bates, the lucky scamp as usual, had a seventeen-inch base with a 35-inch curl. We took both hind quarters and the head and cape of each of the rams. We also took with us some of the loin and then started the climb back for the top of the ridge; Bates carrying the head and cape of his own sheep; each one of the guides two quarters; the cook two quarters; and I carrying two rifles, two pair of binoculars and two cameras. We reached the horses at 5 p.m. and, after a thoroughly enjoyable ride, reached camp again just at dark.

This completed our sheep hunting and in all of my sixteen sheep hunts these were the two easiest stalks and the two best days of sheep hunting I ever had experienced. The first day we secured three record breaking trophies and had fourteen good rams within easy range of our guns for over a half hour. The second day we secured three splendid trophies, much above the average as to measurement. Both stalks brought the hunters out within range of their game and I must modestly admit that both stalks were perfectly conducted. In fact, they were so perfectly conducted and so easy that neither Paul nor Bates appreciated their accomplishments in securing such wonderful trophies with such ease.

The next morning broke cloudy with a cold wind and quite a lot of drizzle, but we were packed up and on the trail by 9 a.m., following the trail made by Prent seven days before.

[269]

Pete Callao holds Snyder's ram.

Our course to civilization lay up what appeared to be a side canyon of the valley in which we were camped, but after we got through the heavy timber at the entrance to this canyon we found we had entered the main valley and had been camped in a side canyon. The valley we were now following carried a really large stream coming from snowcapped mountains to the south of us.

We followed this creek upward for ten miles and camped early, just two miles below the Continental Divide, as we did not want to disturb some likely looking caribou country just ahead, which we hoped to hunt through the next morning. Also, to have pushed on meant another six miles to the next horse feed over the Continental Divide. We could look ahead to a towering snowy mountain, ice capped, with a wonderful glacier that extended in tongues down some of the canyons on the eastern end.

Smith proved to be a curious person. He was known as "Mountain Jim" Smith and seemed to have accumulated sufficient money to allow him to roam the hills all summer alone, spending his winters in Vancouver. He was apparently interested in prospecting, for his mind ran to the geology of the country. In the five days we were with him he seldom spoke and never of himself, so it was difficult to discover much about him. As he rode at the head of the pack train he never looked around but kept his eyes steadily to the front and his mind on something else besides how his companions were making out. One day he and I took a side trip and agreed to meet the pack train at a spot ten or twelve miles ahead. After we had traveled some distance, I got off my horse to take a picture of a particularly fine waterfall that came crashing down a sheer cliff from the foot of a glacier. When I had finished, I pushed ahead rapidly to overtake Smith but lost his horse track in a dense bit of woods. I concluded not to go back to pick up his trail and started straight down the valley toward our rendezvous with the pack train. I had traveled several hours in thick green timber when I came out in a long meadow through which anyone working down the valley would have to pass. I looked for Smith's tracks, and not finding them, concluded I had found easier going in the dense woods than he and was ahead of him. I waited a half-hour but as he did not appear, decided he had gone back to look for me. I therefore fired three shots and shortly heard his answering shot some distance off. When he appeared he told me that he was greatly surprised when he heard my signal ahead, as he had supposed during the past three hours that I was close behind him and had not even known I was not immediately following.

George Bates, Harry Snyder and Carroll Paul, left to right, with rams

Around the camp fire one evening he ventured the opinion that the band of sheep we had hunted was the most westerly and northwesterly of the *Ovis canadensis*; that there were no sheep west to the Parsnip River and that the only sheep of this genus north of this lot were northeast. He contended that the *Ovis stonei* and the *Ovis canadensis* did not interbreed because their range in no place touched. Slim Cowart assured us he had hunted 240 miles along the Parsnip on both the east and west sides, back as far as Vreeland Glacier, and he had never seen a sheep sign north of the Fraser. We were traveling almost due south, parallel to and about fifteen miles west of the British Columbia boundary, and we saw no sheep sign after we left this one band on Fish Creek.

All of this seemed to indicate that the northern limit of the *Ovis canadensis* is south of the Wapiti River and the western limit (north of the Canadian National Railroad) would appear to be between the British Columbia-Alberta boundary and a parallel line not more than fifteen miles west.

Many theories have been advanced why the bighorn did not range at least as far north as the Peace River. On our trip south we had passed some mountains that had every appearance of being good sheep ranges. It was true that a great deal of the country was muskeg but certainly south from the headwaters of Kinuseo Creek the ridges appeared ideal for sheep. Smith advanced the theory that sheep required in their feed certain legumes that only grew on a sandstone formation and as this country was all limestone, the sheep could not find proper food.

I pointed out the fallacy of this by calling his attention to the sheep ranges both in Jasper Park and north along the upper Sulphur River where nothing but limestone was to be found and yet where sheep had ranged since memory of the oldest settler. We had to abandon this theory and found no other except the possible one that since the country north to the Peace was a territory of very heavy snowfall, the sheep found it impossible to either dig down through the deep snow to feed or to find windswept ridges where they could get at their food in winter. After the limits of their ranges are more clearly defined in this territory, it may be possible to arrive at a better reason for their failure to extend farther north.

I was out ahead of the pack train the next morning in order to have a last try at caribou with "Mountain Jim" Smith. We hunted for three hours over some likely looking country and saw seven caribou and a good bull moose but not a head we cared about taking.

[273]

FROM THE PEACE TO THE FRASER

In our travels we climbed a peak 6,200 feet high directly opposite the pass at the head of Sheep River. From this elevation we could look over a lot of country and made a little map of what we saw. There was some fog hanging around the high peaks but gradually it cleared and directly south of us rose Mt. Ida. We took the first picture ever taken of this mountain from the north side. Next to it rose three peaks, which Smith declared were the Three Sisters, not as high as Ida and with but little snow on them. Just to the westward of these three mountains opened the pass through which we were to go. Two lakes separated by only a quarter mile of muskeg nestled in the pass - the sources of Sheep Creek, which flows into the Peace and thence to the Arctic, and of Jarvis Creek, flowing into the Fraser and to the Pacific. The Sheep Creek Lake is about two miles long and a quarter to a half-mile wide. It is fed by a stream from a large glacier on the west and is green gray in color. The Jarvis Creek Lake is clear and limpid and the reflections in it were wonderful of one of the Three Sisters.

As we sat on the summit of this peak and looked over the surrounding country, Smith expressed the hope that somebody would name one of these lakes for him. I told him of my plans to return the following year and map this country and promised to do all I could to attach his name to the lake that drained into Jarvis Creek. The lake that formed the headwaters of Sheep Creek I decided to name for my son, Sherman.

We caught up with the pack train at Sherman Lake (elevation 5,050 feet), and from there we journeyed over a trail cut out by Smith, which for most of its length was a terror. In getting around Smith Lake it skirted a cliff that looked impassable and very nearly was so for some of the horses. After this ordeal was over we plunged into dense timber and dropped straight down to Jarvis Creek. We struck the creek just at the base of the most westerly of the Three Sisters and found that the clear water issuing from the lake had been changed to the greenish gray of a glacial stream by an inflow from the glaciers of the Mt. Ida ice field.

It had become a raging torrent that tore at its banks and made fording difficult, but the character of the soil had changed. The rocks were the granite of the Continental Divide, the soil was sandy and the horses trod the bars of the river without sinking out of sight. Muskeg was gone and its passing left no regrets.

We traveled the banks of Jarvis Creek for a couple of miles and made camp directly beneath a hanging glacier. For the most part we traveled on the gravel bars of the river or the low banks that were densely covered with willow and alder.

We were constantly startled by roars like thunder as masses of ice containing thousands of tons fell from the hanging glaciers. We were fortunate in seeing two of these avalanches and noticed that on hitting the rocks far below, the ice seemed to fly into thousands of pieces, sending up a mist-like spray.

After we had progressed five miles downstream we had to climb high up on the hill to get around a cut bank. It was a nasty bit of trail hardly to be called such but Smith had swamped it out on his way in and hoped that the moose traveling up and down the river would wear it into a usable trail by spring. We found fresh moose signs in it already and he was greatly pleased.

Our travel was a succession of fords. We crossed the main river fourteen times during the day, each time almost belly deep on the horses and with some danger of wetting packs. We forded innumerable side streams and channels of the river so that our progress was more a wade than a ride.

About twelve miles downstream we came out onto a large flat where Black Bear Creek joined the Jarvis, making the McGregor River. Both streams were about the same size and their combination made a really large stream. Here we found our first sign of human visitation. Axe marks, low down, indicated trappers had been here before the deep snows. Smith remembered that several years before two men had been trapping in this valley. We were back into the known. Just below the flats was a low pass leading over into the Herrick River and through this pass we had our last view of the high peaks. We were getting down too low into the foothills to expect to see these magnificent mountains with their ice caps much longer.

As the sun played on all the ice tops around us it sent down an added volume of water in the streams and Jarvis Creek rose fully a foot during the daytime. It fell during the night after the effect of the sun's rays had been spent. We made camp early, as we were loath to leave the sight of these snowy peaks. We wanted to spend one more night watching their glistening tops against the stars, and see them turn a rosy hue as the first light of the morning reached them while the valleys were still in darkness.

Our trail the next day lay along the banks of the McGregor River for ten miles. Sometimes we were following the bars of the river but most of the way we were bucking alder and willow brush on the bank. Occasionally we pulled back from the stream and cut over a ridge that forced the river to make a wide bend. Here the

The country north of Peace River had heavy snowfall.

going was better, as we traveled through green timber; and aside from jumping a few fallen logs, we progressed easily.

We had, however, descended to the elevation at which "devil's club" grew in profusion. While it had been frosted and lost its leaves, it had lost none of its spines and every time we got off our horses to lead them around a bog hole or to stretch our legs we would get our knees and hands full of these devilish prickles. Our cotton gloves and woolen trousers were no protection - they only seemed to gather up more spines that jabbed us in a new place after we were back in the saddle.

At noon we stopped five minutes to eat our sandwiches on a flat where we left the McGregor and crossed the divide to Clearwater River, or the Torpy, as it was called on the newer maps. It was supposed to be twelve miles from this flat to the Torpy and for ten miles of it the forestry service had cut out a trail six feet wide. When Smith told us of this we were overjoyed, but while the brush was cut out, no work had been done underfoot and no horses had been over it to beat it down. The going was therefore very slow and it was after 5 p.m. when we reached the Torpy at its forks and camped for our last night in the open. Frank started a real dinner while I took a bath and brewed a hot rum punch to make us forget the wearisome ten hours on the trail. We cooked about everything left in the grub box, and it was after 9 p.m. when we crawled into our blankets.

We were up before four the next morning and by 7 a.m. were on the trail for our last run. We left our tent, extra stores and trophies, as Joe Callao was to wait at this point for Snyder since there was no horse feed nearer the railroad.

Three hours and a half of fast travel took us to the railroad over a trail, for the most part, through a magnificent stand of cedar and hemlock. The size of the trees made Joe's eyes stick out, as in his country all the timber was smaller and these were the first cedar or hemlock trees he had ever seen.

We struck the railroad about a half-mile from Dome Creek and a mile and a half from Bend. As the telegraph office was at Dome Creek, I proceeded there but the pack train could not ford the Fraser River and the railroad bridge was not passable for horses, so they went to Bend.

We had covered 108 miles by auto, 110 miles by boat, 344 miles on the trail on horses, and 6,044 miles by rail, a long distance; but the thirty days in the woods, to say nothing of our trophies, made up for the many weary miles and compensated in part for the muskeg and downed timber.

Pack horses take a grass break.

CLOTHES

2 - Filson Suits
2 - Unionsuits heavy underwear, wool
2 - Unionsuits light underwear, wool
1 - Slicker and pants
3 - Flannel shirts
1 - Pair pajamas
6 - Pair wool sox
2 - Pair cotton gloves
1 - Pair leather gloves
1 - Pair leather and wool mitts
1 - Pair high boots
1 - Pair shoes
1 - Pair rubbers
1 - Pair rubber-soled boots
3 - Pair moccasins
1 - Belt
1 - Mackinaw shirt
1 - Eiderdown coat
1 - Hat
12 - Khaki handkerchiefs
1 - Toilet kit

Mount Ida and the Three Sisters Peaks

CAMERA OUTFIT

1 - Akeley camera with 2-inch, 6 1/2-inch, 12-inch, & 17-inch lenses
1 - Una camera
1 - Graflex camera with 18 cm. Zeiss lens
1 - Soho camera with 23-inch & 37 1/2-inch lens
1 - Eyemo camera with 2- and 6-inch lens
2 - DeVry camera with 2- and 6-inch lens
1 - Small wooden tripod
2 - Metal tripods with ball and sockets
1 - Akeley development tank
1 - Still development tank
3 lbs. Hypo
3 - Packages Rytol
4 - Extra film magazines
1 - Thermometer
1 - Screw driver
12 - Film clips
1 - Camera pack saddle
1 - Changing bag
1 - Scene book
2 - Justapod meters
1 - Telepeconar lens

Sherman Lake provided fresh water for tired horses and men.

EQUIPMENT

2 - Pair binoculars
2 - Collapsible lanterns
2 - Balls twine
200-foot Sash cord
2 - Rucksacks
1 - Rubber tub
2 - Carrying straps
2 - Cans boot grease
1 - Flask
1 - Tobacco pouch
2 - Pipes
2 - Saddle bags
1 - Eiderdown sleeping bag
1 - Pneumatic mattress
1 - Pneumatic pillow
1 - Fishing rod, flies, line, reel
1 - Carborundum stone
1 - Pocket tool kit
1 - Sewing kit
1 - Sewing palm
2 - Sack needles
1 - Mirror
Toilet paper
12 - Paraffin bags
2 - Towels
6 - Cakes soap
2 - Tubes vaseline
1 - Flashlight
2 - Extra batteries and globes
2 - Marble matchboxes
2 - Knives
1 - 8-inch steel tape

1 - Aneroid barometer
1 - Compass
1 - Metal glasses case
1 - Extra pair glasses
1 - Gun cleaning outfit
1 - Diary
1 - Sewing awl
1 - Holster

———————

Col. Harry Snyder was American by birth, Canadian by adoption. A successful industrialist, he followed the principle that two months of each year should be devoted to big game hunting around the world. His book, Snyder's Book of Big Game Hunting, *published in 1950, contains references to the trip described in this chapter.*

Elmer Keith, who was cook on the trip described in this chapter, went on to become one of the best known and respected gun editors of all time, as well as a renowned big game hunter. He described the trip with a chapter in his book, Keith, An Autobiography, *published in 1974, as well as in his life story entitled,* Hell, I Was There, *published in 1979.*

Muinok Creek means in Cree, "Peaceful, placid and beautiful."

On the trail to Barbara Lakes, the eight men used twenty-six pack and saddle horses. Here, a portion of the pack string is shown.

The Trail to Barbara Lakes
1928

The thirteenth journal Prentiss N. Gray wrote becomes the ninth chapter of this book. The original journal about his extensive trip to Barbara Lakes along the border of British Columbia and Alberta was written in 1928 and includes discoveries of geographic features never mapped by Canadian officials. The scenic photography of Canada will amaze the reader with its beauty and detail. This journal is bound in navy blue cloth and leather and trimmed in gold ink. The printed marbled endsheets include the colors of navy blue, pink and cream. Newly documented geographic features of Canada are photographed in this journal.

Sexsmith and Grand Prairie, passing rapidly by the car window, brought us to the end of steel at Wembley and we climbed off the train in the center of the Peace River wheat belt in northern Alberta where the last settlement of the West was in progress. Miles of wheat fields ready for the harvesters surrounded this little town. The main street was lined with new agricultural machinery that had arrived in carloads to take care of this crop. It was a bumper wheat year and everyone we met positively radiated prosperity and happiness.

Jim Ross met us here with a truck to haul our duffle out thirty miles to the end of the road where the boys were holding the pack train. After supper at the Wembley Hotel we started and by 8:30 a.m. had dropped off the end of the well-traveled road and bumped our way over a mere trail to the last homesteader's cabin, five miles beyond Rio Grande. Here we found the pack outfit and a mountain of supplies. After greeting Joe and Pete Callao, our guides of last year, and meeting the new boys, we crawled into our blankets.

All the next morning was passed in making up packs and adjusting loads but by noon our pack train was strung out along the trail headed for the Wapiti River. Our party consisted of H.G. Dimsdale, civil engineer of Edmonton; Bob Potts,

Wembley, Alberta, in 1928 - heart of the wheat belt

rodman, woodsman, graduate of the University of Toronto and short story writer of High Prairie and almost every place else in the Northwest; Jim Ross, trapper of Hudson's Hope and outfitter of our party; Pete Callao, Cree Indian from Jackfish Lake; Joe Callao, Cree Indian from Jackfish Lake; Johnny Napoleon, Cree Indian from Dawson Creek; Dan Mosher, cook from Sexsmith; and twenty-six pack and saddle horses.

Our trail lay southwest over gently rolling country covered with a scant growth of cottonwood, jack pine and willow. All this land will eventually be brought under cultivation and already has been surveyed and staked for the homesteader. Shortly after our start we passed one new settler who had begun his fencing and plowing but was still living alone in a little five- by seven-foot tent.

We crowded the horses hard and at 6 p.m. after nineteen miles, made camp on a little lake about four miles north of Calahoo Lake. The poor cook, although in size a fine testimonial for his art, was not a horseman, and the ride had about finished him. A good jolt of Scotch helped him to get dinner, after which he rolled into his blankets and was seen no more. We only just had turned the horses loose to feed when a moose stampeded them and it took half an hour to get them back to camp.

No matter what time you get up in the morning, no pack train ever seems able to leave camp before 9:30 a.m. Our crew was no exception, so Dimsdale and I started ahead at about 8 a.m. and rode slowly down the trail to Calahoo Lake. This lake is named for the father of the boys who were with us and the spelling probably should be "Callao," but as neither of the brothers could read we decided not to alter the name on our map. We located a porcupine up a tree and took his picture much against his will, because he refused to pose properly and required a certain amount of poking up with a stick, which he nearly knocked out of our hands by slaps of his tail.

At the lake the pack train caught up with us and for the next three hours we bucked muskeg with a vengeance. About 3 p.m. we reached the edge of the canyon of the Wapiti River and dropped rapidly down 450 feet to a bench where we found splendid feed and an excellent campsite by the side of a clear spring. We were still 240 feet above the river and directly opposite the junction of Chinook Creek and the Wapiti. It was a pleasure to make an early camp, as it gave us a chance to take some pictures and clean up thoroughly before dark.

Prent Gray loads Akeley camera in specially designed wooden box.

THE TRAIL TO BARBARA LAKES

For a year I had been planning this trip in order to map the territory that still remained blank on the government maps. In 1927 we had penetrated this white spot and traversed it but our time had been limited and we had not the instruments to produce a proper map of the country. After my return that year I had spent several months searching without success in all the government offices for any records of travel in this country and had collected all the data that was available on the surrounding areas. This I had put together but there remained a large blank space that cried aloud for rivers and mountains and lakes. The main purpose of this trip was to supply this information and the secondary reason was to get a good moving picture of rams. In 1927 I had killed a full bag of game, (grizzly, moose, goats and sheep) so I did not expect to shoot except for meat, but pictures and a map I wanted badly.

The next morning there was a lot of shifting of packs as two horses had developed sore backs and Jim Ross was taking two mules back to Wembley with him.

At 9:30 a.m. we went down the hill to the Wapiti and made an easy ford without wetting a pack. This stream in any but the lowest stages of water had a bad reputation and this appeared merited as it ran in a narrow gorge with steep hills 1,000 to 1,100 feet high on each side, which could drain a volume of water into the river very quickly.

The climb out of the gorge was steep but an hour put us well on top at an elevation of 3,400 feet or 900 feet above the ford. We climbed 740 feet more before noon. That was our high point for the day - 4,140 feet.

We struck the British Columbia-Alberta boundary at Station #65-6 and followed the boundary trail that zigzagged across the line to Station #65-2, a distance in an airline of four miles. The trail, of course, was longer and we estimated our run for the day at sixteen miles against 13 1/2 miles in an airline.

We left the boundary at Station #65-2 and traveled southwest to Mistanusk Creek, which is called Goat Creek on Murray and Copley's map. Here we made camp comfortably at 5 p.m. and were just eating supper when a thunderstorm broke, which for a few minutes threatened to wash us away.

The next morning was clear so we were away on time. We tried setting up a flag on a high tree as a back sight for the surveyors, but this proved of no avail for when we reached the next ridge we were unable to locate it in the timber. However, about 2 p.m. we did get a back sight to the boundary where it cut over a hill and the

Coffee, conversation and camp

surveyors stopped a couple of hours to figure our position while we pushed ahead with the pack train.

Our trail all day was a real old-fashioned muskeg and downed-timber trail, hard in spots with some chopping and most of it pretty tiresome for the horses. About 4 p.m. we dropped down to Huguenot Creek, which apparently flowed into Muinok Creek two or three miles below where we crossed it. We cut over the intervening divide working a good deal south to a camp on Muinok Creek. I started fishing as soon as we made camp and shortly landed a 16 1/2-inch Arctic trout. As it was Saturday night I bathed and shaved, relinquishing the rod to Pete, who up to dark had caught nothing.

A shower at supper time proved to be snow on the high ridges to the south of camp, and it turned decidedly colder. We made for this day fourteen miles by trail.

Muinok Creek appears on only one map (Murray and Copley's Compass Reconnaissance), as we could find. Its outlet into the Wapiti is approximately correctly placed but its course is entirely wrong on the map and no indication is given of a large lake through which it runs. It is called Fish Creek on the map but as there are hundreds of Fish Creeks we decided to change the name to Muinok (pronounced Mew-in-oak), which means in Cree, "Peaceful, placid and beautiful."

We started the next day over a good trail that had been cut out ten years before by a trapper, but it soon petered out and left us undecided which bank of Muinok Creek to follow. Both looked equally brushy and after investigating for an hour we decided to zigzag across the creek bed and try both.

It was a hell of a road, lots of brush, downed timber and innumerable fords belly deep on the horses. I don't believe we made ten miles all day. Just at 5 p.m. I spotted a big mule deer watching us from a willow thicket. He was soon down and fresh meat for which we had been yearning was assured. We camped where he dropped and soon had his liver in the pan.

Ahead of us we could see the real mountains and after the previous night's snow the higher summits were white. We had apparently reached game country. Bob saw a black bear; Pete, a bull moose; Joe, a bull moose, and what he claimed were four elk, but I think more likely caribou. I saw the mule deer that we dropped and a cow moose, which we photographed although the light was about gone.

We decided to spend an extra day in this camp and to send the three Indians ahead to cut out the trail. Dimsdale and Bob put in the time carrying their traverse

[293]

Fording the Wapiti River to penetrate uncharted Canadian wilderness

on Muinok Creek ahead a few miles, working above timberline to avoid cutting brush. The cook and I held down the camp with nothing to do but loaf, fish and straighten broken pack saddles and gear.

The surveyors came back at 5 p.m. reporting a large lake only four miles away and rough, brushy country in between. They had a most satisfactory day tying into all their former points as far back as the boundary and shooting ahead to beyond the lake. They saw three moose and a calf. The Indians returned at 9 p.m. and reported they had cut the trail through to the lake. They saw five moose and one deer enroute.

The next day we found the trail relatively easy because of the work the boys had done on it. It was bad in spots and in one place the camera horse rolled down the hill and snagged himself badly. He bled a good deal but we finally stopped it and got him into camp. At 2:30 p.m. we reached the shores of a lovely lake that we now christened Muinok Lake. The lake was about 1 3/4 miles long and a half mile wide surrounded by high rugged hills. We camped at the northeast corner and at the southeast corner where the creek left the lake. The creek entered at the southwest corner and through the gap in the hills we could see the high ridge back of our last year's sheep camp and the knife-blade ridge where Snyder, Bates and Paul shot their sheep. It was streaked with snow, and made a wonderful background for the sheet of blue water before us. As we reached the shore of the lake, a mule deer doe was feeding at the edge of the water on one of the timbered points that stuck out from the south shore. Soon after, she fed back into the woods. Another doe appeared and watched the arrival of our pack train with evident annoyance.

We started a more or less permanent camp as we expected to remain here several days while Pete and I explored the surrounding country and the surveyors worked out the trip so far.

As one of our first moves toward a good camp we fired the cook and sent him back to Wembley with Joe Callao. He was too unspeakably dirty for any use, and could ruin more good food than any person I ever saw. The rest of the outfit had worked out splendidly and was most congenial.

The whole atmosphere of the camp was altered the next day after Bob took charge of the kitchen. Most ardent prayers were offered at breakfast that Joe would ride our ex-cook to death getting him back to Wembley, and as he was not much of a horseman and Joe had suffered greatly from the bad food, we all felt our prayers

[295]

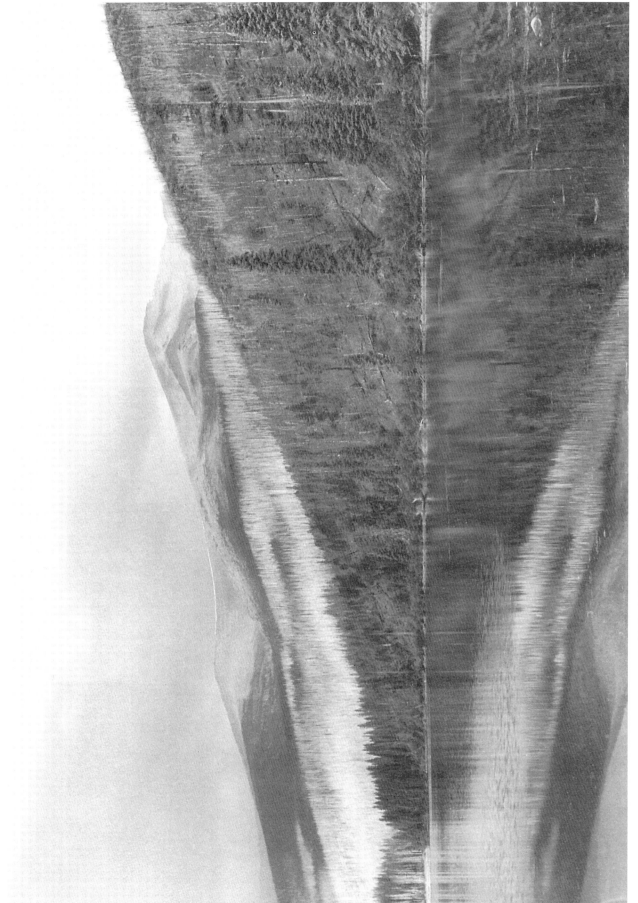

Muinok Lake became the site of a permanent camp in Gray's 1928 travels.

had a good chance of being answered.

Bob immediately started to clean up the mess and before night he had things in order and a lot of bread baked. Lunch gave us a taste of what good camp cookery could be and dinner was a revelation with both trout and venison, cake and a lot of trimmings. Everything was spotlessly clean; it was a real joy.

I put in the morning building a raft and after lunch we circumnavigated the lake, letting Dimsdale take shots with the transit at various points to determine the configuration of the shoreline. It was a quiet day devoid of any excitement but just what this sort of a peaceful scene called for and just what we all felt like after the first strenuous days on the trail.

Inaction even in this lovely spot finally bored us so the next day Pete, Johnny and I started to cut a trail up the Muinok toward our last year's sheep camp. Just as we left camp a cow moose came out on the lake shore and surveyed us carefully for about half an hour. We progressed easily for four miles to a junction of Muinok Creek and a good-sized stream coming from the southwest, which carried fully ten feet of water, six inches deep.

As we were riding along we saw three blue grouse and with a piece of fishline on the end of a pole I noosed two in short order. Johnny had never seen this done before, as he had usually thrown stones or sticks at them and was tremendously pleased at the idea. He noosed the third amid peals of laughter and asked me a dozen times where I had learned the trick as he could not believe a greenhorn knew anything an Indian did not know.

At the forks, after eating our grouse roasted on pointed sticks, we separated and Johnny continued the cutting of the trail toward the sheep camp while Pete and I turned up the side valley to look for game in the basin below the knife-blade ridge.

We had a hard climb through green and downed timber but finally, after leaving the horses, we reached timberline and came out on the talus slopes of the mountain. We soon began to locate goats and before long had found five single billies feeding on different slopes. They were all very dirty in color and as hard to see as sheep.

Suddenly Pete yelled, "Good God, what is that, a grizzly bear or moose?"

It was neither, but a splendid bull caribou with a real set of antlers. We studied him carefully for half an hour and his shovels and tines and tops appeared perfect and evenly developed. He was certainly a fine specimen but his antlers were still in the velvet and we were forced to conclude it was too early to kill him.

A boat slips by on Muinok Lake - named by Gray's exploration party

THE TRAIL TO BARBARA LAKES

We came down off the hill and reached camp at 8 p.m. Johnny came in at 10 p.m. and reported seeing a grizzly, five moose and two goats, while from camp they had seen a second moose and a deer.

With only two Indians left it was a hard job breaking camp and packing eighteen horses; but by 11 a.m. we were on the trail.

The first three hours of travel along the lake and up Muinok Creek we were familiar with as we had covered it the day before. After that we struggled for two hours through muskeg and downed timber. Then suddenly we ran out into green timber and for four miles the trail was lovely. I say trail, for it was a veritable road worn deep by the moose and caribou. It wandered through sunny openings in the forest where the ground was covered with purple lady-slippers and asters with here and there a flash of fireweed. Tall spruces cast long shadows across the smooth-flowing waters of Muinok Creek.

Johnny kept pointing out to me where he had seen the grizzly and the various moose the day before, but not a bit of game did we spy till we entered the valley where our camp of last year had been located. Then a cow caribou stood out on the hillside and watched our pack train go by, vainly sniffing the wind for a warning scent that would confirm her eyesight. It was lacking, as the wind blew from her to us and she settled down again to quiet grazing.

We camped at 8 p.m. in the open meadow at the forks of this valley amid familiar scenes. Just above us on the north was the grassy slope up which I had toiled to kill my first bighorn sheep. A little farther east was where I had waited for a band of sheep to approach for the camera. It recalled the two happiest days of my hunting experience.

Our camp was ideal, on a flat where feed for the horses grew knee deep, the vista broken by clumps of spruce among which you could wind about in the meadows for two miles and surrounded by magnificent peaks rising 3,000 feet above us to snow line. We went to bed happy.

Pete called me from the eiderdown by a yell of "grizzly bear!" In my pajamas I watched an old fellow circle the hillside above us and disappear into the timber. Every time I started back to the tent to dress Pete found something else for me to see till we had looked over four caribou - one a big bull - and a goat on the south slope. About 10 a.m. the clouds began to break away from the high peaks and we decided to get up on top.

Camp near Muinok Lake

THE TRAIL TO BARBARA LAKES

With Dimsdale, armed with the transit, we started up the high ridge to the north of camp that lay between us and Muinok Lake. We were on top by noon but a strong biting wind made surveying on the ridge-crest cold work. We found a point that gave us a straight shot to our campsite on the Muinok Lake and with a short offset a straight shot to our new camp. We left Dimsdale working out the distance by triangulation while Pete, Johnny and I headed for the knife-blade ridge. On the way we spied a caribou cow but our efforts to stalk her with the camera were a failure.

About 5 p.m. we reached the top of the knife-blade ridge but all we could locate were two goats. It was late and getting too dark to stalk them so we headed back to camp.

On the way we spied a caribou cow and calf and set up the cameras on the trail we believed they would take. Then we sent Johnny around to start them and he was all too successful. He scared them out of a year's growth and they came tearing past us not thirty-five feet away. My effort to locate them as they flew past in the finder of the Akeley was not successful, so we packed up the cameras and headed back to camp.

The next morning Pete and I were about to start up the pass to the Herrick River to photograph caribou, when we spied a big bull and five cows about 1 1/2 miles below camp on the south slope. We decided to have a look at the bull, as he appeared to have a fine head even from this distance.

We went down the valley till we were about opposite his position when it became apparent that he had an exceptional head and we decided to kill him. We were bothered in our stalk by the five cows who insisted on staying to leeward of the bull, which was the direction from which, of course, we wished to approach.

We decided, as he had fed a little way apart, to try to run off the cows without scaring him and this, after a good deal of maneuvering, we succeeded in doing by giving them our scent. As they went over the top of the hill without him we breathed a sigh of relief and started our final approach. He fed down the hill just to the edge of the scrub.

We had begun to fear that he had slipped away from us into the timber when Pete grabbed my arm and pointed to a waving antler tip that just showed above the brush. We thought he was lying down and Pete wanted to roll a rock down hill to make him jump up but I stopped him just as the bull stepped out from behind a

Pete, a Cree Indian guide, cleans a caribou rack.

bush in a hollow. I fired and hit him a raking shot in the top of the neck. We ran down to where he lay and stood beside him admiring his antlers when suddenly he scrambled to his feet and dashed off. A shot in the ham as he was headed away from us dropped him again, but as we approached he got to his feet again and started off. Another raking shot in the stern knocked him over and without approaching I ran parallel to him along the hillside. As he got to his feet the third time I hit him in the spine and put him down for good. I never saw a caribou carry so much lead. Any one of the four shots from my .300 Mag. were properly placed to have been fatal.

When we had a good look at his antlers we were more pleased than ever. They measured thirty-nine points with a spread of twenty-eight inches and a height from tip to the frontal bone of 28 1/2 inches. The shovels were almost perfect; both fully developed. As a whole it was the most symmetrical head I have ever seen. The beast itself was a splendid specimen, weighing, when dressed, 404 pounds with hide and head on, or 472 pounds live, allowing one-sixth for blood and entrails. He measured seventy inches from the base of his antlers to root of tail and stood forty-nine inches high at the shoulder.

We took the usual photographs and after skinning out the head were back in camp by 2 p.m. The rest of the day was spent in cleaning out the feet and fleshing the head skin. While we were away Bob reported seeing eleven caribou from camp and Pete and I saw seven.

In 1927, returning across the mountains from Wapiti Lake, Pete and I thought we had seen spray rising from a point in the Valley of the Red Deer. We felt we could hear the roar of falling water but no one had ever even whispered of any falls on the Red Deer River. We were without food and could not take the time to investigate but I promised myself to make this one of the reasons for this year's trip.

Pete, Bob and I with three pack horses and our saddle horses left camp the next day to find the falls of the Red Deer River, if they really existed. We followed last year's trail, which brought up a wonderful flood of memories. At the little lake at the foot of the first pass we saw a porcupine waddle down to the water and strike off for the opposite shore. As it was the first time any of us had ever seen a porcupine voluntarily swim, it was a great surprise and had to be photographed. As we climbed up the last pass leading over into the Red Deer River, we located three goats on a side hill about 600 yards away. We put in an hour photographing them and kept

[303]

Nearing Potts Falls

exposing films till they had climbed to the top of the ridge and disappeared.

As the next day was cloudy we decided not to stop to photograph goats. We pressed on to the falls and hoped for better weather on our return trip.

It was not long before we reached our permanent camp of 1927 and followed a succession of bad trails. First two miles of windfall down to the Red Deer River; then three miles of fairly decent green timber trail along the river; then 5 1/2 miles of just plain hell in green timber full of windfalls where every foot had to be cut out ahead of the pack train. At 6 p.m. we camped in a flat just above the head of a narrow gorge where we believed the falls must be, for now we could hear the roar of falling water.

It rained hard during the night so that we were pretty damp when we crawled out of our blankets the next morning. The clouds hung low in the valley and there was very little light for photographs. We loitered through breakfast and waited for the sun.

About 9 a.m. it showed signs of breaking so we started for the gorge. After an hour's travel in thick brush and downed timber, we left the horses and with the cameras loaded on our backs, pushed ahead. We were traveling high up on the mountainside to keep out of the dense timber and suddenly came out on a magnificent view of a rocky gorge where the Red Deer River cut through a mountain ridge of hard rock. It was a splendid sight but to our horror disclosed the river tearing its way along in a series of rapids but no falls. We sent Pete posthaste down to the lower end of the gorge to see if it ended in a fall. Bob climbed higher up the mountain and I sat down to puzzle it out. Last year I could swear I had seen spray rising from this river as we topped the ridge from Wapiti Lake. Then, and last night, and this morning as we came along, I had felt the vibration rather than heard water falling into a deep pool. Meanwhile Pete had arrived at the lower end of the gorge and vainly we watched him through our glasses for the signal that the falls existed and that we were to come on with the cameras. We saw him turn and start back without giving the signal.

I consulted the aneroid and puzzled that we were now at the same elevation as our last night's camp although a half-mile downstream and yet the river was 300 feet below us. How could it normally fall 300 feet in half a mile unless the bottom dropped out some place? The falls were between us and camp. It was unquestionable, so back we started through the heavy timber staying close to the riverbank and in

A splendid sight, but where are the falls?

half an hour heard again the heavy zoom of falling water. Suddenly we came out on a rocky ledge directly above the river and there was seventy feet of sheer drop where the river plunged into a gorgeous pool, hemmed in by towering rocks. It paid for all the trip as we gazed at that silvery ribbon that no one but possibly the Indians had ever seen before, as far as I know.

We had an orgy of photographing and the sun obligingly broke through and gave us splendid light. Pete tried fishing but the numerous big trout in the pool would not take hold of his unbaited hook even though it was decorated with a piece of his red flannel shirt.

About noon we left and visited the second falls a quarter mile above, which is a drop in the form of a cascade of about thirty feet. A hearty drink and lunch and we were on the back trail, which we traveled for 4 1/2 hours till darkness and a driving rain forced us to camp just a mile beyond our last year's camp.

While at breakfast we saw a goat on the hillside above camp. He appeared to be in a God-given place for photographs and we thought all we had to do was to climb above him and shoot his picture. But we had not counted on the goat. He kept moving his position and for three hours we climbed with all the camera stuff on our backs. My pack weighed fifty-two pounds and it was not the heaviest. Finally we were above him and thought surely we had his picture. Incidentally, we were above about everything else and from the top of the ridge could see over all the surrounding country. All the lakes of the Red Deer River were clear below us and only to the south the high peaks from Sherman Lake to Mt. Ida appeared higher than we were.

The goat was on a ledge straight down below us and Potts from the opposite ridge signaled to us that he was lying down. We waited an hour, but then becoming impatient, started to investigate. The goat heard us and left for parts distant, running along a perpendicular cliff directly below us. We caught only a glimpse of him as he complacently trotted along ledges that you would not think a bird could light on, scaling jagged points you could hang your hat on. We could no more keep up parallel with him on the rough going than we could run alongside an auto at sixty miles an hour. So after a vain effort we gave it up and the last we saw of him he was trotting over a ridge two miles away.

We were almost completely out of grub and as the weather had turned rainy we decided to return to the base camp the next morning for a good clean up and real food. After all, a fly-camp trip has its limitations, especially as the men forgot the

Towering rocks and a deep pool at Potts Falls made for "an orgy of photographs."

fly and we had been sleeping under spruce trees with saddle blankets to keep off the rain. Each day since we left, it had poured in the late afternoon or evening and sleeping had been rather damp. The men also forgot the oatmeal so breakfast and every other meal consisted of caribou, bannock and tea. We made a fast run as far as the second pass but right in our road lay nine goats that looked as if they needed photographing.

As we had messed every goat stalk to date, we decided we would make this one a success if it took all day. We left Bob Potts to move the goats upwind to us while Pete and I hurried on ahead to set up the cameras where we figured the goats would pass. Our aim was a series of close-ups, as I had all the long-distance pictures of goats I wanted.

Pete and I traveled a mile and a half along the foot of a precipitous cliff that offered the goats no chance to get up on top. We found a cleft in the rocks, which we figured they might turn and just beyond this in a jumble of rocks we planned to set up the cameras. The only flaw was that it required a climb of 600 feet straight up the talus slope with the cameras on our backs to reach the position we had chosen.

I never want to even think of that climb again. Bob was to start the goats an hour after we left and when we reached the foot of the slope we had only twenty minutes of the allotted time left in which to make our position. Pete's load was the Akeley camera, weighing with the box fifty-five pounds. Mine was the still camera and the two tripods weighing sixty-eight pounds and making as top-heavy a pack as possible.

The allotted hour passed and we were still several hundred feet below our station. An hour and twenty minutes had gone by before we put down our loads and, with lungs crying for air and leg muscles aching, lay down to rest before setting up the cameras.

For two hours we sat there waiting for goats. Finally Bob arrived and told us of his trouble in trying to start them in the right direction. He had climbed till exhausted but the goats had broken back and headed just the opposite direction. It was now 3 p.m. and to add to our joy a cold rain poured down till we were drenched.

We gathered up the cameras and dropping down to timberline boiled a cup of tea and started for camp content in the idea of dry clothes and a good supper. At 6:30 p.m. we arrived but no tent greeted us; only a burnt-out fire and a note on one

Bob Potts cleans pots in camp. Gray named the falls for him.

of the tent stakes explaining that the day before they had moved camp twelve miles farther south. It still poured but we sought a sheltering clump of spruce and soon had a roaring fire that took the edge off our disappointment.

All night the downpour continued and we were very damp at breakfast but soon the clouds began to lift and the sun struggled through. While we were packing, three caribou, a two-year-old bull, a cow and calf, came almost into camp. While they were trying to make up their mind what we were, we took several camera shots of them. Our lack of food for breakfast was made up in part by the beautiful morning and also by the thought that the boys were camped only twelve miles away on the trail to Sherman Lake following up Muinok Creek.

I figured Joe would camp where we did last year as that was the last horse feed before crossing the divide. He had, and at 1 p.m. we rode up to the tents to find everybody out except a new wrangler, Bill Taylor, whom Joe had brought back from Red Willow in place of the cook. They had pitched camp just under the towering rock that so impressed us last year and never was a sight more welcome than food, clean clothes, a bath and shave. It took us all afternoon to clean up. Then we plotted our trip of the past five days and found that our compass bearings checked out all right. After that it was time to eat again.

It seemed that Joe did give our ex-cook a rough ride back to civilization as he took him back in three days over the trail it had taken us five days to cover. He reported the cook near dead on arrival but the pathetic recital of the trip brought forth no tears.

Dimsdale came in at 6 p.m. and described an encounter with a grizzly that did not want to give them the trail. He and Johnny had located the bear a mile away feeding in a meadow. They wanted to see how close they could get although they had neither gun nor camera. They rode to within a hundred yards before the bear paid any attention to them at all, and then he started toward them to investigate.

They thought it time to move when the bear was fifty yards away but as they rode off the bear came on faster. They turned and faced the bear and he stopped and regarded them, advancing slowly step by step with all the hair on his neck bristling. Each time they turned to retreat he came faster so they decided to face it out and for ten minutes tried to stare down the grizzly who was advancing slowly one step at a time. Dimsdale said he looked four feet wide and they thought he would never stop. Finally, at twenty feet, he turned to the side and ambled off into

Prentiss Gray shoots footage of wildlife on a rocky cliff.

the brush.

At daybreak the next morning I saw from camp two goats on the mountain above us. Pete and I wanted to break our jinx on goats that had held up to now, so we headed in their direction with the cameras. A 1,000-foot climb put us above where we had seen them but when we tried to locate them they had departed for other parts.

We returned to camp sore and tired and as the afternoon had clouded up we stayed in camp until nearly 4 p.m., when we rode a couple of miles to a beaver pond where Joe had reported seven beaver working. We sat for an hour on the shores of this beautiful pond in the heart of the dense spruce woods and watched the beaver swim about. However, they did nothing to make a film of as only their heads showed above water as they swam. We had hoped one might crawl out on the shore or on the top of their house but they disappointed us and at 6 p.m. we returned to camp.

The next day we started south again and Dimsdale, Pete and I pulled out ahead of the pack outfit in the hopes of getting a bear picture in the meadows on the headwaters of the Narraway River.

It was the first absolutely perfect day we had had on the trip. Not a cloud in the blue sky - a warm sun fast dispelling the hard frost that coated every leaf. Above us towered glacier peaks glistening in the brilliant sunlight.

We soon topped the divide between Muinok Creek and the Narraway and started down the meadows where Dimsdale had met the grizzly. All was perfect except that the bear was busy elsewhere. However, we began an orgy of film exposing on the scenery that lasted till we reached the shores of Sherman Lake.

The pack train caught up with us as we were photographing the falls at the head of the Narraway and we rode on together till we reached the hill above the lake. Here with Mt. Ida, the Three Sisters Peaks and Mt. Alexander-Kitchie before us we forgot all else except exposure, focus and films. When we had shot our last film we came on down to the lake where the boys already had made camp in a lovely spot. The boys insisted on calling the high peak (8,000 feet) to the north Mt. Gray and the pass, where the Sherman Lakes nestled, as Gray Pass. The place was somewhat spoiled by the discovery of a cache of grub of considerable size put up this summer by Jim Smith, who guided me out from here last year.

I sent Pete and William off to the northeast to locate sheep, as for some reason

Headwaters of the Narawa River where grizzly were found

the band of sheep we had hunted on Muinok Creek the previous year had quit the country. We had the men out four days trying to locate them but they did not find a track. Up to date we had not seen even a sheep sign. Goats around the headwaters of the Red Deer River were scarce while the year before the place fairly crawled with them. However, both these places were now full of caribou. Dimsdale headed down the Narraway to connect it with the part they had already traversed north from its big bend toward Muinok Creek.

Joe and I started with the camera horse to investigate the outlet of Sherman Lake. To our surprise, just where the water left the lake, it dripped over a ledge 130 feet into a second lake that was over a half mile long. So we had to call them Sherman Lakes and not lake.

The falls at the foot of the main lake were a lovely thing but very hard to photograph. They had worn a deep gorge for themselves into the rock, which was very dark while all the surrounding cliffs were flooded with sunlight.

Just at the head of these falls we found a big moose and caribou wallow and built ourselves a blind. We did not attempt to hide there as the wind was wrong and it would have been useless. We left it for another day. We saw two small caribou near the wallow and a bull moose swam the narrow tongue of the lake as we stood watching him.

We were back in camp early for a lazy afternoon. About 6 p.m. Dimsdale arrived, having definitely connected the Narraway River with the water flowing out of Sherman Lakes. We now had everything cleaned up behind us and knew positively all about the mythical Sheep Creek and Fish Creek that nobody could put on paper and which Murray and Copley had all wrong on their map.

At 7 p.m. Jim Smith arrived with the Bergland brothers of Wilmington, Delaware, and twenty horses. They were not at all pleased to see our camp but after a drink with us they became more chatty. Pete and Bill arrived at 9:30 p.m. after a trip ten miles down the Narraway looking for sheep. They reported no sign, so we decided to move camp the next day.

We were late in leaving the Sherman Lakes camp as Dimsdale and I were trying to pry information about the topography out of Mountain Jim Smith. He was worse than the proverbial clam and we gained nothing. However, we were enroute by 11 p.m. and found an easy trail down to the Narraway along whose banks we travelled for about two miles. Here we turned south again up a branch that gave

[315]

Lower Sherman Lake - named for Prentiss' young son

promise of affording a pass at Mt. Ida. We topped the divide at 5,400 feet and below us straight down was a creek, which flowed along the north side of Mt. Ida and the Three Sisters Peaks. This we named Barbara Creek. As it was getting late and an easy descent was not apparent, we decided to camp in the pass by a little lake. It was above timberline and only a few stunted spruce afforded firewood. Also the wind howled and it was so rocky we could hardly get stakes in the ground to hold the tents. It was also damn cold up among the glaciers.

We could start our sheep hunting from on top and not from 2,000 feet every time we wanted to hunt. Further, Dimsdale could sit in camp and sight on mountain peaks with his transit to which he had tied in from three camps back. It also gave him a straight path for the boundary. We made the best of a poor campsite and soon after supper crawled into our blankets to get warm.

From this camp Dimsdale and Johnny started for the boundary to tie in our survey. I sent Joe and Bill north to locate sheep with orders not to come back till they found them. Pete and I started due east up the valley on our own account to locate sheep. Poor Bob was left alone in camp and while he had a lot of baking to do it was lonesome and he was mighty glad to see us return at 7 p.m.

Pete and I hunted hard but all we saw was one small caribou a long way off. We were somewhat compensated by the magnificent views of Mt. Ida and Kitchie rising to the south of us. The tremendous ice fields that flow down from both these mountains make the country both rough and picturesque. We came back to camp pretty downhearted at the lack of sheep sign. The country looked deserted by animal life as not even a goat greeted us from a lofty perch.

Our camp was windblown and uncomfortable but there was nothing to do but keep everyone out looking for sheep and hunt as hard as possible myself. This we did for two days and then our party began to straggle in from the brush. Johnny showed up first, having lost Dimsdale and all his horses. They had been overtaken by darkness the previous night just over the ridge and had slept two miles from camp. Their horses had strayed during the night and Johnny had walked in. They reported a big party guided by Stanley Clark of Entrance camped three miles from us at the base of Mt. Ida. They had been to the boundary and tied in our position, which was out only fifteen hundredths of a mile. Our calculations were that we were 10.85 miles from the boundary, whereas we were exactly eleven miles. Joe and Bill next appeared, not having eaten since the previous noon. They had seen sheep

Mountain sheep located overlooking a grassy flat

to the northeast but no big rams.

When we were all assembled we held a council of war and decided that Dimsdale would take one party southwest down Barbara Creek. This stream had its source in four lakes just east of Mt. Ida and was joined by the stream flowing south from Gray Pass. We decided to call the lovely lakes at its source Barbara Lakes.

Dimsdale was to follow this down the trail to Sherman Lakes. After going up to the lakes in Gray Pass to finish his survey there, he was to travel down Barbara Creek to its junction with the Big Salmon where we expected to join him the night of September 7th. The rest of us planned to go east to the boundary and follow it north to the Narraway. Here we hoped to find some rams to photograph.

It was 3 p.m. before we pulled out of camp and 4 1/2 hours later we made camp on the larger of Barbara Lakes under the shadow of Mt. Ida. We had found no such beauty spot in all our travels; four lovely lakes, the forest pressing close to the water's edge, the placid surface reflecting the needle spire of Mt. Ida (10,135 feet) with mirror-like precision. As we stood on the shore a band of four caribou cows and a young bull came out of the woods a quarter of a mile away and started their swim across the lake.

No scene could be more peaceful and yet on its surface stood clear the rugged heights of Mt. Ida that had battled a million storms. For the moment, soft fleecy clouds hung about her head but before we left they became dark and lowering and still the lake smiled up at Mt. Ida. It was so like Barbara.

Below the larger lake the stream ran out in a series of cascades whose roar came to us as an undertone in the forest stillness. There Barbara Creek tumbled in rapids and found its way through long pools till it joined the Big Salmon to form the MacGregor.

We found camped on the shores of the lake Mr. and Miss Wright and Mr. Bingham of Toledo, guided by Stanley Clark of Entrance. We swapped yarns with them and Eyemo cameras, as Bingham's camera refused to work.

I was up at 5:30 a.m. in order to photograph the first daylight on Mt. Ida reflected in Barbara Lake. I took a whole flock of movies and stills and at 10 a.m. moved camp toward the British Columbia/Alberta boundary. In Jarvis Pass, after six miles of trail, we turned sharp north up one of the tributaries of Jarvis Creek, traveling parallel to the boundary.

Our course took us through a considerable amount of jack pine timber, gradually

Scaling cliffs in search of game at 8,000-foot elevations became commonplace.

climbing until we reached an elevation of 6,000 feet. We passed timberline at 5,925 feet, which was very high for this country. We came out on grassy slopes and after topping the ridge, dropped down a little to camp at 5 p.m. on the watershed of Torrens River. Just north of us was a range of mountains 7,000 feet high that were grass nearly to their tops; it looked like real sheep country. I sent the three Indians out immediately while Bob and I unpacked the twenty horses and made camp. The boys came in after dark and all reported seeing sheep. I gave them each a big jigger of rum and before supper was over every ewe they had seen had bighorns and the ram Bill had met had at least a twenty-inch base. They were sure we would get 10,000 feet of ram pictures the next day.

With the three Indians, Pete, Johnny and Bill, I left early the next morning as their reports of the previous night led us to believe we were at last in sheep country. About 10 a.m. Johnny located two ewes on a ridge overlooking a wide grassy flat. We planned our approach to take us high above them but while we were climbing we found three ewes and three lambs and got a picture of them at 400 yards without their even knowing we were about. While we were doing this, however, the two ewes on the ridge moved, and as it was getting along toward noon, we decided to move down to timberline for wood and water for lunch.

As we were pushing through a small basin we almost ran over a bunch of sheep and retraced our steps as fast as possible, hoping they had not seen us. We climbed the ridge above them but they were in a position that was hard to get at. As they were feeding our way we decided to set up the cameras and wait. There proved to be sixteen ewes, lambs and one five-year-old ram in the bunch and while we were sitting there Johnny spotted two young rams high up on the ridge above them bedded down where they could survey all the world in the way of rams.

We sat there for an hour while the sheep nibbled their way slowly in our direction. Suddenly, on the very top of the ridge opposite appeared ten goats. They were two miles off and we paid no particular attention to them until they had covered half the distance straight toward us. Then we realized that possibly they too might come within photographic range. Over a period of three hours we lay in our windswept position on the ridge crest and watched those goats come across the basin, mingle and feed with the sheep and gradually feed within 150 yards of us.

Then the camera got busy and films were reeled off apace. It was a perfect garden of Eden, sixteen ewes and lambs, two rams and ten goats all before us.

[321]

Bill Taylor, Johnnie Napoleon and Pete Callao, left to right, carry state-of-the-art camera equipment in 1928.

THE TRAIL TO BARBARA LAKES

Unfortunately, not all within reach of the cameras but the eye picture was there to be long remembered. The statement of many natural history writers that sheep and goats do not range the same mountain was here completely disproved. We were back in camp at 7 p.m., tired, but well- pleased with our first day's work on sheep.

Smoke from a forest fire to the east hung low in the valley when we awoke the next morning, and there was little promise of a breeze to blow it away. The sun rose as a ball of fire but had not even strength enough to throw a shadow. We moved up the valley toward the high ridges, hopeful that the weather might become clear enough to make photography possible.

About noon the visibility improved a little and we spotted two small rams high up on a ridge above us but they were inaccessible and really too young to even make a decent picture, so we left them alone and hoped for more and bigger rams.

All afternoon we toiled up one ridge and down again and at 8,000 feet elevation that was not as easy as it sounds. Once the sight of five ewes and lambs cheered our hearts but darkness came down before we reached camp after a blank day pictorially. Then came the last day that we could devote to getting a picture of a big ram. The boys were all keyed up to do their utmost to make it a success but they were stumped as to where to go. The only country that we had not covered lay to the northwest so we decided to hunt there.

After an hour's ride we really started to climb, which means we reached hillsides up which we could not ride but must lead our horses and struggle upward on foot. Finally, we wanted to cross over one divide that the horses could not negotiate. So the boys cheerfully shouldered the cameras and we scrambled up on foot.

For the next six hours we crawled uphill and slid down trying to get pictures of a bunch of twelve ewes and lambs, and hoping in vain to locate a ram. In neither were we successful and finally at 7 p.m. we started back to camp. Twelve hours on a hunt does not sound long unless you realize that every minute of it is sixty seconds full of climbing or sliding downhill with a pack on your back. Sheep hunting is the very hardest work I know and I fear the day is soon coming when I cannot carry my camera pack of fifty pounds over these mountains.

We started our homeward trip the following morning but the packing dragged so that the pack train was not on the trail until 11 a.m. Everything seemed to go wrong. The horses could not be located. When driven into camp they refused to be caught; one had even stuck his nose into a porcupine and had to be roped and

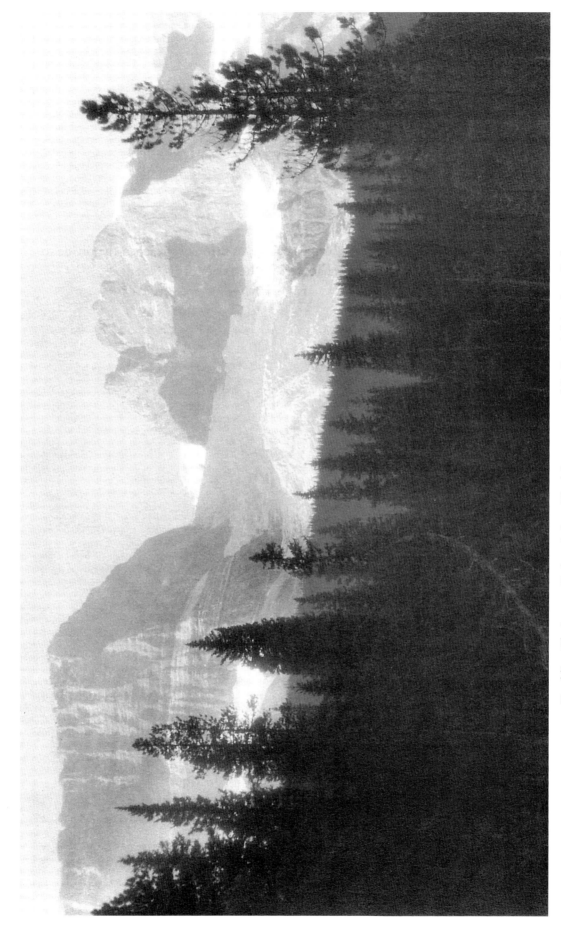

Tumbling Glacier near Barbara Lakes - The lakes were named for Prentiss' daughter, Barbara.

thrown before we could extract the quills - a most painful process. Then they bucked and kicked and struggled against being packed and just as things settled down a bull caribou appeared 300 yards off and we opened fire on him and stampeded the whole bunch of horses again. We did not get the caribou and when the pack train finally left they went out of camp every man jack bucking his head off. Three days of idleness had been too much for them.

It was as well that they had surplus energy, as before we reached the divide to Jarvis Creek a snowstorm broke that took the heart out of everybody.

Wet clinging snow came down steadily for the next five hours making the trail slippery, the bog holes softer and depositing a load on every spruce bough to descend on our unsuspecting heads. It was hard, cold, wet going and by 6 p.m. we were ready to camp although still four miles from our objective. We passed along the shores of the Barbara Lakes and saw them in a different mood from the sunny glistening smile they gave us when we left. But now they were lovely, too. The dark spruces on their shores were tipped with white and through the gently falling flakes of snow their water appeared a dark green. Camping was no fun but soon supper was over and our clothes drying out over a huge fire, while we lay in our blankets and smoked. We left this cheerless, snowy camp in a hurry. Either a thorough dislike for the place or the effect of my few well-chosen remarks about an outfit that could not get packed before 11 a.m. had a marvelous effect on the boys, for we were on the trail at 8:30 a.m.

We were trying to break out a trail down Barbara Creek from Barbara Lakes to the Sherman Lakes trail and while the distance by air was only nine miles, by trail it was certainly fifteen heartbreaking miles. We figured to reach the previous year's camp by noon and possibly camp with Dimsdale on the Big Salmon at night. We did not reach the Sherman Lakes trail till 6 p.m. and camped at 7:30 p.m. after eleven hours on the trail.

The previous day's snow hung heavy on all the branches so that we were soaked before we had been on the trail ten minutes. However, the day was clear and warm and the scenery around the base of Mt. Ida and along the Three Sisters Peaks was the very finest we have seen - glaciated, rocky peaks towered above us and from beneath the snowy ice cap, white ribbons tumbled down the mountainside through the dark spruce forest to mingle their waters with Barbara Creek.

Just ten minutes before we reached camp we struck a sandbar by the river and

Gray found a low pass through the mountains for the Canadian National Railroad.

some of the horses decided to roll. The packs on two of them turned in a minute and such a display of bucking and kicking you never beheld - canned goods, shovels, grates and whatnot flying in all directions and the whole train in a turmoil; Result: Two busted pack saddles and a half-hour spent gathering up the stuff.

We awoke to again see the sunrise on a wonderful hanging glacier just above camp. It was another clear day with bright sunlight reflected from the ring of glaciers around us. We had lost a day in the snowstorm coming down from Barbara Lakes, but we knew Dimsdale was somewhere downstream. At 4 p.m. we reached the Big Salmon to find his camp abandoned. There was no doubt he had gone downriver since it was nine miles farther to where the crossing left the MacGregor for the Torpy. There was no decent camping ground. In spite of the eighteen miles behind us we pushed on another three hours and camped at dark on a sandbar within two miles of the crossing. There was just not light enough to make those two miles and the outfit was done in with twenty-seven miles to its credit for the day and a lot of fording and many bog holes.

Our great surprise of the day was that from the mouth of the Big Salmon and for several miles south we had a wonderful view of Mt. Alexander-Kitchie. Mountain Jim Smith, who never spoke unless he had to, let me go past it last year and never told me what mountain it was. Dimsdale had figured its elevation at 10,980 feet, making it the highest peak of the Rockies north of Mt. Robson.

An hour's travel the following morning put us into Dimsdale's camp at the divide between the MacGregor and the Torpy. We were glad to see him again and particularly anxious to know how his work had turned out. Since early in our trip, it had begun to dawn on us that Muinok Creek offered a low grade and easy construction route for a railroad into the heart of the mountains. We all knew the crying need of the Peace River country for an outlet by rail to the west. We also knew the frantic efforts of the Canadian National Railroad and the Canadian Pacific Railroad engineers to find a pass to the Pacific. Monkman Pass out of the Wapiti and Pine Pass were costly construction and could only be used as a last resort. Dimsdale kept asking me questions about the country ahead and at many a campfire we discussed the possibility that either the Muinok River or the Narraway might lead to a low-grade pass at Sherman Lakes. At the end of every day we talked over what the trail had developed. Each day our hopes grew but we could not believe that all the money that had been spent on reconnaissance by the various railways

Mt. Ida from Barbara Lakes - A parting glimpse of mountain peaks as Gray returns to Bend, Oregon

with their best engineers had not found this route, which was almost a straight line between Steel and Bend on the Canadian National Railroad line. My personal fear, expressed every time we found ourselves getting too optimistic, was that the drop off on the Pacific side of Sherman Lakes would prove too steep.

We developed that the Muinok did not head in Sherman Lakes. They were the real source of the Narraway. These lakes, at an elevation of 4,250 feet, could be reached easily with almost prairie construction by following up the Narraway from the Wapiti. When we left Dimsdale at Barbara Lakes he was to find a way down the Pacific side of Gray Pass at Sherman Lakes. We already knew we had solved the Arctic side. Everything hinged on his work in the next few days.

Therefore, when I rode into his camp we wasted few words on the state of each other's health, but he whispered, "It's OK, maximum eight-tenths percent grade," and quickly produced a bottle of Scotch.

Our problem remaining was to get over from the MacGregor to the Torpy. We could go down the MacGregor and hit the main line at Hansard but that was sixty miles farther and no better in mileage than the Pine Pass route. Within an hour we were away and before noon had found a route that was ideal. That put us onto the slopes of the Torpy and fourteen miles on easy grade from the main line. The line was possible and we hoped probable.

Just as we were leaving Dimsdale's camp, "Deafy" Daton and his trapping partner, Bob Wiley, appeared. "Deafy" was all excitement. Two days previous he had killed a big grizzly on whose trail he had assiduously camped since the preceding winter. It seemed that his partner of the winter before had shot a moose near their cabin. He returned to the cabin for a packsack and later in the day went up for some meat, leaving his gun behind.

When he did not return that night, "Deafy" went to look for him and found him dead, badly mauled, near the carcass of the moose. From the tracks it was apparent that he had found a grizzly at the carcass and his efforts to scare the bear off had resulted in a charge wherein one blow only was struck by each. As there was blood on the man's axe it was hoped that he had hurt the bear badly but "Deafy" lost the blood trail after a mile or two and a snowstorm then blotted out further tracking. "Deafy" spent the rest of the winter, the spring and summer hunting that bear. He had only just killed a big grizzly with a deep scar on his jaw and nose. The upper jawbone was cut through and the teeth on one side driven out. "Deafy" was sure it was the same bear and he felt he had accomplished a full revenge.

A short run of ten miles from Dimsdale's camp put us at Haines' cabin on the Torpy. Bob Wiley had accompanied us to the Torpy and offered to take us by boat down this river and the Fraser to Bend. We were glad to accept anything to get out of the saddle and we wanted to see the last miles of our proposed railroad route. We let the outfit take the trail to Bend and had a wonderful ride down river in Wiley's boat.

It was a joy to watch the changing lights on the placid surface of the river, a joy to rest and still progress and to just sit back and revel in the changing panorama of autumn color and sunlit hills.

And, so we came to Bend, which spelled the end of this wonderful trip. The outfit was to return by trail and Dimsdale was to go back to check and recheck the route we believed we had found.

Sherman Gray, 12, and his sister Barbara, 16, caught twelve grayling on Birch Creek with a stick fishing pole.
Here, Sherman stands on the banks of the creek.

Ketchikan totem poles stand tall and proud.

Alaska
1930

The final chapter of this book and the eighteenth journal Gray wrote describes in writing and full-page photographs the travels of Gray, his son Sherman and daughter Barbara to Alaska in the summer of 1930. The remaining three journals of Gray's travels to Central America, Egypt, Palestine and Florida from 1933 to 1935 are not included in this book.

The original journal of his trip to Alaska is bound in red leather and cloth and contains printed marbled endsheets of red, blue, green and cream colors. Sherman was 12 years old and Barbara was 16 years old when the two teenagers visited Alaska with their father. Sherman in 1994 is 76 living near New York City. Barbara just celebrated her 80th birthday at her home in Washington, D.C. This was an adventure of a lifetime for these young people, and their memories of their beloved father are forever etched in their adult consciousness. Photographs of Prentiss, Sherman and Barbara hunting big game highlight this final chapter of the book.

We sailed early in the morning of August 9th, 1930, on the "S.S. Yukon." We traveled all day through Puget Sound and Georgia Straits in gorgeous sunlight, which was quite unusual for these waters.

We awoke the next morning just as the ship was starting across Queen Charlotte Sound, which has the reputation of being a rough piece of water. But to us it was kind. The sea was smooth as glass and clear weather gave us a chance to see the tops of the mountains. As it grew dark we passed into Graham Reach, which has always seemed to me the first bit of typically southeastern Alaska scenery. Dark spruce-covered hills rose precipitously from the water's edge topped by snow fields and jagged peaks.

The following morning we reached Ketchikan, our first port of call, at 7 a.m. and soon scrambled ashore to visit a lumber mill and a salmon cannery. While the ship was unloading, we wandered about the town taking pictures of totem poles and watching some boys snag salmon in Ketchikan Creek. We sailed at 3:30 p.m. and stopped at Kasaan before dark.

Wrangell came at 2 a.m. but I was sound asleep. I had no great desire to see Wrangell after spending thirteen days there in 1904 waiting anxiously for the steamer to sail up the Stikine River. I did crawl out at 4 a.m. to see Wrangell Narrows and dragged out the kids midst loud protest, but typical Alaskan weather had set in with mist so low on the mountains that we could see nothing besides the channel dead ahead.

In a driving rain we landed at Juneau shortly after noon and motored out to the Mendenhall Glacier. As soon as we stepped out of the closed car we were drenched and the trail up to the face of the glacier had turned into a small river. However, the kids loved it and waded along gaily until we were close to the ice. A large piece as big as a California bungalow fell off into the river so we had all the thrills and I believe the cloudy day intensified the deep blue of the crevasses.

Our last port of call in southeastern Alaska was Port Althorp and I, like a fool, must get up to see it at 2:30 a.m. This cannery was the largest in Alaska, running six lines, but they just that night had closed down for the season, having packed 186,000 cases. Every nook and corner of the buildings were piled to the roof with salmon in tins, despite the shipments all summer on every passing boat. We spent the rest of the day, which began so early, plowing across the Gulf of Alaska, in a choppy sea that put most of the passengers to bed.

After twenty-seven hours we arrived at Cordova and soon left in a special train for Childs Glacier. A forty-two mile run put us at the foot of this tremendous body of ice, which extended along the Copper River for three miles and whose face towered 300 feet above the river. It was a beautiful, clear, sunshiny day and the glacier was fairly active. Huge masses of ice broke off and fell into the river with thundering roars, creating waves in the river that nearly washed overboard one of our party who was perched on a rock at the river's edge. Miles Glacier, a little farther upstream, was also very impressive, but the railroad did not approach so close, so our view was too distant to be interesting.

We sailed from Cordova at noon and in three hours were off the Columbia Glacier. We saw it under perfect conditions with the sun glistening on the perpendicular glacier face that rose from the sea for 350 feet and extended along the seafront for three and a half miles. The bay was dotted with icebergs that had broken off and for several miles we pushed through ice pans and slush ice, which the wasting of the glacier had dumped into the sea.

Valdez at 6:30 p.m. was a mournful sight with its many deserted houses slowly falling into decay. After a short stop at Latouche, we entered Resurrection Bay at daylight and at 7 a.m. docked at Seward. Within an hour we pulled out on the train for Anchorage and our hunting trip was really started. We made a stop at Nellie Neal's, where we looked over some splendid moose, sheep and bear trophies and listened, with our tongues in our cheeks, to her graphic story of their killing. At Anchorage we purchased a few neglected necessities and sailed at 9 p.m. on the motorboat "Discovery" for Kasilof. The quarters on the boat were not very commodious as there was but a single cabin with four bunks. However, we did get some sleep interspersed with dreams of carbon monoxide leaking from the motor exhaust, which went up through the center of the cabin.

At daylight we entered the mouth of the Kasilof River and landed at a deserted cannery where Bob Bragaw, field manager of the Alaska Guides, Inc., met us and gave us a splendid breakfast. We soon loaded some of our duffle in a twenty-foot boat with an outboard motor for the fifteen-mile trip up the Kasilof River to Lake Tustumena; the balance of our equipment started off by pack train. There were a few bad rapids in the river and as it was running full, due to heavy rains, it was slow going. It was six hours before we entered the lake. We still had a fifteen-mile run up the lake to the cache where we were to camp and it was not until 6 p.m. that we arrived. Here we found camp all made for us and had a wonderful twelve-hour sleep.

The pack train that left Kasilof at the same time was not due for another day so we put in the time fishing and targeting the guns. Sherman and Barbara caught twelve grayling in Birch Creek amid wild shrieks. I lay on the bank in the warm sunshine and roared with laughter at their excitement. The stream was full of salmon on their way up to spawn and Sherman shot several with the .22 rifle. When they found an eleven-inch bear track on one of the bars, they were ready to start back to camp. The pack train came in about 4 p.m., and we had all our stuff together again. As we had been two days without a toothbrush, we were glad.

We pulled out of camp on Lake Tustumena at 9:30 a.m. after the usual delays of a first day's start. Our trail lay straight back from the lake, crossing Birch Creek and then over the divide to a point on Funny River. The day was clear and beautiful,

Child's Glacier, Alaska, in 1930

and from the hills we had a splendid view of Lake Tustumena, Cook Inlet and, beyond, Iliamna Volcano and Redoubt Mountain of the Aleutian Range. Behind us we could see Skilak Lake and between lay the famous moose country where we hoped to kill a big head. Northeast of us lay the Kenai Mountains where at the head of Funny River we were to hunt sheep.

With all the noise of the pack train we hardly expected to see any game but one cow moose stood and watched us go by. We covered more than thirteen miles by shortly after 3 p.m., although the trail was wet and boggy in spots.

Our outfit consisted of four riding horses and nine packhorses. Our personnel was Hank Lucas, chief guide; H.A. Anderson, guide; Duncan Little, cook; and Henry McKinnon, horse wrangler.

We broke camp before 9 a.m. and traveled up Funny River for ten miles until 1:30 p.m., when we pitched camp just at the timberline. Above us stretched the open tundra gradually rising to the rocky slopes of the Kenai Mountains. It was only a two-mile ride from our camp to sheep country and fortunately the footing was good, so we could take the horses up to snow line. We spent the rest of the day making camp, for this was to be our permanent camp, at least until September 1st. We erected a ten-by-twelve-foot cook tent and three seven-by-nine-foot sleeping tents, one for Barbara, one for Sherman and myself and one for the men.

The next morning we awoke in a downpour but two of the men went out early to swamp a trail through the alders of the steep riverbank to the tundra plateau above timberline. About 11 a.m. it began to clear and after a hurried lunch we left to look for a black bear that the boys reported having seen far up on the hill. We traveled up the bed of the Funny River till it became little more than a trickle and then started to climb up onto the bench to the south. The hillsides were covered with berries, and we hoped Mr. Bear had a good appetite and had remained feeding for the five hours since the boys had seen him. He was, however, not in sight and while we were resting after our climb, Hank Lucas spotted two other bear a mile and a half away. We started after them, but had not gone far when we happened to look behind us and there was our bear just emerging from a clump of alders in which he evidently had been taking a nap, hidden from us.

We retraced our steps and after waiting a half-hour for him to feed behind a little knoll we crossed an intervening creek and climbed straight up toward him. We peeked over a little ridge and there was the bear feeding busily just eighty yards

Sherman crawled into position, and at the crack of his gun, the bear dropped.

away. Sherman crawled into position and at the crack of his gun the bear dropped as if he had been pole-axed. I had not expected anything like this and was lying prone, holding a bead on the bear ready to shoot if Sherman crippled him. Bruin never moved a foot, and when I realized he was down and dead I let out a yell, and with Sherman ran forward. Sherman had drilled him right through the back of the head into the brain. A nice workmanlike job. We measured and skinned him out in a biting cold wind.

Length - tip of nose to tip of tail ....58 inches
Height of shoulder ....34 inches
Hind foot length .... 6 7/8 inches
Length - squared skin ....66 inches

I got a greater kick watching Sherman kill this bear than I ever got from a shot that I had fired. Sherman would not believe he had killed the bear until he had carefully examined my gun and found it clean. Even then I think it took him some hours to get used to the idea that he had really killed it alone.

We were off early the next day and as it was a bright clear day we decided to hunt sheep. We had hardly reached the upper bench before we saw a bear and while we were watching him a solitary ram appeared moving down the ridge about two miles away. We decided unanimously on the ram as our objective, but it looked like a difficult job, as he was high above us and there appeared to be no cover at all. We left Sherman and Anderson with the horses while Hank, Barbara and I started the two-mile stalk. We took turns watching the ram through the glasses, and when his head was down two of us crawled ahead until signaled by the one behind that the ram had lifted his head. We progressed alternately in this way until we were under the brow of the hill and out of sight. Then we crawled up a ravine that was nearly straight up. After a half-mile of this we felt we were on a level where we had last seen the ram, so we started to round the hill. We had not gone 200 yards when I heard Barbara gasp, and there, just over a rock ledge, showed the ram's white back, about thirty yards away. Fortunately, he had his head down and had not seen us. As he fed up the hill into full sight, Barbara cracked him through the heart -- a perfect shot and all that was necessary. He dropped where he stood and we came up to find a very old ram, with most of his teeth gone, but a good head for the Kenai.

Barbara Gray stands with her first Dall's sheep in 1930.

ALASKA

It measured:

Base	12 1/2 inches
Length of curl	34 1/2 inches
Spread	18 inches

When Barbara shot we heard Sherman yell far down in the valley below. Then he and Anderson started up with the horses, but it was fully three-quarters of an hour before they arrived. Meanwhile, we looked over the country and counted seven black bear feeding on berries. Not far off was a very good bull moose. Certainly there was game enough to satisfy anyone in this country.

It was only a short job to skin out the head and load the meat onto a horse, so we were back in camp by 2 p.m. and had the rest of the day to clean up and bathe.

When we reached the upper bench the next morning it was foggy and as we approached the sheep hills the fog seemed to lower until we could not see across the little draws. We decided to sit down for an hour, as it only stirred up the country to blunder about in the fog. As we sat on the hillside a black bear came into view across the valley, scuttling about in his search for berries. Now and again he was blotted out by the fog but gradually he drew near until he was only 600 yards away. Barbara could stand it no longer, so she and Hank went off to collect his hide. They dropped down into the bottom of the valley and crept up on him till it looked to us on the hillside as if they intended to get close enough to strangle him, not shoot him. Then we saw Barbara settle down for the shot, a puff of light smoke, the bear spun around chasing his tail and as he fell the report reached our ears. It was a perfect shot at forty yards, straight through the foreshoulder into the heart. The bear proved to be good-sized and very old. It measured:

Length - tip to tip	62 3/4 inches
Height at shoulder	34 1/2 inches
Hind foot	8 inches
Skin squared length	78 inches

We left Barbara and Anderson to skin out the bear while Hank, Sherman and I went on to find a ram for Sherman. We had only traveled about a mile toward

[341]

A black bear for Barbara

ALASKA

Killey River when I spotted a ram lying down among the rocks. He had seen us, but we tried the old ruse of one staying with the horses to hold his attention, while Sherman and Hank tried to sneak around behind him and get closer. He was more than 300 yards from us and we feared the shot too long for Sherman.

Our scheme did not work, for the ram started up the hill, followed by another that appeared out of a hollow.

When they had moved off what appeared to me a very long way Hank said, "That second ram is a very good one. Why don't you try a shot at him?"

Without any hope of hitting, I lay down and fired two shots, both of which were high. The third shot dropped him and we went up to find a fair head that measured:

    Circumference .... 13 inches
    Length .... 34 inches
    Spread .... 17 1/4 inches

The bullet entered back of the foreshoulder, low down, ranging up, and tore the top off his heart and went to pieces in the foreshoulder. We skinned out the head, and, carrying the hams, stepped off the distance that measured 458 steps.

We moved on into a basin where the very headwaters of Funny River start and there saw more than 100 sheep scattered over the hillside. As there appeared to be at least two good rams in the bunch, we tried a stalk, waiting for them to go over the pass into Killey River before we moved up.

As we peaked over the top of the pass we were disappointed to find the sheep had traveled up onto one of the side peaks, but the herd gave us a magnificent picture as seventy-five of them stood grouped on a field of snow.

We returned to camp against a terrific wind that blew up a storm and kept us in camp for two days. Finally, on August 25th it cleared, and we were soon out of camp. It was late afternoon, however, before we located a bunch of rams with a "shootable" head and then they were across the valley and high above us. Sherman and Hank started the stalk, while Barbara and I sat on the hillside and watched every move of their progress.

There were eleven rams in the bunch and they were feeding quietly. Gradually they all lay down except three, which to our consternation fed uphill about fifty

Prentiss Gray's first Dall's sheep

yards before settling down on a commanding point of rocks. Slowly, Sherman and Hank, with a lot of crawling, got within 150 yards of the bunch before the three rams above spotted them. The rest were still lying down when these three started to run. Immediately the whole bunch was off. Sherman had to take a running shot and just as he fired at the largest ram, a smaller six-year-old stepped in front and took the shot in the belly. That meant a long chase, but finally the animal fell a half mile away on the slide rock. Its horns measured:

Circumference .... 12 1/2 inches
Length .... 26 1/4 inches
Tip to tip .... 18 1/4 inches

We skinned out the head, took all the meat we could carry and started for camp, where we arrived at 6:30 p.m., very tired.

We made an early start the next morning although it was raining. Our course took us through the pass into Indian River and from high up on the ridge we could see Lake Tustumena and the mountains beyond Cook Inlet. To the east lay Tustumena Glacier, with its many drainage tongues. We made an unsuccessful stalk to look at a small ram near the top of the ridge, but he caught our scent in the varying wind that was swinging into all four points of the compass. As he went off we had an easy shot, but he was too small and we let him go.

We found eighty-two sheep in a basin after an hour's travel and located five rams far up on the hill to one side. After lunch we started the stalk and found it hard work to get past the ewes and lambs without driving them straight up to the rams. While we were working slowly toward them, the fog came down so thick we could not see fifty feet, and we were soon entirely lost in it. I suggested we sit down and wait and while we were smoking and talking I heard a rock fall and slowly out of the fog emerged a white shape. We froze, and as the fog lifted a little, we made out a small ram watching us. We could not move a muscle and to add to our difficulty, four more appeared and fed in under a ledge about thirty yards away. The little fellow had had his suspicions aroused and stood looking at us, so that for twenty minutes we lay there without daring to move a muscle. Finally, we decided to try to move Sherman into position to shoot at the big ram, which was among the four below the ledge. The first movement, however, started the small ram and his

Sherman stands as Barbara and Prentiss skin Barbara's bear.

flight alarmed the others. They all melted into the fog before Sherman could get his sights on them. We made our way back to camp in the next three hours -- cold, wet and tired. But, we had a good laugh watching a black bear, who must have sat on a porcupine. He appeared, running full tilt around a side hill. When he reached a large patch of snow he galloped to the top, slid to the bottom on his tail, galloped up again and rolled and somersaulted down. This he did half a dozen times until suddenly he left for the other side of the mountain at full speed.

When we awoke the next day it was pouring again, but soon it stopped, and before we had finished breakfast it was all clear and the sun was beautifully bright. As it was late we decided on a bear hunt and journeyed to the top of the ridge where we lay in the sunlight and loafed. From time to time we looked over the country and at considerable distances saw four bear. They were all a long way off and we decided to eat and then look over the next valley. After lunch Hank, Andy and I left Barbara with the horses and strolled up the ridge a quarter of a mile.

When we returned both the horses and Barbara had gone so Andy took up their trail while Hank and I went after a good-sized bear that had appeared a half mile below us. We dropped down below the bear and approached within sixty yards but the sun was directly behind him and as he had not the slightest idea we were about, we shifted our position to get the sun out of our eyes. We waited for him to come out of some tall grass he had entered and as he stepped clear, forty-two yards away, I let go at his shoulder. He made one frantic jump into a bunch of alder. We had no way of knowing how badly he was hurt so I ran to a little hummock to see that he had not come out below the alders. It was not necessary, for he had dropped dead at the end of his one frantic leap. We pulled him out of the brush and measured him:

Length from tip to tip .... 63 inches
Height at foreshoulder .... 34 inches
Length of back foot .... 8 1/2 inches
Squared skin length .... 78 inches

Just as we started skinning, Barbara appeared and reported she had chased the horses half-way home but had not been able to catch them. She was completely tired out. Hank went off to see if he could find them and an hour later appeared

Barbara Gray in camp near Tustumena Glacier

with the horses and Andy. Meanwhile, I had skinned out the bear and we started camp.

The next morning was windy and cold but not raining so we made an early start for sheep. About 10 a.m. we located fifty-four sheep in a bunch just through the pass at the head of Funny River. We could see no way to approach them so we lay still and watched. We ate an early lunch and still watched, but the sheep peacefully fed on or lay down. About noon the inaction wore us out so we sent Andy around to the windward side of the sheep to try to quietly move them into some place more approachable. It was highly successful for the sheep started straight for us. They were not long in getting to us and the rams fortunately stayed well down the hill. We were all ready for them and Sherman knocked down the biggest ram at ninety-six yards. I expected all the rest to run but after a short dash they stood about and some even started feeding again. This gave me a chance to pick out the second-best head and he fell to a heart shot.

Sherman's ram, which was the largest obtained on the trip, measured:

Circumference	13 7/8 inches
Length - Left	36 1/4 inches
Right	35 3/4 inches
Spread	19 3/8 inches
Live weight	300 lbs.

My ram measured:

Circumference	13 3/4 inches
Length - Left	34 1/4 inches
Right	34 1/4 inches
Spread	16 1/2 inches

Our shooting on sheep was finished, as Barbara did not want another sheep, so we decided to spend a day just looking at game. The wind had pulled into the north bringing bright sunshine and a clear day. As we reached the top we could see all the mountains on the west side of Cook Inlet from Iliamna and Redoubt north to Mt. Susitna. Dimly we could make out Mt. McKinley, 200 miles away. It was

Sherman Gray, 12, with his Dall's sheep

such a gorgeous day we just rode around or lay on the hillside in the warm sun, hoping for an easy chance to take pictures.

During lunch two wolverines trotted along the hillside above us and Hank and I emptied our guns at these destructive devils at 300 yards without damage to either. They had been visiting our sheep kill of yesterday and our arrival had interrupted their feast.

We loaded the two sheep on a couple of packhorses and slowly started them home. We stopped long enough to stalk two rams to photograph them at 150 yards and reached camp at 6 p.m. We had seen in our eight days hunting more than 400 sheep and forty-five bear. We had only failed to get game on one hunt and best of all we had left no cripples.

The following day it was still clear and beautiful so we decided to move to the moose country. We broke camp and by 11 a.m. hit the trail for the ten-mile ride down Funny River to the Moose Camp. The wind was straight down the river, so we had little expectation of seeing game, but as we came down into the timbered slopes, first a cow moose ran off ahead, then a mile farther a splendid bull with a head that looked like church spires slowly trotted up the hill. Before long a cow with twin calves went away in a great hurry. One of the calves, evidently too preoccupied with the tender feed to see us, loitered behind until we were within fifty yards. Then it discovered that its mother and brother had departed and that great danger was at hand. It raced and floundered up the hill in apparent terror.

We were certainly in moose country, for on the opposite hillside 300 yards away were feeding four big bulls and higher up a bull and two cows. We stopped and watched these four magnificent heads feed slowly up the hill. They were all still in the velvet but just starting to peel. It was a sight to inspire any hunter and cheered our hearts mightily for the three-day hunt ahead of us. In any other place in the world it would have been ridiculous to try to get a good moose head in three days, but here there did appear to be plenty of game.

We were in the greatest moose country of the world, where the animals were most abundant and grew to the greatest size. We did not dare hope for a trophy approaching the giant head in the Field Museum of Chicago with its 78 1/2 inch spread, but we felt sure we would not have to take home any small heads with all these moose to look over.

This country formerly was known as caribou country, but about fifty years ago

Moose camp was struck ten miles down Funny River.

it was burned over and the first moose appeared shortly after that, attracted no doubt by the succulent feed of willows and low bushes that sprang up after the fire. It is within the memory of the old Indians (about 1873), when the first moose was killed near Kenai village and caused a sensation among the natives who had never before seen an animal like it.

Gradually more moose came in or the increase was so enormous that the caribou were driven out. The winters in the Kenai Peninsula are fairly mild, tending to reduce the terrific starvation ordeal that comes with deep snow. Natural enemies such as wolves are scarce and all conditions seem to have cooperated to make this the greatest moose pasture of the world.

The number of shed antlers seen on every hand was prodigious. As standing timber is scarce, these shed antlers are used by the hunters to blaze the trails. A horn propped against a stump or hung on a willow or alder bush makes an excellent trail marker. When the government surveyors passed through this country they named the main trail on the map "Moose Horn Trail" because it was so marked throughout its entire length.

Waiting for the season to open is always tiresome, but neither brown bear nor moose opened until September 1st, so we spent the time washing our clothes and ourselves and oiling the guns. We sent off five packhorses to Birch Creek for more food as we were completely out, except for sheep meat and ten pounds of flour.

A bright clear morning with a southwest wind provided encouragement, if we needed any, for an early start. Within an hour we were on top of a rise from which we could look over a considerable area of flat country along the north bank of the Funny River. For three miles before us stretched flat marsh and tundra, dotted by clumps of spruce, willow and alder.

Gradually through the glasses we began to see moose. We kept strict count up to fifteen but then we could not always tell whether it was the same moose we were counting twice or a new moose, so we gave it up. It would be safe to say, however, that we saw more than thirty moose from our lookout. About 10 a.m. the moose began to lie down and it was hard to locate them, so we all took a bath in citronella and stretched out for a nap. Mosquitoes and black flies were annoying but not unbearable. About 2:30 p.m. we headed down into the flat to look over at closer range a bull whose newly peeled antlers were flashing in the sunlight. Here we found the walking very bad. Swamps covered most of our way and the dry ridges

Barbara, sitting on log, "glasses" for big game.

were strewn with downed timber.

Our hunt for the bull was abortive as we jumped him from his bed and he went off before we could get a good look at his antlers. On the way home we saw a freak head and would have taken it if we could have made the approach. The head showed a good left palm. The right was not as good, but it bristled points, at least forty, and probably had a spread of more than sixty inches. However, the wind was shifting and the bull left before we could get up.

Next morning we started in a pouring rain and by 3 p.m. after a continuous downpour we decided we had had enough. Meanwhile we had seen eleven moose, one of which had a good enough head to take.

We started this hunt by jumping a two-year-old bull and cow out of a spruce thicket. They ran off but we decided to look over the thicket to see if any had stayed behind. Sure enough there was a little spike bull, and he let me walk up to within fifty feet of him and take pictures at that distance before he slowly walked off.

A little later we jumped a bull with about a fifty-inch head and, before he left, we made out three others with him. But the rain was coming down to mist up our binoculars and we could not tell which was the best head till they were 150 yards away and running fast. Barbara took one shot but missed clean. It was a hard shot and we should have all dropped dead with surprise if she had made it. After this we built a fire and dried out a bit, which with lunch, cheered us up despite the downpour, so that we started on again. We jumped one bull moose in dense timber but as he had a poor head we made no attempt to follow. Camp finally looked awfully good, with a chance to get dry clothes and a cup of tea.

The rain was still coming down in torrents when we awoke the next day and we thought we were in for a wet, miserable hunt again. It was our last day and we felt we could not stay in camp. We had only been on the trail an hour before it began to clear in the east and by 10 a.m. we discarded our slickers. Except for a few misty showers it did not rain again all day, till just after we reached camp at night.

Our first sight of moose came early when Hank, who was on foot ahead, motioned us to get off our horses and come quick. There, not thirty yards from us, was a bull lying down but an examination of his head showed only a small one with poor palms. In the hope there was another bull with him, we circled downwind and soon saw two pink, freshly peeled antlers waving slowly in the alders. We

Barbara takes a trophy moose. She shot like a veteran.

moved up to within forty yards, as this bull was also lying down. This head looked all right and Barbara sat down to shoot. We cautioned her to wait until the bull stood up, which he did in a couple of minutes.

She was just about to fire when Hank called out, "No good. Don't shoot."

As the bull had turned we saw he did not have spread enough and one palm was not as good as we had thought. It was a terrible letdown after all the excitement of the stalk, but I had repeatedly told Hank we preferred no head at all to a mediocre head, and he was very wise not to let Barbara shoot.

During midday we saw but few moose as they were all lying down in cover. By 3 p.m. we began to run into cows and soon located some bulls as they came out of the alder thickets to feed. We looked over two heads at a hundred yards, but although one carried at least a sixty-inch spread, the left palm was too small.

It was getting on toward 5 p.m. and worst of all the wind had changed so we had to travel with it to reach camp. It looked like a blank day and we were all blue.

Suddenly Hank announced, "There's your head."

With great difficulty, we made out a palm glistening in the alders a half mile away. We could only see one palm but that was immense and it warranted a closer look. We made a most careful stalk and at 110 yards looked the head over carefully. The palms were excellent, brow points good, but the spread was a little narrow. However, it was by far the heaviest head we had seen and if we had been in Quebec it would have been a record. Barbara sat down and aimed. Just then the bull got up out of his bed and she drilled him. He took two steps and down he went, dead as a doornail. Her shot went in behind the foreleg, ranging forward, and broke up on the offshoulder. It was all over after a hard day and after taking off the head and cape, we could only just make camp by dark. But we were awfully proud of the job Barbara had done -- she had shot like a veteran. Her moose measured:

Spread .... 57 inches
Left palm length .... 46 inches
width .... 18 1/2 inches
beam .... 9 1/2 inches, 15 points
Right palm length .... 44 1/2 inches
width .... 19 inches
beam .... 9 1/2 inches, 14 points

Packing out moose - last hunt in Alaska for Prent, Sherman and Barbara in 1930

Weight with lower jaw off and skull cut to span at eyes - 82 lbs.

The next morning the boys started out for the moose head at 5 a.m. and were back in camp with it before 9 a.m. We were all packed and ready, but the usual delays of breaking camp kept us until after 10 a.m., so that we did not reach Birch Creek camp on the shore of Lake Tustumena until after 3 p.m. It had been a beautiful clear day and a gorgeous full moon made perfect our last night under canvas.

An aeroplane was to call for us sometime during the next day but at what hour we did not know. Therefore, we were up at the first crack of dawn and had everything packed and ready before 7 a.m. The cook outdid himself for our last breakfast and as the day was beautiful all the signs were auspicious. About 11:30 a.m. we heard the low droning of the motor and soon the plane appeared following the shoreline of the lake looking for our camp. When he picked out the white tents in the green forest he swooped down in a graceful curve and taxied up to the beach at our tent door. A few minor motor adjustments, a bite of lunch, and we, with all our duffle, were stowed away in the plane. At 12:30 p.m. the motor roared and we left the surface of the lake, which in a final fit of kindness was as smooth as glass. We circled over the camp twice, while we gained altitude, then cut back over the swamps directly to our moose camp. We covered in ten minutes the distance that had taken us five and a half hours the day before. On we went to Skilak Lake, and thence through a pass in the mountains and down the Resurrection River to Seward. Fifty minutes was all it took us as opposed to two full days that we had spent to reach Lake Tustumena by rail and boat.

The "S.S. Aleutian" was late so we had to put up at the Van Gilder Hotel in Seward for the night, but it gave us ample time to square up our accounts and buy six live mink for the ranch. Five more days at sea and we landed at Seattle after a run down the Inside Passage to Dixon's Entrance. Because of fog, the ship put out to sea here and skirted the west side of Vancouver Island to the Straits of Juan de Fuca. On the night of September 12th we stepped ashore.

Last job of the day for Barbara - rifle cleaning

This book was:

Produced with the able assistance of:
David Dillman
Sandra Poston
Jack Reneau
Julie Tripp

Book design and layout by: Susan C. Reneau
                             Donna Elliott

Cover and dust jacket designed by: Walker Graphics
                                     Great Falls, Montana

End sheet photographs by: Prentiss N. Gray

Typesetting by: Meerkat Graphics Centre
                  Lolo, Montana

Printed and bound by: Publishers Press
                        Salt Lake City, Utah